The Political Future of
Social Security in Aging
Societies

The Political Future of Social Security in Aging Societies

Vincenzo Galasso

The MIT Press
Cambridge, Massachusetts
London, England

MIT Press books may be purchased at special quantity discounts for business or sales promotional use. For information, please email special_sales@mitpress.mit.edu or write to Special Sales Department, The MIT Press, 55 Hayward Street, Cambridge, MA 02142.

This book was set in Palatino on 3B2 by Asco Typesetters, Hong Kong and was printed and bound in the United States of America.

Library of Congress Cataloging-in-Publication Data

Galasso, Vincenzo, 1967–
The political future of social security in aging societies / Vincenzo Galasso.
    p. cm.
Includes bibliographical references and index.
ISBN-13: 978-0-262-07273-1 (hardcover : alk. paper)
ISBN-10: 0-262-07273-4 (hardcover : alk. paper)
1. Social security—Case studies. 2. Social security—Forecasting. I. Title.
HD7091.G34 2006
368.4′3—dc22   2006022065

10 9 8 7 6 5 4 3 2 1

to Paola and Chiara

Contents

Contents

List of Tables

List of Figures

Preface

What is the future of social security in our aging societies? Will the growing number of elderly be able to rely on publicly provided retirement income for their old age consumption? And will these pension benefits be sufficiently large to support the needs of individuals whose life expectancy continues to increase? A large literature has addressed these questions from a pure economic perspective in an attempt to provide some qualitative—or even quantitative—predictions on the future development of the current social security systems. The expectation is that population aging will substantially undermine the financial sustainability of most European pension systems. As more retirees draw from the systems while fewer individuals pay in, contribution revenues will soon fall short of the pension benefits awarded under the current rules, and our graying societies will hardly be able to honor their commitment to pay social security benefits to future retirees. This gloomy prospect has led economists, academics, and supranational institutions to propose several social security reform options that may easy the future financial troubles of these systems. Yet few major reforms have actually been implemented in European countries.

This book argues instead that social security policy decisions go beyond economic theory into the realm of politics. Since the effect of aging on our unfunded pension systems calls for either higher contribution rates or lower pension benefits, the political process will have to reconcile the conflicting interests of different generations. The crucial insight of this *political economy* approach to pensions is that the effect of aging on social security and the success of any reform proposal depend on political factors. Economically sound, clever reform projects that do not gain sufficient political support just do not represent a feasible option for policy-makers. In democratic countries a social security regime or reform is *politically sustainable* if supported by a majority in the Parliament or, more directly, in the electorate.

This book provides a quantitative comparative analysis of the future *political sustainability* of social security in six aging societies—France, Germany, Italy, Spain, the United Kingdom, and the United States—that differ in the magnitude of the aging process, in the current level and design of the existing social security systems and in their political dynamics. Not only has the aging of the population significant economic effects on social security, it also modifies the age composition—and hence the preferences—of the voters. Indeed, an older electorate will put more pressure on the policy-maker for keeping or even rising pensions' generosity, despite the adverse economic effects of aging. Using a common approach to all countries, I evaluate how these political constraints shape each social security system under population aging. The quantitative assessment of the economic and political effects of aging on social security may depend on country-specific characteristics, such as the magnitude of the aging process, the redistributive feature of each pension system and the existing retirement policy in each country. Overall, political constraints seem to magnify the impact of aging on the pension spending. Yet postponing retirement mitigates this effect while leading to more generous pension, and hence represents the only viable solution to pension system problems in the face of population aging. Simulations on the political feasibility of this policy show encouraging results.

This book is primarily intended for economists and political scientists who are interested in analyzing the future of social security system from a political economy viewpoint. Advanced undergraduate or graduate students may also benefit from this exercise as it presents a quantitative application of the political economy approach to economic policy—namely to social security issues. Finally, to policy-makers and to the public at large, this book may provide a different angle on social security problems: rather than handing over more recipes for reforms, I present a positive analysis of how social security systems may evolve in the future and discuss *politically sustainable* measures to revert the process.

My decision to embark on a large research project on the political economy of pensions in OECD countries came while participating at the conference Pensioni. Davvero una verifica? held at the Italian Economic Ministry in Rome in fall 2001. My presentation of a paper analyzing the future political sustainability of the Italian pension reforms of the nineties gave rise to a heated debate among academics and policy-makers, who were somewhat skeptical regarding the possibility that future politicians might alter the newly reformed system for electoral purposes. As I expected, that scepticism is rapidly fading away.

Some of the material in this book draws on joint published work with Marcello D'Amato, Paola Profeta and Jose Ignacio Conde-Ruiz. I am grateful to them for their collaboration on these papers and for their feedbacks on the whole book. In particular, Marcello D'Amato co-authored a paper that constitutes the backbone of chapter 6, while Jose Ignacio Conde-Ruiz collaborated on chapter 8. I am greatly indebted to Paola Profeta for her involvement in two joint papers that gave rise to many of the ideas in chapters 2, 4, and 11 and for her continual support throughout the project.

I also want to thank many colleagues either for useful discussions on these topics that helped me to gain a better understanding of these issues or for their comments on single chapters or on the whole book, in particular, Alberto Alesina, Costas Azariadis, Giuseppe Bertola, Tito Boeri, Henning Bohn, Michele Boldrin, Agar Brugiavini, George Casamatta, Marco Celentani, Richard Disney, Elsa Fornero, Jonathan Haskel, Arye Hillman, Tullio Jappelli, Florence Legros, Georges de Ménil, Franco Peracchi, Pierre Pestieau, Andras Simonovits, Guido Tabellini, Silke Uebelmesser, and Jaume Ventura. I also benefited from comments at several seminars and conferences in which parts of this book were presented, but in particular, at the European Commission DG Ecfin internal seminars and the fall 2003 Economic Policy Panel in Rome. I would also like to thank my editor, John Covell, for his kind encouragement. Some of the material underlying this book was used in courses given at Bocconi University, Universidad Carlos III de Madrid and CORE. Andrea Asoni, at an initial stage, and Giuseppe Cappelletti later on, provided excellent research assistance. My largest debt is to Paola and Chiara, for being so patient while this project crept in several summer vacations. I gratefully acknowledge financial support from different institutions. In particular, this research was supported by Università Bocconi (Ricerca di base), MIUR, Fundación Ramon Areces, Fundación BBVA, and US Social Security Administration—through the Sandell Grant of the Center for Retirement Research at Boston College. The views herein expressed are exclusively mine and do not represent the opinions of the SSA or of any other US federal government agency.

The Political Future of
Social Security in Aging
Societies

1   Introduction

The world population is aging fast. In 2000 individuals aged 65 years or more represented about 7 percent of the world population, up from 5.2 percent in 1950. Yet United Nations projections suggest that this share of the aged will double to reach 16 percent in 2050. The population aging is even more pronounced if one considers only the more developed regions of the world. The fraction of elderly individuals—those aged 65 years or more—in Europe, Northern America, Australia, New Zealand, and Japan has already increased from 8 percent in 1950 to 14 percent in 2000, and is forecasted to reach 26 percent in 2050.

This dramatic demographic dynamics is the result of a contemporaneous drop in mortality and fertility rates. The reduction in mortality seems to represent a long-lasting trend, which has already generated substantial longevity gains during the last fifty years. UN data indicate an increase in the average world life expectancy at birth from 46.5 years in 1950 to 65.4 years in 2000, yet further longevity gains are forecasted, with the average life expectancy reaching 74.3 years by 2050. Also the drop in fertility seems to follow a trend, although in the more developed countries the large fall in the number of births has mainly occurred during the eighties and nineties and is now expected to stabilize. According to these forecasted demographic dynamics, aging will hence continue.

Population aging bears significant implications for the economic environment. The structure of production may have to adjust to accommodate a labor force with a different age composition. Individuals may respond to their increased longevity by saving more for old age consumption, thereby leading to higher aggregate savings and to a larger stock of physical capital. The composition of the aggregate demand may also change, since a graying society will express different needs, and presumably higher demand for goods and services for the old, such as recreational entertainment and long-term care. The relative importance of the different schemes in the welfare state will also be affected, with more emphasis being posed on programs targeted to the elderly, such as social security, health insurance, and long-term care.

Aging has also dramatic consequences for the functioning of unfunded, or pay-as-you-go (PAYG), social security systems. In an unfunded system, contributions imposed on the labor earnings of covered workers are used to provide pension benefits to current retirees. Thus aging has a direct impact on the financial solvency of social security, since it tends to increase the fraction of recipients—the retirees—while reducing the proportion of contributors—the workers. To restore the financial balance of the system, either pension benefits have to be reduced or the tax burden on the workers has to be increased. The magnitude of this phenomenon is captured by the changes in the old age dependency ratio, which is defined as the ratio of elderly (aged 65 years or more) to adult individuals (aged between 18 and 64 years). In Italy and Spain this ratio is projected to double in less than fifty years, increasing respectively from 27.9 and 26 percent in 2000 to 64.5 and 63.5 percent in 2050. Together with these changes in the age composition of the population, most OECD countries have also experienced a large drop in the labor force participation of middle-aged and elderly workers. These early exits from the labor market, which were induced by the introduction—since the late sixties—of generous early retirement schemes, have further increased the number of retirees—hence contributing financial distress to the systems.

The scale of population aging, and its dramatic effects on the unfunded pension systems, have captured the attention of economists, media, and policy-makers—giving rise in several European countries to a flurry of pension reforms. During the eighties and nineties, in fact, incremental policies that extended the coverage and generosity of the welfare state were progressively abandoned, while mild retrenching measures were instead adopted. Most reforms amounted only to moderate variations in the parameters of the systems, which did not modify their underlying unfunded nature or defined benefit[1] structure. Yet sometimes these conservative changes to the benefit calculation criteria, to the eligibility requirements, to the indexation rule, and particularly to the effective retirement age managed to reduce the generosity of these systems—often along a lengthy transition period—and thus to enhance their long-term financial sustainability. To summarize these different scenarios, EU official projections on the future financial sustainability of European social security systems forecast changes in pension expenditure for the next fifty years to range between a small reduction in the United Kingdom—from 5.1 percent of GDP in 2000 to 3.9 percent in 2050—and a large increase in Spain—from 9.4 to 17.7 percent, depending on the different magnitude of the aging process, of the initial status quo and of the reforming experience of the last decades.

These calculations, however accurate, fail to consider that the design, the rules or the crucial parameters of the social security systems may further be modified. For instance, will the legislated—but yet to be introduced—retrenching measures ever be implemented? Or will policy-makers decide to renege on reforms adopted by previous governments—as in Germany during the nineties—and thus to stop their phasing in? In other words, how will further aging affect the development of these unfunded pension systems?

Conventional economic wisdom suggests that further aging will require additional retrenchment efforts to limit the growth of pension spending. Indeed, even if per-capita pension benefits are reduced, aggregate pension spending—and hence social security contributions—is still likely to rise, due to the increasing proportion of retirees. Yet, unlike welfare state expansion measures, retrenchment policies are extremely unpopular. Welfare states enjoy extended support among pensions' recipients and bureaucrats, who strongly oppose any benefit reduction. Electoral concerns—and political pressure by unions and lobby groups—may thus dictate the social security policy decisions of policy-makers, who face a political plea not to retrench.

This book acknowledges that social security policy decisions often go beyond economic theory into the realm of politics. The crucial insight of this political economy approach is that social security policies—also in response to demographic shocks—need not to enhance economic welfare, but only to be supported politically. In democratic countries, this typically amounts to obtaining the support of a majority of the Parliament or, more directly, of the electorate, although a broader consensus may be needed to overcome the existence of de jure or de facto political veto players. This intuition carries an additional powerful consequence: normative economic analysis may fail to provide useful policy recommendations, unless they lead to the design of *politically* sustainable reform packages.

The task set up for this book is to provide a *quantitative assessment* of how these electoral—and more generally political—concerns by the policy-makers will shape the response of the existing social security systems to the expected demographic dynamics in six aging countries —France, Germany, Italy, Spain, the United Kingdom, and the United States. How will social security systems be modified to obtain the political support of an older electorate in a graying economy? Will the retrenchment policies advocated in the economic literature— for instance, a reduction in the pension benefits' generosity and the increase in the effective retirement age—be politically feasible? Throughout the book, the focus of analysis will hence be on the *political sustainability* of social security regimes or reforms in aging societies. Since policy-makers are recognized to have electoral concerns, political sustainability of social security will indicate the existence of a political majority, in the Parliament or among the electors, that is willing to support the system in all its provisions—such as retirement age, contribution rate, eligibility criteria, and benefit calculation rules.

The choice of these six countries enables to gain a broad perspective on the political response to aging in developed economies. In Italy and Spain, the Mediterranean welfare state—largely centered on the social security system—will be exposed to a dramatic hike in population aging, whereas in the United Kingdom and the United States, a less pervasive welfare system, featuring a shared private and public responsibility in the provision of retirement income, will face less extreme demographic dynamics. Between these two polar cases, the analysis of France and Germany depicts the reaction of large continental welfare states to a sizable demographic challenge. The different social security status quo, the unequal magnitude of the aging process, and the variety of political systems and institutions among these countries will result in quantitatively different future social security scenarios; the qualitative message will, however, coincide.

The economic and political literatures have produced a wide body of research on the determinants of the initial introduction of these unfunded social security systems and on the motivations of their rapid development into the most relevant welfare state program. Paternalistic and equity principles may have played a crucial role, as social security prevented elderly people from falling into poverty, but this public intervention may also be justified by private markets' failure in providing life annuity. Political theories associate the industrialization process and the appearance of left parties and unions with the initial establishment and the large growth of welfare policies, while diverse welfare scenarios in equally developed economies are often attributed to the effect that different political institutions may have on the policy-makers' decision process. Yet the analysis of the expansion of the welfare state may prove of little help in understanding a possible retrenchment phase induced by the aging process. The extension of the coverage and the rise in the pension benefits' generosity that characterized the growth in social spending since World War II are popular measures that typically generate positive electoral returns. The politics of welfare state retrenchment is instead an exercise in electoral blame avoidance —since retrenching measures tend to impose large costs on specific groups of voters, while creating only dispersed and uncertain gains. Exploiting external constraints to reduce the political accountability of these policies or adopting "divide-and-rule" strategies may help to minimize electoral backslashes, but the relevance of electoral concerns remains crucial.

An analysis of the political sustainability of social security under aging thus needs to examine the individuals' position on social security issues in order to assess the political relevance of these vested interests. Preferences over social security typically depend on an individual's age—since different cohorts of people face different remaining periods of contributions and benefits, but also on the redistributive design of the system. Retirees who receive a pension benefit at no current cost, middle-aged individuals who consider past contributions to the system as a sunk cost, or low income young individuals who benefit from within cohort redistribution may experience an increase in their economic well-being, thanks to social security. These individuals, who represent the constituency of the welfare state, will thus oppose retrenchment, and their electoral push may lead policy-makers to refrain from reforming the system. These electoral considerations are at the heart of the theoretical framework used in this book to assess the political sustainability of social security and can easily be embedded in a simple majority voting model—or in its widely used median voter's application.

The aging society hands over to the policy-maker a crucial trade-off between economic efficiency and political accountability. In fact demographic dynamics affect the individuals' preferences over social security—through changes in the average return from the pension system—but also the political process—through the aging of the electorate. In an environment with a stable employment the average internal rate of return of a PAYG social security system is equal to the sum of the population and the productivity growth rate. Yet individual returns are also affected by the survival probabilities that determine the length of the retirement period. Aging thus reduces the average return, although longevity gains may dampen this effect, and should induce the agents to reduce their support for social security. In the political arena, however, the aging society augments the political relevance of the elderly voters—those close to retirement. As the identity of the pivotal voter changes—and the median voter becomes older—the political support for social security increases.

The impact of the demographic process on the long run political sustainability of social security depends also on some characteristic features of the system. For instance, pension schemes enabling massive early retirements, as in France and Italy, amplify the negative impact of aging on the average profitability of the system, since the growing share of middle-aged individuals will be induced to retire early rather than continue to contribute to the system, while countries with high pension spending, such as Italy, may already experience too severe economic distortions because of the large social security contribution rate.

The simulations of the political economy model used in this book portray a grim picture for the future of these systems—well beyond the typical predictions by several international institutions, which forecast moderate to large increases in pension spending. Under population aging the political push—corresponding to the aging electorate—is forecasted to dominate the economic elements—consisting of the reduction in the average profitability of the system. Pension spending is estimated to rise sharply in all six countries, albeit with some relevant quantitative differences. The largest increases are expected to occur in Spain, the fastest aging country, but also in the United Kingdom, with contribution rates rising respectively from 21.3 and 14.5 percent in 2000 to 45.5 and 33.2 percent in 2050. Yet Italy would still experience the largest contribution rate, 50 percent. These significant rises in the social security contribution rate, and thus in the overall pension spending, would nevertheless be accompanied by some retrenching measures, with pension benefits' generosity falling—in France, Germany, Italy, and Spain. In the United Kingdom and the United States, higher social security contribution rates would instead be associated with more generous pensions.

The book introduces an additional specification of the political economy model, which considers economic distortions in the labor market, by allowing workers to reduce their labor supply in response to large increases in the social security contribution rates. These simulations suggest that, even in presence of labor market distortions, the political forces dominate and social security spending is still forecasted to increase, albeit less than in the previous case. Under this scenario, for instance, the Spanish and British contribution rates would be estimated to reach respectively 37.5 and 31.7 percent, while the largest contribution rate would be 46.2 percent in Italy.

Despite the bleak scenario portrayed by these simulations, a strong policy implication emerges. Postponing retirement represents an effective measure to limit the increase in pension spending induced by population aging—as measured by the social security contribution rate— while typically increasing the generosity of the system. The intuition is straightforward. A rise in the effective retirement age moderates the political demand for more social security, since it reduces the expected retirement period, while increasing the contribution period for the decisive voter. This policy measure is particularly successful in those countries with a low initial effective retirement age, such as France and Italy, in which a rise in the retirement age to 65 years would reduce contributions by around 12 percent. In all other countries the effect would be smaller, but still sizable.

However, is this policy measure politically feasible? Would individuals be willing to work longer years? Simulations on the political support to postponing retirement give an encouraging picture. In all countries a majority of voters is expected to support an increase in the retirement age. In fact aging tends to decrease the individuals lifetime income—due to the presence of a large social security system whose profitability will largely drop—while lower pension benefits will reduce the incentives to retire early. These two effects will hence induce the electors to postpone retirement.

A key message of the political economy approach of this book is that an aging society leads to large increases in pension spending, because of the political accountability of the policy-makers. Policy-makers will likely determine the pension policy in order to favor their aging electorate and hence to increase the probability of being re-elected. Delegating part of the responsibility for the pension policies to a supranational institution, such as the European Commission, could help relaxing these political constraints, as the national policy-makers could blame the supranational institution for any unpopular reforms.

The nonelected supranational institution could thus give voice—
and votes—to young or yet to be born individuals who will largely
be affected by the future consequences of the current policies. Yet
the recent failure to approve the European constitution in the
Dutch and French referenda shows the drawback of this strategy:
when given the opportunity, voters may oppose this economic policy
delegation.

After this brief introduction, chapter 2 provides a detailed overview
of the social security systems in six countries—France, Germany, Italy,
Spain, the United Kingdom, and the United States—that encompasses
their main institutional features, the reform measures implemented in
the last decade, a discussion of the OECD official pension spending
projection and an analysis of a labor market trend—early retirement—
typically induced by the design of the system. This chapter includes
also a brief overview of the main aspects of population aging common
to the six countries and of its impact on the political representation.
Chapter 3 summarizes the main economic and political theories of welfare state expansion, and discusses the crucial differences between
theories of expansion and of retrenchment. Chapter 4 provides a
formal definition of political sustainability, describes the theoretical
framework used throughout the book and discusses the calibration
and simulation issues, whose results are then presented in chapter 11.
Chapters 5 to 10 address the political sustainability of social security in
each of the six countries.

Each chapter begins with a brief historical detour and a detailed description of the system, then reports on the country's demographic
dynamics, and finally concentrates on the main focus of this book, by
examining how the system is expected to change to retain its political
sustainability in 2050. Most chapters include an analysis of recent
reforms, based on the theoretical framework presented in this book,
but also on alternative theories. Chapter 7 on Italy devotes space to
explaining the Amato and Dini reforms of the nineties, and to examine
their effects on the long-run political sustainability of the system.
Chapter 8 discusses a "silent" reform of the Spanish system perhaps
agreed upon in the Pacto de Toledo. Chapter 9, on the United Kingdom, provides an evaluation of the 1999 Blair reform, which substituted the earning related pension scheme (SERPS) with a nearly flat
benefit scheme (S2P), while chapter 10 discusses some of the redistributive feature of the US social security system and the recent Bush re-

form plan. Finally, chapter 11 provides a comparison of the simulated changes in the social security systems of these six countries, which will be needed to retain the support of a majority of the aging electorate. A discussion of the political feasibility of the main policy implications arising from the simulations—postponing retirement age—and of the opportunity of delegating pension policies to a supranational authority concludes chapter 11.

2

Crucial Features of the Social Security Debate: A Cross-country Analysis

Most industrialized countries feature an unfunded social security system that collects contributions from the workers' labor income and uses the revenue to provide pension benefits to current retirees. The actual size and generosity of these programs differ widely across countries—even at comparable stage of economic development: in 2000, pension spending ranged from 4.3 percent of GDP in the United Kingdom to 14.2 percent in Italy.

The first section of this chapter presents a brief comparison of the unfunded (or pay-as-you-go) social security systems in six countries—France, Germany, Italy, Spain, the United Kingdom, and the United States. Their main characteristics are summarized along five dimensions: social security contribution rate, effective and statutory retirement age, pension's eligibility requirement, pension benefits' calculation criteria, and benefits' indexation method. A concise overview of the more recent pension reform measures—aimed at restoring financial sustainability in these countries—is also provided.

Although most social security systems date back at least to the post–World War II period, they have recently taken center stage in the public debate, with economists, media, and policy-makers closely scrutinizing their financial solvency under population aging. The current demographic process has in fact a direct effect on pension programs, by increasing the proportion of recipients from the system—the retirees—while reducing the proportion of contributors—the workers. Section 2.2 shows the forecasted demographic trends for these six countries, by placing a special emphasis on the role of the old age dependency ratio—the ratio of elderly individuals to young and adult individuals—as a synthetic indicator of the impact of aging on the demographic balance of unfunded pension systems.

Over the last three decades population aging has been accompanied, in several OECD countries, by a dramatic fall in the labor force participation of elderly workers (aged between 60 and 64 years) but also by a substantial decrease among younger workers (aged between 55 and 59 years). The magnitude of this phenomenon varies extensively across countries, being particularly large in France and Italy—where the participation rate of men aged 60 to 64 has decreased respectively from more than 70 percent in 1960 to less than 20 percent in 2000 and from around 60 percent to around 30 percent—but less remarkable in the United Kingdom and the United States. A consequence of these labor market trends is the reduction of the average effective retirement age, which in turn exacerbates the direct impact of aging on the demographic balance of the PAYG social security systems. Yet these early exits from the labor market are known to depend—at least in part— on the incentives provided by the pension system through generous early retirement provisions (see Gruber and Wise 1999). Hence the designs of the pension systems contribute to their own financial distress. Section 2.3 introduces a relative measure of the relevance of these effects by computing the difference between the pension dependency ratio—defined as the ratio between actual workers and retirees—and the old age dependency ratio.

Because of the joint effect of an aging society and labor market trends, under current social security rules, the amount of collected revenue will eventually fall short of the entitled pension benefits in several countries. Then either a greater financial burden is placed on the working generations or pension benefits are cut. Several international institutions—such as the World Bank (1994) and the European Commission (2003)—have provided detailed normative analysis with the aim of designing sensible reform measures to cope with the aging process. The desiderata is a PAYG pension system that is financially sound vis-à-vis the expected demographic dynamics, that retains economic efficiency by avoiding waste of resources and minimizing individual distortions, and that is equitable. Additionally the system should be designed to hedge demographic, economic and political risks. Yet these reforms may prove difficult to undertake, as also the relevant political actors are aging. The last section in this chapter discusses the aging of the voters. The theoretical framework to analyze the political sustainability of social security in graying societies will be introduced in the next two chapters.

2.1   A Comparison of PAYG Social Security Systems

Although unfunded social security systems represent a pervasive institution, their characteristics vary extensively across countries. In France,
Germany, Italy, and Spain, a large PAYG system covers all employed
individuals, and provides them with more than 75 percent of their total
retirement income. In the United Kingdom and the United States, this
first pillar of the pension system is less sizeable (accounting respectively for 65 percent of retirees' income in the United Kingdom and 45
percent in the United States); and additional retirement income stems
from occupational and private pension plans. In the United Kingdom,
for instance, employees may choose to partially opt out of the public
unfunded system to join funded occupational schemes or private
personal pension funds. In the other countries, funded schemes—
occupational and private plans—only exist in an embryonic form.

2.1.1   Institutional Characteristics

Despite sharing some underlying common elements, PAYG social security systems differ along several dimensions, such as contribution
rates, benefit formula, benefit indexation, eligibility requirements and
official retirement age. Table 2.1 summarizes the main features of
PAYG schemes around the year 2000 for these six countries.

Contribution Rates   Italy has the highest contribution rate—32.7 percent of earnings (8.89 percent paid by the insured person and 23.81
percent by the employer)—followed by Spain with 28.3 percent (4.7
percent paid by the insured person and 23.6 percent by the employer).
France, Germany, Spain, and the United States have a ceiling on the
taxable labor earnings. The contribution rates are 19.5 percent in Germany (equally levied on employers and employees) and 14.75 percent
(8.2 percent paid by the employers and 6.55 percent by the employees)
of insurable earnings plus 1.6 percent of total payroll for the main system (*régime général*) in France.[1] The United States and the United Kingdom enjoy lower contribution rates. In the United States, the tax rate is
12.4 percent of the income below a ceiling (equally levied on employer
and employee). In the United Kingdom, the primary national insurance contribution rate, due by the employee, is 10 percent of the income between the Primary Threshold (GBP 87 per week in 2001) and
the Upper Earnings Limit (GBP 575 per week), and it is reduced to 8.4

Table 2.1
Principal features of the PAYG social security systems

Country	Contribution rate	Benefits formula and indexation	Eligibility requirements	Official retirement age
France	*Régime général* (main scheme): 14.75% (8.2% by the employers and 6.55% by the employees) below the social security ceiling plus 1.6% on the entire salary (due by the employers) Complementary mandatory schemes: ARRCO: 6% (plus a temporary 1.5% to achieve financial balance) below a ceiling for managers and professional staffs, below 3 times the ceiling for other employees ($\frac{3}{5}$ due by the employers and $\frac{2}{5}$ by the employees) Above the social security ceiling (or 3 times the ceiling): between 15 and 20% depending on the firm's longevity	*Régime général* pension: $T \times (N/150) \times R$ T = replacement rate, based on the age of the insured person and the number of years of contribution; ranges between 25 and 50% N = number of quarters of contribution to the scheme; maximum 150 R = reference wage; equal to the average annual wage below the ceiling over the 19 best years (to become 25 in 2008) Complementary schemes (AGIRC and ARRCO): old age benefit is determined by the accumulation of points during the working life *Indexation: consumer price index*	*Régime général*: Eligibility depends on payment of at least one-quarter of contributions (acquired when the earnings equal at least the amount of 200 hours of the minimum wage)	*Régime général*: 60 years, but several early retirement programs exist ARRCO and AGIRC: 65 years Early retirement: 55 years, without penalizations if the conditions to retire with the maximum pension in the *régime général* are satisfied

	Contributions	Pension formula	Qualifying conditions	Retirement age
	AGIRC: 16% (plus a temporary 4% to achieve financial balance) applied on income between the ceiling and 8 times the ceiling (12.5% due by the employers and 7.5% by the employees up to 4 times the ceiling; afterwards the split is contracted upon)			
Germany	19.5%, equally levied on employers and on employees, below a social security ceiling	Pension: $PEP \times C \times AR$ PEP: personal earnings point, depends on number of years of contribution and on the individual's wage level relative to the average wage in the economy C: adjustment factor, depends on pension type and retirement age AR: average current pension value—corresponding to the monthly pension paid to an average earner for each insured year *Indexation: gross wage growth*	Minimum 5 years of contributions	Normal retirement age: 65 years Early retirement: 63 years old (60 for severely handicapped) after 35 years of service Women: 60 years with 180 months of contributions

Table 2.1
(continued)

Country	Contribution rate	Benefits formula and indexation	Eligibility requirements	Official retirement age
Italy	32.7%, of which 8.89% due by the insured person and 23.81% by the employer	Category 1 (persons whose insurance period started after January 1, 1996): pension benefits are calculated as 33% (20% for the self-employed) of taxable base income, reevaluated on annual basis, multiplied by a conversion coefficient Category 2 (persons with more than 18 years of contributions at December 31, 1995): pension benefits are equal to 2% of reference wage (equal to the average wage in the 5 years before retirement) times the number of years of contributions Category 3 (all others): pro-quota combination of the two schemes *Indexation: consumer price index*	*Old age pension* Category 1: 57 years old and 5 years of contributions Category 2: 65 years old (men)/60 (woman) and 15 years of contributions prior to 1992 Category 3: 65 years old (men) or 60 (woman) and 20 years of contributions prior to 2001 *Seniority pensions*: 57 years old and 35 years of contributions or 37 years of contributions, regardless of the age (increase to 40 by 2008)	New system: 57–65 years (amount of benefit decreases for lower retirement ages)

| Spain | 28.3% of the earnings between a floor and a ceiling, of which 4.7% due by the insured person and 23.6% by the employer | Pension: $R \times T$
R = reference wage, equals the average of social security contribution base during the 15 years prior to retirement
T = replacement rate, equal to 50% for the first 15 years of contributions, plus 3% for each year between 16 and 25, and 2% for each year beginning with the 26th, up to 100% (since 2002, this amount may exceed 100% for those who retire at 66 or later with at least 35 years of contributions)
Indexation: consumer price index | 15 years of contributions (of which at least 2 during the 8 years immediately before retirement); 35 years of contributions for a full retirement pension | Retirement age: 65 years
Transitory measure: persons insured under the system abolished in 1967 may retire at 60

Special early retirement provisions for workers in particular sectors and professions |

Table 2.1
(continued)

Country	Contribution rate	Benefits formula and indexation	Eligibility requirements	Official retirement age
United Kingdom	Primary national insurance contribution rate of 10% of income between the Primary Threshold and the Upper Earnings Limit, due by the employee; reduced to 8.4% if the insured person opts out of SERPS Secondary national insurance contribution rate of 12.2% for the earnings above the Secondary Threshold, due by the employer; rebated by 3% if the employee opts out of SERPS	BSP (basic state pension): flat rate pension related only to the contributory years; maximum level of BSP achieved (for a man) with 44 years of contributions SERPS (state earning related pension system): pension benefit equal to the average indexed surplus earnings (after 1978) between the lower and upper earnings limit multiplied by the number of valid contribution years and by an accrual rate of 1.25% per year (for persons retiring after April 2000, the accrual rate is reduces to 1% for a 10 years transitional period) *Indexation: consumer prices legislated annually*	BSP: 11–12 years of contributions SERPS: earnings above the lower earning limit (LEL) for at least one year since April 1978	65 years old for men and 60 for women (to be raised to 65 between 2010 and 2020). No early retirement. Pension increases of 7.5% yearly if pension age is deferred

United States	12.4% of wage income up to a ceiling, equally shared by employee and employer for OASDI	Pension benefits based on the indexed average earnings over 35 years (AIME) and on a redistributive formula, according to which the normal monthly pension benefits (PIA) are equal to the sum of 90% of the AIME below a lower bend point, of 32% of the AIME between the bend points and of 15% of the AIME above the higher bend point *Indexation: consumer price index*	10 years of contributions and minimum retirement age	Retirement age: 65 years (62 for reduced benefits); postponing retirement from 65 up to 70 provides delayed retirement credits

Sources: Social Security Administration data available at ⟨www.ssa.org⟩, EC DG Employment and Social Affairs (2002), and EC Economic Policy Committee (2000).

percent if a person "opts out" of the second tier of the public system. The secondary national insurance contribution rate, due by the employer, is equal to 12.2 percent for the earnings above the Secondary Threshold (GBP 87 per week) and is rebated by 3 percent if the employee opts out.

Pension Benefits and Eligibility   All countries—with the exception of Italy after the 1995 Dini reform—feature a defined benefit PAYG system. Benefits are based on the number of years of contributions and on a reference wage, which typically depends on the worker's past wages. However, even countries with a defined benefit system differ in how pensions relate to the reference wage and in how this reference wage is obtained. France, Germany, and Spain feature a tight link between wages and benefits. In these so-called Bismarckian systems, the benefit formula is constructed so as to entitle the retirees to a pension income that replaces a certain share of their previous labor income. This replacement rate—namely the proportion of the last wage income paid out as pension benefit—may depend on the number of years of contributions, but it is typically not related to the retiree's lifetime income. In these schemes the reference wage plays a crucial role in the pension benefit calculation. In France, the reference wage corresponds to the average annual salary, capped by the social security ceiling, calculated over the 19 best years (they will become 25 by 2008). In Spain, the reference wage is taken to be the sum of the wage during the 180 months prior to retirement divided by 210. The pension benefit replaces 50 percent of this amount if the contribution period is 15 years, plus 3 percent for each additional year between 16 and 25 and 2 percent for each year from the 26th up to a maximum replacement rate[2] of 100 percent. In Germany, individual's pension benefits are obtained as the product between the average current pension value—corresponding to the monthly pension paid to an average earner for each insured year—and the individual's personal earning points. The earning points depend on the number of years of contribution and on the individual's wage relatively to the average wage in the economy.

The United Kingdom has a redistributive system (see Disney 2004). The basic state pension is not related to any reference wage; it depends on the number of years of contribution. A second tier of the British public pension—the state earning related pension system (SERPS) until 2002 and the state second pension (S2P)—is linked to the level of earnings, though it retains an element of intragenerational redistribution. Also the United States have a redistributive system, albeit not a pure one, since the reference wage is calculated as the average earnings during 35 years of contributions. A redistributive formula is applied to reduce the high lifetime earners' pension benefits.

Italy presents a different scenario. In 1995 the system switched from a (Bismarckian) defined benefit formula, in which pension benefits are based on the worker's average earnings during his or her entire career, to a notional defined contribution scheme, in which pension benefits are instead linked to some notional returns on the worker's social security contributions. After this reform, pension entitlements began to be calculated as 33 percent of labor earnings revaluated on annual basis and multiplied by a transformation coefficient, which depends on the average longevity and on the retirement age. This new scheme applies entirely to the workers who joined the system after January 1996, and only pro-quota to those who had less than 18 years of contributions in December 1996. The old formula continues to apply to the remaining (elderly) workers.

At the turn of the twenty-first century, all countries but Germany indexed their pension benefits to inflation. In Germany, benefits were instead indexed to net wage growth, though this adjustment was temporarily suspended in 2000 and 2001. In 2004, however, a new indexation criterion was introduced—on a proposal formulated by the Rürup Commission—which linked indexation to the pension dependency ratio, calculated as the ratio between actual retirees and workers, in an attempt to retain the advantages of wage indexation, while coping with the aging process.

Eligibility to old age pension benefits may depend on the years of contributions and/or on a minimum retirement age. The minimum contribution period varies from one quarter in France to 20 years in Italy (5 for the new workers who joined the system in 1996). It is equal to 5 years in Germany, 15 in Spain, 11 to 12 in the United Kingdom (for the state pension) and 10 in the United States.

Retirement Age   All countries feature an official retirement age, when people are allowed—indeed sometimes forced—to exit the labor market and receive their pension benefits: 60 years in France, 65 in Germany, from 57 to 65 in Italy under the notional defined contribution system[3] introduced by the Dini reform, 65 in Spain, 65 for men and 60 for women in the United Kingdom, and 65 in the United States. Most countries have also early retirement provisions that allow workers to retire before the official age on a reduced pension benefit.

2.1.2 Recent Reforms

The challenges of a graying population led several OECD countries to implement some reforms of their social security systems—or at least to legislate them, since their actual complete phase-in will only occur after long transition periods. Most of the reforms have been "parametric," to the extent that the unfunded nature of the system has not been modified. According to the OECD (2002), the recent measures have pursued three main objectives: (1) a rise of the effective retirement age, through a reduction of the incentive to retire early and an increase in the labor market employability of elderly workers, (2) a reduction of the pension benefits—in order to improve the financial sustainability of the systems—through their indexation to prices, rather than to wages, and through changes in the benefits calculation formulas, and (3) an increase of the private pension arrangements aimed at modifying the current mix of public-private provision of retirement income, through tax incentives to private pension contributions and the establishment of new regulations for the relevant financial institutions.

Table 2.2 summarizes the main reforms in these six countries over the last ten years. These reform measures aimed at postponing the retirement age—France (2003), Germany (1992, 1997, and the 2003 proposal), Italy (1992, 1995, and 2004), Spain (1999), and the United Kingdom (1986)—and at developing a private second pillar (occupation funds) and a third pillar (individual funds). The latter type of reforms has characterized virtually all countries. Complementary—albeit unfunded—pension schemes already existed in France (Arrco and Agirc), and were strongly regulated in 1997. In Germany, the 2001 Pension Reform Act (also known as the Riester reform) provided additional advantages in the tax treatment of pension funds. In Italy, the 1992 Amato reform established occupational schemes, while subsequent legislative interventions introduced special tax treatments for nonmandatory funded pensions (their returns are taxed at 11 percent, rather than the standard 12.5 percent on returns from other financial activities) in 2000 and facilitated the investment of an end-of-career severance payment (TFR or "trattamento di fine rapporto") into occupational pension plans in 2004. Despite the existence of a well-

Table 2.2
Recent reform measures

Country	Year	Reforms
France	1993	Benefit calculation: reference wage's base period extended from 10 to 25 years Contribution period: extension to access full pension from 37.5 years to 40 years Benefit indexation: from wage to price indexation
	1997 Thomas Law	Framework for second pillar: contribution to optional private retirement funds exempted from income taxation and social security contributions (later suspended by the Jospin government)
	1998	Partial retirement: elderly workers may opt to reduce their working hours until reaching retirement age in exchange for a partial pension Retirement age: reduction of the disincentives for early retirement and introduction of incentives to postpone retirement
	2003 Fillon reform	Contribution period: extension to access full pension from 40 years to 41 in 2012 and to 42 in 2020 Benefit indexation: possibility of a *coupe de pouce*—one time increase every three years Private plans: Introduction of voluntary individual pension plans with tax incentives
Germany	1992	Retirement age: progressive increase to 65 for both men and women; early retirement at 62 with actuarial adjustments Benefit indexation: net income indexation
	1997 Pension Reform Law (Blum reform)	Eligibility: restricted accrual of pension rights not based on contributions Benefit calculation: replacement rate reduced from 70 to 67% (in 30 years) Pension funding: more transfers from the federal budget covered by higher VAT rate
	1999	Suspension of the Pension Reform Law Benefit indexation: temporary shift from net wages to inflation
	2001 Old Age Provision Act (Riester reform)	Introduction of personal pension plans through subsidies and tax breaks Eligibility: establishment of individual right of workers to an occupational pension Benefit calculation: replacement ratio decreases from 70 to 67%
	2004	Benefit indexation: introduction of a "sustainability factor" linking pension benefits to the system dependency ratio

Table 2.2
(continued)

Country	Year	Reforms
Italy	1992 Amato reform	Introduction of occupational private schemes (with tax incentives) Retirement age: increase from 55 to 60 for women and 60 to 65 for men Benefit calculation: reference wage's calculation period gradually increased to the entire working career Eligibility: minimum contribution period to obtain a pension increased from 15 to 20 years Benefit indexation: from wages to inflation
	1995 Dini reform	Retirement age: flexible, from 57 to 65 for both men and women but with penalties for early retirement Benefit calculation: from defined benefit to notional defined contribution (see table 2.1) Eligibility for seniority pension: to be increased to 40 years of contributions or 35 if aged 57 by 2008 Fiscal incentives for contributions to private pension funds
	1997 Prodi reform	Retirement age: increase in the early retirement age Harmonization of public and private pension regimes and increase in pension contributions paid by the self-employed Temporary measures: postponement of access to early retirement benefits and suspension of inflation adjustment for high pensions Eligibility for seniority pensions: more stringent requirement Increase of contributions for self-employed workers and other categories Increase of the amount of social and minimum pensions Tax deductions for pensioners with lower income Tax incentives to convert the TFR (end-of-career severance payment) into supplementary pensions
	2000	Tax incentives on pension funds' returns (taxed at 11% instead of the standard 12.5% for returns of financial activities) and for TFR to be invested in pension funds
	2004	Retirement age: increase in the minimum retirement for the individuals still under the DB scheme to 60 years beginning in 2008 Automatic investment of the TFR in pension funds
Spain	1997 Toledo Pact	Benefit calculation: gradual extension from 8 to the 15 years of the time period over which the reference wage for the pension benefits is computed Benefit Indexation: automatic price indexation Reserve fund built with contribution surplus Retirement age: reduction of the incentives to retire early

Table 2.2
(continued)

Country	Year	Reforms
	1999	Retirement age: new partial retirement scheme aimed at keeping older workers on the job
	2000	Creation of a fund for the transition to a mixed system combining PAYG and funded elements
United Kingdom	1986	Retirement age: flexibility up to 70 years Benefit calculation: for the public earnings related schemes, reference wage from the average wage over 20 years to the entire working carrier Benefit calculation: for the public earnings related schemes, replacement rate from 25 to 20%
	1995 Pension Act	Retirement age: State pension retirement age gradually increased for females from 60 to 65 years Introduction of a personal pension and regulation of the occupational schemes
	1999–2002 Welfare Reform and Pension Act	Introduction of minimum income guarantee and of a pension credit aimed at rewarding savings Benefit calculation: SERPS replaced by the new state second pension (S2P) to provide higher transfers to low-income individuals Introduction of the new stakeholder pension scheme (SPSs) for middle-income earners with no existing private pension provision
United States		No significant reforms

Sources: EC DG Employment and Social Affairs (2002), Economic Policy Committee (2002), and Rodolfo Debenedetti Foundation Report (2000).

developed second pillar, in 1986, the United Kingdom passed a Pension Act that introduced the possibility of opting out of the second tier of the state pension system and of contributing to personal pension funds.

In addition to these reform measures, there has been a common trend to switch from wage to price indexation of pension benefits. Other, more limited reforms led to small increases in the contributory tax rates (Germany), in the years of contributions and in the reference salary period to compute pension benefits (France, Spain, Italy with the 1992 Amato reform). More comprehensive measures have instead been introduced in Italy in 1995 with the Dini reform, which radically modified the benefit formula from defined benefit to notional defined contribution.

Table 2.3
Official projections of old age pension spending over GDP

| | | | Contributions to changes from 2000 to 2050 | | | |
| | | | Aging | Policy measures | | |
Country	2000	2050	Old age dependency ratio	Employment rate	Benefit formula	Eligibility
France	12.1	15.9	7.6	−0.5	−3.4	0.4
Germany	11.8	16.8	6.4	−0.7	−2.7	2.1
Italy	14.2	13.9	10.1	−3.2	−5.5	−1.5
Spain	9.4	17.4	8.6	−2.6	0	2
United Kingdom	4.3	3.6	1.7	0.1	−2.5	0.1
United States	4.4	6.2	2.4	−0.1	−0.2	−0.3

Source: OECD (2002).

2.1.3 Official Projections

An official assessment of the long run financial sustainability of the system, and hence of the need for further reforms, has been carried out in a joint effort by the European Commission and the OECD—together with the member countries. The aim of the project was to produce projections of pension spending as percentage of GDP for the next fifty years. Table 2.3 shows the official projections provided by each country's institutions, as reported in OECD (2002). This study evaluates several effects: the demographic dynamics, namely the increase in the ratio of recipients from the system—the retirees—to contributors; the employment rate, with a particular emphasis on the goal in terms of employment of the elderly (a 70 percent employment rate for workers above 50 years old) agreed upon by the country members at the Lisbon meetings; and the policy measures, with specific reference to the policy reforms being legislated in the 1990s, and yet to be entirely implemented.

Italy stands out as the most striking case: despite featuring the largest demographic effect—capable of increasing spending by 10 percent of GDP—pension expenditure is expected to decrease in the year 2050, due to the projected increase in the employment rate of elderly workers and to the positive impact of the retrenching measures introduced by the Amato-Dini reforms. Also the United Kingdom is expected to reduce its pension spending, as policy measures counterbalance a mild aging effect. For all other countries, an increase in the amount of

Table 2.4
Demographic trends

Country	Fertility rate		Life expectancy at birth (males)		Life expectancy at birth (females)		Share of very elderly[a]	
	2000	2050	2000	2050	2000	2050	2000	2050
France	1.73	1.8	74.8	80	82.8	87	3.58	10.04
Germany	1.4	1.5	74.7	80	80.8	85	3.53	11.28
Italy	1.22	1.5	75.5	81	82.0	86	3.89	13.00
Spain	1.19	1.5	74.9	79	82.1	85	3.68	10.96
United Kingdom	1.72	1.8	75.2	80	80.0	85	3.92	9.16
United States	2.05	1.95	73.9	79.1	79.6	83.5	3.30	7.82
OECD[b]	1.55	1.66	74.1	79.3	80.6	84.7	n.a.	n.a.

Sources: OECD (2002) Health Data, and EC (2000).
Note: Fertility rate is the number of children per every woman between 18 and 45 years.
a. Individuals aged 80 years old or more.
b. Average of main OECD countries.

resources devoted to pensions is expected. In Spain, the strong demographic effect is even magnified by a policy that extends pension eligibility, while in Germany and France reform measures are not sufficient to neutralize the aging problem. Not surprisingly, the United States are expected to feature a lower increase in spending than an average of the OECD countries.

According to these official projections, Italy and the United Kingdom do not need additional reform measures to limit their pension spending, whereas in France, Germany, and Spain, effective reforms ought to be implemented in order to mitigate the increase in pension spending. The next chapters will address a complementary issue, by analyzing how political constraints may shape size and generosity of these systems.

2.2   Demographic Trends: Population Aging

The current aging problem is the consequence of an increase in life expectancy and a decrease in fertility rates. This is a characteristic common to all countries in the sample. However, while further longevity gains are expected, fertility rates should slightly recover. Table 2.4 summarizes these demographic trends. The increase in longevity is a pervasive feature, with little cross-country variation. In fact the life expectancy at birth for the year 2050 is forecasted to range between 79

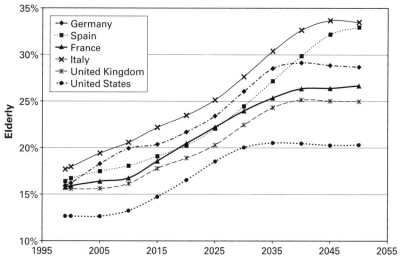

Figure 2.1
Share of elderly in the total population (Sources: Eurostat and US Census)

years in Spain and 81 years in Italy for males; and between 83.5 years in the United States and 87 years in France for females. Fertility rates in 2050 are instead expected to vary more widely, from 1.5 children for woman in the low-fertility countries (Germany, Italy and Spain) to two children on average in the United States.

Higher longevity and lower fertility produce a substantial increase of the share of elderly people in a population. As shown in figure 2.1, the proportion of elderly individuals (aged 65 years or more) over the total population will rapidly increase until 2035, and will remain constant or increase at a lower pace thereafter. The aging problem will be particularly large in Germany, Italy, and Spain, where by the year 2050 individuals aged 80 years or more will account for more than 11 percent of the total population, but less dramatic in the United Kingdom and the United States.

A graying population puts pressure on the functioning of a PAYG social security system, by modifying the relative proportion between contributors—the workers—and recipients from the system—the retirees. The magnitude of this effect may be quantified by the changes in the old age dependency ratio, which is defined as the ratio of persons aged 65 years or more to the persons aged between 20 and 64 years. Variations in this ratio characterize the demographic dynamics;

Table 2.5
Dependency ratios and retirement ages

Country	Old age dependency ratio		Effective retirement age	Pension dependency ratio[a]		Required retirement age[b]
	2000	2050	2000	2000	2050	2050
France	25.9	48.8	58	40.4	76.1	68
Germany	25.0	51.5	61	36.0	67.7	70
Italy	27.9	64.5	59	44.0	91.7	71
Spain	26.0	63.4	61	34.2	80.2	73
United Kingdom	25.3	44.3	63	29.2	50.9	71
United States	20.5	36.3	63	23.4	41.5	68

Source: Eurostat, US Census, and EC (2000, 2003).
a. The pension dependency ratio is equal to the ratio of retirees to workers, with age division being the effective retirement age in 2000.
b. This is the retirement age required to keep the pension dependency ratio at its 2000 level.

however, they do not exactly capture the changes in the proportion of retirees per worker. If all individuals were covered by the social security system, all workers retired at age 65 and every individual in working age was employed, the old age dependency ratio would coincide with the ratio of retirees to workers—the pension dependency ratio. Yet occupational decisions, unemployment and early retirement behavior create a wedge between these two measures (see the next section). Despite these shortcomings the old age dependency ratio still represents a useful measure to isolate the demographic effect.

According to OECD projections, the average old age dependency ratio in the OECD countries will increase from 23.8 percent in the year 2000–corresponding to more than four people in working age for every elderly individual–to 49.9 percent in 2050–amounting to only two individuals in working age for every elderly person. This demographic process is expected to differ across countries (see table 2.5): Spain and Italy will experience the largest rise in the dependency ratio, France and Germany will be close to the OECD average, while the United Kingdom and the United States will be well below average.

2.3   Labor Market Trends: Early Retirement

In several countries, the population aging problem has been accompanied by a dramatic reduction in the labor force participation of middle

Table 2.6
Labor force participation of males aged 55 to 64 years

Country	1960	1970	1980	1990	2000
France	80.3	75.4	68.5	45.8	41.1
Germany	83.0	82.2	65.5	60.5	55.2
Italy[a]	60.5	48.2	39.6	36.0	31.4
Spain	n.a.	84.2	75.7	62.4	60.3
United Kingdom	94.2	91.3	81.8	68.1	63.3
United States	84.7	80.7	71.2	67.8	67.3

Source: OECD, Labor market statistics at ⟨www.oecd.org⟩.
a. Males aged 60 to 64.

aged and elderly workers. This phenomenon has been particularly strong in France and Italy, where in 2000 participation rates fell well below 50 percent, but less remarkable in other countries, such as Spain, the United Kingdom, and the United States (see table 2.6).

These labor market trends have important effects on social security systems, which can be characterized by a reduction in the average effective retirement age (see Latulippe 1996), or in the average age of transition to inactivity (see Blöndal and Scarpetta 1998). In particular, Latulippe (1996) calculates that the average retirement age for males in the OECD countries dropped from 67.9 years in 1950 to 61.7 in 1990. Blöndal and Scarpetta (1998) and more recently Duval (2003) obtain similar results. According to their estimates, the transition from work into inactivity of a French male worker occurred on average at age 66.1 in 1950, while already at age 59.2 in 1995. Although the legal retirement age—when elderly workers are required to exit the labor market and collect their pensions—has not been lowered in the last few decades, the effective retirement age has indeed fallen.

A comprehensive study on eleven OECD countries edited by Gruber and Wise (1999) suggests that the generous early retirement provisions featured by several social security systems are largely responsible for these labor market trends. Gruber and Wise (1999) and Blöndal and Scarpetta (1998) identified some crucial features of early retirement schemes that are strongly related to the exit of the elderly workers from the labor market. Unsurprisingly, they show that the statutory early and normal retirement age are important determinants of the timing of the workers' exit decision. In most OECD countries the (conditional) probability of a male worker to exit the labor force—the so-called hazard rate—peaks at the early and at the normal retirement age, as most individuals leave the labor market as soon as they are entitled to collect a pension benefit.

Both studies emphasize that in several countries (Germany, Sweden, the Netherlands), these early exits do not follow the official route of early retirement schemes, but rather alternative programs, such as disability or unemployment benefits—whose eligibility has often been made contingent on labor market conditions. Gruber and Wise (1999) report the proportion of males drawing disability or unemployment benefits at age 59—hence typically below the early retirement age—to be 21 percent in France, 24 percent in Sweden, 27 percent in the Netherlands, 33 percent in the United Kingdom, and 37 percent in Germany. In contrast, it is only about 12 percent in Japan and the United States.

This retirement behavior may be due to workers' bad health status, or may simply be driven by a large valuation of their leisure by the elderly, or by adverse employment perspectives. Yet Gruber and Wise (1999) and Blöndal and Scarpetta (1998) identify another crucial economic determinant of this retirement behavior: the existence of a large implicit tax imposed on continuing to work after the early retirement age. By this evidence, workers' decision to retire early represents their optimal response to the economic incentives provided by the social security system.

Because of the widespread use of these early retirement provisions, the old age dependency ratio—a demographic indicator—differs quite dramatically from the pension dependency ratio (the ratio of retirees to workers). The pension dependency ratio represents a synthetic measure of the balance between contributors and beneficiaries in an unfunded social security system. Table 2.5 reports the old age dependency ratio and the pension dependency ratio, which is calculated by using the 2000 effective retirement age (according to the European Commission, 2003) to partition the population between workers and retirees.[4] Clearly, countries with a low effective retirement age, such as France and Italy, feature the largest difference between the old age and the pension dependency ratio. For instance, in France the old age dependency ratio suggested the existence of one elderly person for every four young and middle aged individuals. Yet, if retirement decisions are accounted for, the actual proportion becomes two retirees for every five workers.

These data show how early retirement provisions exacerbate the impact of aging on the demographic balance of the PAYG social security systems, but are also suggestive of some possible reform measures. Postponing retirement in fact goes in the direction of counterbalancing the effect of aging, by reducing the ratio of retirees to workers. Table 2.5 reports the retirement age needed in every country to keep the pension dependency ratio at its 2000 level. The required increases in the retirement age are sizable, as they range from five years in the United States to twelve years in Italy and Spain—the two fastest aging countries.

Another measure of the impact of this early retirement behavior on the financial sustainability of the social security system is provided by the average length of the retirement period. Since longevity has increased, while the effective retirement age has decreased, the average number of years spent in retirement—and hence receiving a pension benefit—has expanded over time. Figure 2.2 suggests that the combined effect of longevity gains and early retirement have dramatically expanded the average length of retirement—defined as the difference between the average longevity computed at age 60 and the effective retirement age—hence requiring more resources to be devoted to pension spending.

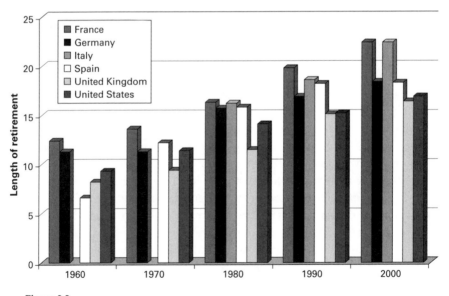

Figure 2.2
Average length of retirement (Sources: Latulippe 1996 and OECD 2002)

2.4   Political Representation in an Aging Society

As a population ages, so do the electorate and other relevant political players, such as the unions' members. In democracies population aging leads to an increase in the political representation of the elderly, who gather a larger share of votes. As politicians seek re-election—in order to pursue their ideologies or to enjoy some pecuniary or ego rent from being in office—incumbents may use their role as policy-makers to increase their probability of re-election. In particular, policy-makers will try to address the needs of this crucial voting group—the elderly—with generous social security policies. Aging will thus increase the relevance of pension spending on the political agenda.

The political influence of the elderly is magnified by their homogeneous preferences in terms of economic policies. In fact, while young and middle-aged individuals typically differ along several dimensions, such as employment status, economic conditions (income and wealth), or family profiles, and hence have conflicting preferences over many economic policies, all elderly individuals—if retired—care mostly about social security issues. The elderly are single-minded (see Mulligan and Sala-i-Martin 1999): they are all concerned about their pension benefits, which, for a majority of retirees, represent the largest—if not the unique—source of income. Due to these homogeneous preferences, elderly individuals are a crucial target for politicians. Their votes can easily be swayed with appropriate pension policies (see Profeta 2002a).

Furthermore the elderly individual voting behavior contributes to augment their political relevance. In several countries, in fact, elderly voters tend to have higher turnout rates at elections—defined as the percentage of people who actually vote among those who are entitled to—than the young. This voting behavior may be justified by lower opportunity cost of voting for the elderly, who enjoy more free time, or by their single-mindedness, which increases the elderly's willingness to be represented politically. Since the aggregate impact of this voting pattern may be sizeable, population aging may lead to a disproportionate political representation of the elderly. Table 2.7 shows that in the United States the turnout rate among individuals aged 60 to 69 years is twice as high as among the young (18 to 29 years); however, significant differences appear also in other countries, such as France, where the turnout rate among the elderly (60 to 69 years) is almost 50 percent higher than that among the young (18 to 29 years).

Table 2.7
Turnout rate at elections by age

Voters' age	France	Germany	Italy	Spain	United Kingdom	United States
18–29	63.2%	84.8%	95.4%	80.6%	81.0%	35.6%
30–39	79.8%	90.5%	97.0%	85.1%	88.4%	50.0%
40–49	83.9%	92.1%	97.8%	89.9%	89.4%	58.7%
50–59	86.4%	93.6%	98.7%	88.8%	88.7%	64.5%
60–69	91.9%	93.0%	96.7%	90.5%	90.0%	69.2%
70 and over	93.6%	93.4%	89.3%	83.4%	89.4%	66.8%

Source: IDEA (1999) and US Census at ⟨www.census.gov⟩.
Notes: Turnout rates correspond to the percentage of voters among the entitled individuals. For the United States, 1996 presidential election data; for EU countries, survey data.

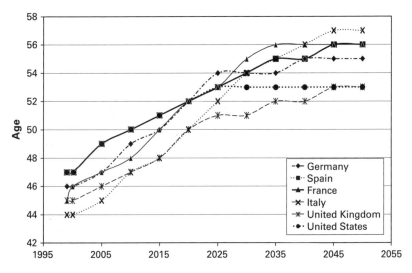

Figure 2.3
Median age among voters (Sources: IDEA 1999, Eurostat, US Census, and author's calculation)

A synthetic measure of the aging of the electors is given by the median age among the voters. In 2000 the median age among the voters—adjusted for the different turnout rates at election by age—ranged between 44 years in Spain and 47 years in France and the United States. The evolution over time of the median age among voters is displayed in figure 2.3. The expected increase is striking. In 2050, the median age will vary between 53 years—in the United Kingdom and the United States—and 57 years in Spain. Unsurprisingly, Spain and Italy, which undergo the most dramatic population aging, will also face the largest change in the median age, respectively 13 and 11 years, whereas in the United States and in the United Kingdom, where the demographic dynamic is more moderate, the median age will rise respectively by 6 and 8 years.

Theories of Welfare State Expansion and Retrenchment

A good starting point to assess the future evolution of social security is to understand the reasons behind the initial institution of this system and its development into the most widespread and generous welfare program. The first unfunded public program of retirement income was introduced in Germany in the late nineteenth century; several other countries followed at the beginning of the twentieth century—often with the creation of small funded systems targeted to workers in specific sectors (e.g., in the public sector). By the end of WWII, most systems had become unfunded. Since then, their relevance as providers of retirement income has constantly grown, mainly because of the extension of the coverage among workers and of the increase in pension benefits' generosity. The rapid expansion of the social security system came to a partial halt at the beginning of the nineties, because of mounting concerns about the rising social spending and—in some countries—also because of the financial difficulties to meet short-term pension obligations with the current social security contribution revenues. An increasing awareness about the long-term financial effect of the aging process fueled the debate on the need to impose retrenching measures, aimed—at the very least—at reducing the level of pension spending per retiree.

Several contributions in the economic literature have analyzed the determinants of the creation of the welfare state and of its evolution into one of the most influential government interventions in the economy. The initial institution of these programs is often viewed as a policy response—inspired by equity principles—to rescue elderly individuals who have fallen below the poverty line because of dramatic negative economic shocks—as during the US Great Depression. A paternalistic view, which emphasizes the shortsightedness of the individuals—as opposed to the policy-makers—in taking their economic (in particular, savings) decisions, and the failure of private insurance markets to provide reasonably priced life annuity, has also been cited as economic rationale for public intervention in the provision of retirement income.

Section 3.1 summarizes these economic theories on the expansion of the welfare state, while providing an overview of a parallel literature that attributes the existence of social security systems to political forces. The latter approach originates the initial establishment of welfare policies and the large growth in social spending in the social and political responses to economic factors—such as the industrialization process at the end of the nineteenth century, but also in the upsurge of political phenomena, such as the appearance of new social and political actors (e.g., left parties or unions). The dissimilar expansion paths followed by countries at comparable stages of economic development are instead tied (by this "new institutionalism" approach) to the role played by different political institutions in shaping the policy-makers' incentives, and in creating crucial veto players in the decision process over welfare policy.

A recent political economy approach—presented in section 3.2—also emphasizes the political determinants in investigating social security issues but retains from the economic literature the methodological approach based on individual rationality. The individual agent remains the central focus of analysis; and the relevance of a social security system is evaluated according to its impact on each agent economic well-being. Several economic channels for social security to enhance the welfare of (at least some) young individuals are considered, with particular emphasis on the effects induced by the redistributive design of the system. Only after a complete representation of each agent's individual preferences over social security, these models turn to the political and social arena, where these competing individual preferences have to be mediated and converted into a policy outcome. A corporatist approach highlights the relevance that unions and lobbies have received in the welfare expansion and in the specific design and fragmentation of the social security system; whereas an electoral view underlines the role of the electoral push in the policy-makers' decisions of expanding social spending.

The demographic dynamic of the last few decades and the forecasts of further population aging have, however, shifted the focus of the policy debate towards retrenching measures, aimed at reducing the generosity of the pension benefits, to compensate for the increase in the share of retirees. Yet, as convincingly argued by Pierson (1996), welfare state retrenchment does not constitute the mirror image of welfare state expansion. Along its development path, the welfare state in fact creates its own diffused constituency—composed of benefits' recipients and bureaucrats—which will then oppose any reduction of its entrenched interests, quite independently of the political and social actions taken by unions and lobby groups. While the corporatist approach was reasonably successful in accounting for the rapid growth in social spending, electoral concerns assume a prominent role for policy-makers, who observe the political push for more social spending turning into a political plea not to retrench. Section 3.3 identifies the politics of welfare state retrenchment with the politics of electoral blame avoidance. The external constraints and the political scenarios that may facilitate a reform are emphasized, and the "divide-and-rule" strategy that may minimize the possible electoral backslashes induced by a reform is discussed. These electoral concerns will be at the heart of the theoretical framework presented in the next chapter and will be used to assess the political sustainability of social security in France, Germany, Italy, Spain, the United Kingdom, and the United States for the next fifty years.

3.1 Theories of Welfare State Expansion

Why were welfare states—and in particular, PAYG social security systems—introduced? What are the main determinants of their continuous expansion since WWII? Why do social security systems differ so widely—for instance, in their generosity—across countries at similar stages of economic development? How do they interact with other public expenditures, such as health care and education, among other redistributive programs of the welfare state? This section provides a short—and admittedly incomplete—overview of some economic and political theories of welfare state expansion.

A wide body of literature has been produced in an attempt to provide economic motivations for the initial institutions of pension systems (e.g., see Diamond 1996; Gramlich 1996; Feldstein and Liebman 2002a). A paternalistic view suggests that a pension scheme, which effectively forces individuals to transfer resources from youth into old age, is required to prevent shortsighted individuals, who may also lack information about their future, from saving too little for their old age consumption. An explanation complementing this view is that—

even if individuals were indeed able to plan for their old age necessities—reliable savings instruments to transfer resources into the future may fail to exist. Historical episodes validate this observation. Several systems have in fact been transformed from fully funded to PAYG, after that existing savings had been wiped out either by stock market crashes—as in the United States after the Great Depression— or by high inflation—as in France, Germany, and Italy after World War II. Equity considerations may also justify the institution of welfare states. Even when markets reach an efficient allocation of resources, governments may still want to intervene—perhaps by introducing a pension system—in an attempt to lower the degree of income inequality in the society or to reduce the share of the population below the poverty line, particularly among the elderly. Social security systems may also have emerged in response to the need for old age insurance against the longevity risk (i.e., the risk of depleting all the personal resource while still alive). Old age insurance, although historically provided within the family, emerged after the shift from agrarian to urban society. Since private insurance markets may fail to offer convenient life annuity—because of typical adverse selection problems—the introduction of a government-run PAYG system restores this missing market.

While all these economic factors represent valuable contributions to account for the initial establishment of these schemes, they fall short of providing a convincing explanation of the rapid increase in the size of these programs after WWII, and of the large cross-country differences in some relevant features of these systems.

A parallel literature has explored different venues to explain the introduction of PAYG pension systems, and more in general of the welfare state. The underlying idea is that decisions on pension policy, from the initial design of the system to its later expansion, go beyond economic theory into the realm of politics. Large changes in economic conditions, such as the industrialization process at the end of the nineteenth century, may create social unrest, which in turn triggers political responses. Social and political actors may emerge, such as large left wing parties or trade unions, which tilt the balance of political power—hence affecting policy decisions. Contributions to political campaigns, lobbying and the votes of vested interest groups may induce career-oriented policy-makers to sacrifice economic principles to their political goals.

A crucial insight of this literature is to recognize that welfare states (or pension systems) need not to enhance the well-being of all individuals in the society in order to be introduced; they simply need to be sustained politically. In democratic countries, this may amount to obtaining the support of a majority of the members in the Parliament or, more directly, of the electorate. In some political environments, however, de facto or de jure veto players may emerge, which require welfare state policies to be backed also by these political actors (see Bonoli 2000). Large left wing parties and unions represent frequent de facto veto players in welfare state issues because of their power in fostering public attention through national strikes but often also because of their formal involvement in the decision process over welfare state policies. De jure veto players are instead created by the specific characteristics of the political and electoral systems, which may attribute the power to block the legislative process over welfare state (or other) policies to some key political players.

An early political theory of welfare state expansion—the "logic of industrialism"—emphasized the strong positive link between economic development and social expenditure (also known in economics as the Wagner law). This logic attributed to the industrialization process new social needs, which were at least partially accommodated with the introduction of welfare programs (see Cutright 1965; Wilensky 1975). Recent contributions by Acemoglu and Robinson (2000, 2001) identify the political enfranchisement of new citizens as a crucial step toward the creation of a welfare state. The increase in income inequality that characterized the industrialization period and the resulting social unrest forced the political elites to extend the franchise, which in turn led to a poorer electorate and thus to more demand for redistribution. However, critics of this view (see Pierson, 1996) argue that while this logic may account for the introduction of these systems and, to some extent, for the difference in social spending between poor and rich economies, it fails to explain the large disparity observed within OECD countries.

The comparative politics literature has suggested the large increase in social spending and the cross-country variations to be due to the different distribution of political power among social classes. This "left power resource" approach is of the view that strong unions and large left parties contribute to the growth of welfare programs, which in turn greatly increase the bargaining power of the workers. However, although a strong empirical correlation can be found between the strength of the left parties and/or the unions and different measures of social spending in the decades following WWII (see Esping-Andersen 1990; Myles 1984), the recent decline in the power of organized labor and of some left parties has not been accompanied—in these countries—by a parallel reduction of the redistributive programs. Moreover this theory is silent on the reasons leading to the political success of the "left power," which then translates into more redistributive policies.

The "new institutionalism" approach suggests that political institutions matter, as they may largely influence policy outcomes—and thus welfare state programs. According to these theories, political institutions affect the government authority to implement policies by determining its administrative capacity and political strength, and by awarding de jure veto power to crucial political players that may oppose the government policy. De jure veto points may emerge in several political scenarios. Their existence is commonly associated with less social spending, as electoral-rewarding expansions of the welfare state proposed by the governments may be blocked by powerful veto players (see Bonoli 2000). In the United States, for instance, a strong separation between executive and legislative power typically provides the Congress with veto power to oppose the policy designed by the executive, as in the case of the US health reform plan endorsed by President Clinton. Dual executive powers may also constitute a source of veto, as an agreement may need to be reached between these two branches over relevant policies. This may occur, for instance, in France, where the executive power is shared by the prime minister and the president, under the "cohabitation," so called whenever the two politicians belong to different parties. Albeit not directly, electoral systems may represent a major cause of veto points, since proportional representation tends to generate (weak) coalition governments. Indeed, the path of welfare state expansion in several countries suggests that coalition governments—rather than been prevented from increasing social spending by the high density of veto points—may actually tend to overspend, in an attempt to accommodate the political requirements of the different parties or forces in the coalition. The high degree of fragmentation in the social security systems of several European countries may in fact be viewed as the result of this process of enlargement of the political base—at least within the governing coalition—that is achieved through a redistribution of resources to the constituencies of the different veto players.

A recent literature on the political economy of social security systems shares with the previous approaches the key insight on the relevance of political determinants in the institution of unfunded pension

systems and in their development into a widespread instrument of social insurance (see Galasso and Profeta 2002). Yet this new political
economy literature hinges on a different methodological approach
based on individual rationality. These models explicitly derive the individual preferences over social security by analyzing the effect that a
PAYG pension system has on each agent's economic well-being. While
pensions clearly improve the economic welfare of the retirees, there
may exist economic reasons for a social security system to enhance the
well-being of—at least some—young and middle-aged workers. The
crucial role is played by the (intergenerational and intragenerational)
redistributive features of the social security system that determine its
profitability to the agents, as measured by different notions of internal
rate of return. Once determined the individual preferences over policies (e.g., over the size of social security), these models turn to the
political representations of these different, and often conflicting, individual interests and to their interaction in the political system. An electoral approach highlights the democratic role of the electorate in
shaping economic policy. Incumbent politicians or candidates at elections adopt—or commit to—social security policies backed by at least
a majority of the voters. According to this approach, a social security
system is *politically sustainable* if supported by a majority of the members of the Parliament, or alternatively of the electorate, in all its
features—such as contribution rate, retirement age, benefit calculation
criterion and indexation (see Galasso and Profeta 2002). A corporatist
view emphasizes instead the role of veto players—such as the
unions—or interest groups—the retirees' lobby—in shaping the decision process over social security (see Bonoli 2000; Mulligan and Sala-i-
Martin 1999).

3.2   A Political Economy Approach to Social Security

Social security affects the individuals' economic well-being through
several channels. A direct effect emerges as social security tilts the
agents' net income profile toward more resources in old age. In fact
contributions to the system decrease the individuals' net labor income
during their working life, while pension benefits provide income at retirement. This purely mechanical shift is accompanied by behavioral
effects, as individuals adjust their economic decisions to the size and
the characteristics of these systems. A large economic literature has in
fact established that pension systems, by transferring resources from

the working period into old age, affect the individuals' savings decisions, and hence the aggregate stock of capital in the economy (see Feldstein and Liebman 2002a). Individuals are also induced to revise their labor decisions according to the pension system's characteristics. The magnitude of the impact of social security contribution rates on individuals' labor supply decisions—in particular, regarding their weekly working hours, or their exit toward unofficial (black) market— is controversial (see Disney 2004). However, several studies identify social security as the main reason for the huge drop in labor participation among elderly workers experienced by most OECD countries in the last thirty years (see Gruber and Wise 1999; Blöndal and Scarpetta 1998). All these factors contribute to determine the individual agents' economic well-being, and hence their preferences over the pension system.

3.2.1 Economic Determinants

To analyze the impact of the crucial economic factors on the individuals' preferences over social security, it is useful to introduce a simple economic environment.[1] I consider an economy with three overlapping generations of individuals: young, middle-aged, and old. Population grows at a constant non-negative rate n. Hence the demographic structure is easily summarized as follows: in any period for every old there are $(1 + n)$ middle-aged individuals and $(1 + n)^2$ young.

During the first two periods of their lives, individuals—young and middle-aged—work: they receive a labor income, denoted respectively by w^y and w^a, and pay a proportional contribution rate, τ, on their labor income. Old individuals retire and receive a pension transfer, P. To simplify the analysis, I assume that individuals only care about their (remaining) lifetime income, which, for a young individual living at time t, corresponds to the following expression:

$$I = w_t^y(1 - \tau_t) + \frac{w_{t+1}^a(1 - \tau_{t+1})}{1 + r} + \frac{P_{t+2}}{(1 + r)^2}, \tag{3.1}$$

where subscripts indicate the time period and r is the real discount rate. The first term in (3.1) represents the net labor income in youth, the second term is the discounted net labor income when adult, while the third term indicates the discounted pension benefits when retired.

The economy features a budget-balanced PAYG social security system that in every period shares the collected contributions *lump sum* among all current retirees. The pension transfer to the retirees at time t is thus equal to the following expression:

$$P_t = \tau_t[\hat{w}_t^a(1+n) + \hat{w}_t^y(1+n)^2],\qquad\qquad(3.2)$$

where $\hat{w}_t^a$ and $\hat{w}_t^y$ are the average wages at time t respectively among the middle-aged and the young, so that the expression in brackets represents the average labor earnings in the economy. This characterization of the pension system introduces an element of within-cohort redistribution, since individuals contribute a proportional share of their income to the system while receiving a flat pension benefit. Hence, to the extent that agents differ in their labor income, the system redistributes from the rich to the poor.

To highlight the different economic factors at work, it is convenient to consider constant sequences of contribution rates ($\tau_t = \tau\ \forall t$) and to examine the individual preferences over these sequences. This amounts to assuming that—in forming their preferences over the social security contribution rate—young and middle-aged agents expect the financing of the current scheme not to be modified in the future. Workers who do not assume the system to be in place in their old age perceive the current contribution rate as a pure cost, and would generally not be willing to support the system[2].

These political economy models characterize the pension system primarily as a savings device, so individuals' preferences over the system depend on the performance of savings, as computed by the internal rate of return. If all agents earn the same wage, regardless of their type and age, $w = \hat{w}_t^a = \hat{w}_t^y$, and wages grow over time at a constant rate, g, this internal rate of return, i, can be obtained by solving the following expression:

$$-\tau w - \frac{\tau w(1+g)}{1+i} + \frac{\tau w(1+g)^2[(1+n) + (1+n)^2]}{(1+i)^2} = 0,\qquad(3.3)$$

where the two negative terms correspond to the discounted contributions to the system made during the working life, while the (positive) third term represents the discounted pension income, which has been rewritten using the budget constraint at (3.2). The equation above can be solved for the internal rate of return, i, and yields the usual result. The profitability of the system to a young individual depends on the rate of growth of the population and of the wages:

$$1 + i = (1+n)(1+g).\qquad\qquad(3.4)$$

The retirees' preferences over the pension system are easily established. Because retirees bear no current or future cost, they clearly favor the contribution rate that maximizes their current pension benefits. For young and middle-aged agents, an increase in the (constant sequence of) contribution rates has three effects, which can be identified at (3.3): (1) a rise in the labor income tax in the two working periods, (2) an increase of the pension transfer, and (3) a change of the factor prices, meaning wages and rates of return (w, r), due to the variations in the stock of capital and in the average labor supply.

The economic factors behind the support of (some) young and middle-aged agents to the pension system are summarized as follows.

Dynamic Inefficiency   For a long time since Aaron's (1966) and Samuelson's (1958) important work, pensions were known to improve the welfare of every individual in a dynamically inefficient economy. In other words, every young agent would find it more convenient to transfer resources into the future through a PAYG system rather than through alternative savings instruments if the implicit rate of return from social security, i, is larger than the real rate of return from alternative assets, r:

$$1 + i = (1 + n)(1 + g) > 1 + r. \tag{3.5}$$

Reliance on this economic rationale to explain the support for unfunded systems among the young does, however, raise some doubts. Critics of this view suggest in fact that real returns from pension systems do not compare favorably with returns from risk-free bonds (see table 3.1), and that this differential widens if one considers alternative portfolios including risky assets. Yet a fair comparison should also take into account that—unlike the other assets—social security offers an additional service by providing a real annuity to the retirees. The cost of purchasing an annuity on the private market should hence be subtracted from the returns of these alternative assets.

Partial Time Horizon   Later Browning (1975), in another influential work, argued that even in a dynamically efficient economy, adult individuals may still support pensions, since they consider past contributions as a sunk cost and value only current and future contributions and benefits. In other words, forward-looking adult individuals do not consider the entire cost of their pensions but focus only on their remaining time horizon.

Table 3.1
PAYG versus risk-free asset, average real returns, 1961 to 1996

Country	PAYG[a]	Risk-free asset[b]
Belgium	2.95%	3.83%
France	2.98%	3.70%
Germany	2.58%	3.70%
Italy	2.85%	1.65%
Japan	4.85%	2.53%
Sweden	2.23%	3.00%
United Kingdom	2.25%	2.55%
United States	2.90%	3.23%

Source: D'Amato and Galasso (2003).
a. PAYG: average real growth rate of earnings.
b. Risk-free asset: average real rate of return on long-term government bonds.

To isolate this effect, I consider a dynamically efficient economy, $i < r$. The implicit return factor from the pension system for an adult who views previous contributions as a sunk cost is denoted by $1 + i^a$, and this is equal to the ratio between future benefits and current contributions. In a steady state the return is equal to

$$1 + i^a = (1 + g)(1 + n)(2 + n). \tag{3.6}$$

An adult individual is willing to support social security, $\tau > 0$, if the implicit return from the system, calculated on this partial time horizon, is larger than the real return on capital accumulation: $i^a > r > i$.

Since Browning (1975), this insight has been widely used. More recently, Cooley and Soares (1999) have combined this idea with the crowding-out effect described below to replicate some quantitative features of the US social security system. In Galasso (2002), I have instead computed the internal rate of return from "investing" in social security for the median voter at several US presidential elections. These calculations support Browning's argument: for a middle-aged individual—a 44-year-old median voter—the internal rate of return from social security almost always exceeds the return from investing in alternative (risky) assets, as shown in table 3.2.

Within-Cohort Redistribution   Several authors have suggested that some young individuals may support pension spending because of the existence of a within-cohort redistribution element in the system (see Casamatta et al. 1999; Conde-Ruiz and Galasso 2005; Persson and

Table 3.2
Returns from alternative assets for the US median voter

Year	Social security	S&P	DJIA	US bonds
1964	9.8%	0.7%	−0.2%	−3.8%
1968	8.0%	3.8%	3.7%	1.3%
1972	6.7%	6.7%	6.9%	4.5%
1976	6.3%	9.4%	10.04%	5.0%

Source: Galasso (2002).
Notes: Social security returns represent the continuation internal rate of return from contributing to social security for the median voter (family). The returns from the alternative assets (Standard and Poors index fund, Dow Jones Industrial Average index fund and long-term US bonds) are calculated according to a buy-and-hold strategy in which every year the median voter invests in each asset the same amount as contributed to the social security system.

Tabellini 2000; Tabellini 2000). Even when social security systems provide *on average* a lower rate of return than alternative savings instruments, some (low-income) individuals may still enjoy higher returns because of this intragenerational redistributive component. In systems featuring (nearly) flat pension benefits, social security returns depend on the agents' income: high-income individuals pay large contributions—obtaining below average returns—while low-income agents pay lower contributions—enjoying an above average profitability. This redistributive element is indeed present in several systems. For instance, the United Kingdom features a flat pension program (Basic State Pension, BSP) together with an earning related scheme (see chapter 9), and the US social security system is known to redistribute within cohorts across different family types, by yielding higher returns to low-income than to high-income individuals (see chapter 10).

To analyze this redistributive effect, it is sufficient to consider a two-period, dynamically efficient economy, in which agents differ in their labor income w. The pension system collects contributions τw from every worker and provides an old age pension P to every retiree, so the pension's budget constraint at (3.2) simplifies to

$$P_t = \tau_t \hat{w}_t (1 + n), \tag{3.7}$$

where $\hat{w}_t$ is the average wage income at time t. In a two-period economy the individual life-time income at (3.1) becomes

$$I = w_t(1 - \tau_t) + \frac{P_{t+1}}{(1 + r)}. \tag{3.8}$$

By using the pension's budget constraint, the equation can be rewritten as

$$I = (1 - \tau)w + \frac{\tau \hat{w}(1 + g)(1 + n)}{(1 + r)}. \tag{3.9}$$

Because agents differ in their wages, the labor income on which contributions are levied may differ from the average labor income that enters the determination of the pension benefits. This difference is reflected in the internal rate of return from the pension system i^w:

$$1 + i^w = (1 + n)(1 + g)\frac{\hat{w}}{w}. \tag{3.10}$$

Hence individuals with average income, $w = \hat{w}$, obtain the average IRR: $1 + i^w = (1 + n)(1 + g) = (1 + i)$; high-income individuals, $w > \hat{w}$, experience a below average return, $i^w < i$; while low-income individuals, $w < \hat{w}$, enjoy an above-average return, $i^w > i$. Hence the low-income may be willing to support a social security system even in a dynamically efficient economy.

Crowding Out   The existence of a social security system is known to affect the individuals' economic well-being also indirectly, by modifying the labor and savings decisions. Cukierman and Meltzer (1989) first claimed that individuals evaluating public debt policies do take into account the potential effects of their decisions—and hence of the implemented policies—on the stock of capital, and thereby on factor prices. In other words, every individual acts as a monopolist who recognizes that if a preferred policy prevails, then all their decisions will be affected, and stock of capital and factor prices will change accordingly. Cooley and Soares (1999) and Boldrin and Rustichini (2000) extended this idea to social security. They argue that the existence of intergenerational redistribution schemes, such as public debt or pensions, tends to crowd out capital. This reduction in the stock of physical capital leads to a decrease in real wages and to an increase in real returns to capital—hence redistributing in favor of assets-holders (capitalists) and against individuals who rely more heavily on labor income (workers).

Social security systems may also affect factor prices because of changes in the labor supply. In particular, if social security contributions are distortionary and hence reduce labor supply (see Disney 2004), a large system would lead to higher wages, but lower returns on capital—thereby dampening the crowding-out effect.

In a two-period overlapping generations model Boldrin and Rusti-chini (2000) fully characterize political economy equilibria with social security that emerge exclusively because of this crowding out effect, while Cooley and Soares (1999) use a four-period overlapping genera-tions economy to combine this effect with Browning's "partial time horizon" argument. This strand of the literature emphasizes the impor-tance of the crowding out effect in shaping the individuals' preferences for social security, yet its empirical relevance remains to be tested.

3.2.2 Political Institutions

The section above described how different economic features shape the individuals' preferences over social security. Yet, how these individual interests are converted into a social security policy depends on the policy-makers' decisions, and hence on the existing political institu-tions. The literature on political economy of social security has identi-fied two main approaches as sensible ways of describing the decision process over social security issues: an electoral approach—placing electoral considerations at the core of the policy-makers' agenda—and a corporatist view—emphasizing the role of de facto veto players and interest groups.

Electoral Approach   Voting models stress the role of the electorate in determining the economic policy. Policy-makers are typically identi-fied with opportunistic incumbent politicians, aiming at achieving re-election, or candidates at election drafting a political platform. Both politicians have an electoral interest in adopting economic policies that are supported by at least a majority of the voters. In models of direct democracy, agents typically vote—that is, they express their individual preferences—on social security contribution rates, and the outcome corresponds to the policy obtaining a majority of the votes. Alterna-tively, social security may represent an important item on the policy platform of the political candidates, who—once elected—implement their announced policy. Voters then choose between candidates ac-cording (also) to their positions on social security issues.

Since workers constitute a large share of the electorate, their support is crucial for the political sustainability of social security systems. Yet, why should some young and middle-aged agents favour social security—thereby bearing a current cost—if policy-makers are unable to commit to the existence of a corresponding system in their old age? In his important contribution, Hammond (1975) suggested that the workers' apparently altruistic behavior may be induced by an implicit contract connecting successive generations of individuals. Sjoblom (1985), and later Cooley and Soares (1999), Galasso (1999), and Boldrin and Rustichini (2000) extended this insight to a majority voting environment, in which elections are repeatedly held. This idea is simple,[3] yet intriguing. Repeated voting over social security allows a system of rewards and punishments to emerge as a social norm among successive voters. This implicit contract works as follows: If a system has already been established, and a majority of voters—typically composed of all retirees and some workers[4]—continues to endorse it, current retirees receive their pension benefits; while current workers will obtain a corresponding transfer in their old age. If instead a majority of voters fails to comply with the contract—and hence to provide a pension to the current retirees—this voting behavior will trigger a response by future voters, who will be unwilling to support the system. Hence the generation that initially deviates from the implicit contract is punished, as it will not receive an old age pension.

Another strand of this political economy literature has suggested that, in democratic societies, substantive changes to social security policy may require a broader consensus than a simple majority. Politicians may be reluctant to implement policy reforms that adversely affect the vested interests of politically powerful groups—such as the retirees—unless they are backed by a vast majority of voters (see Azariadis and Galasso 2002). Bonoli (2000) emphasizes instead the role played by the veto players induced by the political institutions in place, such as the electoral system. For instance, while majoritarian systems tend to produce strong one-party governments, which are better equipped to survive until the end of the legislation, proportional systems often give rise to weaker coalition governments, whose policy decisions may easily be blocked by small parties in the ruling coalition.

Corporatist View   A corporatist view of the political process suggests that—beyond the electoral considerations described above—policy decisions are largely influenced by de facto veto players and strong interest groups. Union movements represent a good candidate for veto players in welfare state policy. Interstingly union coverage—measured as the percentage of the workforce covered by the contracts bargained for by the unions—has a positive and significant impact on social security spending. Highly representative unions, as in Germany, Italy and Spain, may use their strong bargaining position to support old age spending because of their "seniority bias" in favor of the elderly members (see Brugiavini et al. 2001). The credible threat of nationwide general strikes and the close association of some unions with—typically left-wing—political parties further increase the de facto relevance of the unions. Moreover the role of the unions as veto players in social security policy decisions may derive from their formal involvement in the policy-making and in the administration of the pension scheme (see the French experience in chapter 5).

Interest group models hint instead to the fact that—despite being a minority—the elderly may control the political process. Because of the existence of social security programs also in nondemocratic countries, this literature argues that lobbying and political pressure—rather than voting—are the crucial determinants of the political support for large redistributive policies. Yet, why should the elderly exert more pressure than other groups, such as the young, or the employees, or the firms? Mulligan and Sala-i-Martin (1999) suggest that elderly are single-minded over social security benefits because these constitute most of their retirement income. Other individuals' interests tend to be more diversified and to depend on their family status, occupation, income and so on. Economic and demographic factors also play a role: elderly may have a lower opportunity cost of lobbying, whereas the young, faced with the prospect of becoming old, will exert less opposition to social security expenditures.

3.3   Aging and Retrenchment

The theoretical literature surveyed in the previous sections addresses mainly the rapid expansion, since WWII, of the welfare state, and of its most relevant program—social security. Yet new concerns have taken center stage in the current policy debate as the dramatic population aging in most OECD countries over the last three decades is expected to overburden their economies (see chapter 2).

Population aging increases the number of elderly individuals entitled to old age pensions, while reducing the relative share of workers that contribute to the system. If future pension benefits were calculated according to the current rules, most PAYG social security systems would face severe financial difficulties to meet the existing pension obligations, since the total amount of collected contributions would not be sufficient to cover the benefits. Many leading economists and international institutions (see World Bank, 1994, and European Commission, 2003) have been forecasting this financial solvency problem in the medium to long term. They have called for an effort to reform the welfare state, and particularly those programs that are mainly targeted to the elderly and are closely tied to the demographic dynamics. Since the late eighties several pension reforms have indeed been implemented in many OECD countries (see section 2.1.2 and table 2.2).

Among the major adjustments to the existing social security systems aimed at coping with the aging process, one potential—albeit often criticized—policy measure is to keep the pension benefits' generosity untouched and to finance the extra expenditure associated with the growing number of retirees by increasing the social security contribution rates, or by making additional use of general tax revenues. Alternatively, pension benefits may be reduced, retirement age postponed, and benefits indexed to inflation (rather than to wages). The latter option defines a set of welfare *retrenchment* measures pursuing a reduction of the pension spending per retiree. In an aging environment, however, retrenchment policies may still be associated with a rising aggregate social security expenditure—and hence with higher contribution rates—even when these measures prove effective in reducing the per-capita spending, due to the increasing proportion of retirees.

Yet retrenchment is not the mirror image of welfare expansion—as persuasively argued by Pierson (1996)—and hence the theoretical framework used to explain the growth in social spending may fail to provide valuable insights on possible retrenchment measures. In fact, while increases in the coverage and generosity of the welfare state typically constitute popular policies, which distribute resources to a large group of individuals and encounter little resistance in the political and social arena, welfare retrenching policies are unpopular because they tend to concentrate losses on specific large groups (e.g., the early retirees; see Conde-Ruiz and Galasso 2003, 2005), and to create only diffuse and uncertain gains. Social movements, left parties, and interest groups played an important role in the expansion of the welfare state and contributed to the fragmentation of the social security system by acquiring large private benefits for the individuals they represented. Yet, once established, a welfare state creates its own constituency, formed of different groups of benefits' recipients and bureaucrats, and becomes less dependent on political parties, social movements and unions.

To be sure, unions, left parties, and lobbies may still play a crucial role in the decision process over welfare state policy by informing the public opinion about the consequences of the retrenchment—thereby increasing the visibility and the electoral cost of a reform—and by mobilizing the public at large through national strikes and social unrest against cuts to social spending. For instance, the 1995 Juppé reform plan in France, the 1994 Berlusconi reform proposal in Italy and the 1997 Kohl reform project in Germany had to be withdrawn because of the massive opposition by unions—and left parties. Yet most of these plans were politically ill-designed. They spread the cost of retrenching onto virtually all the current generations, thereby creating a diffused discontent across the entire welfare state constituency. Shortly after the failure of these proposals, in fact, alternative retrenching reforms that concentrated the cost on the young workers—and shifted part of the fiscal burden on to future generations—took place in all three countries,[5] sometimes against the unions' will, as in Germany in 2001 (see chapters 5, 6 and 7).

Because of the strong vested interests created by the existence of a large welfare state, not only do retrenchment policies fail to create a constituency, they replenish support for the welfare state and may result in large electoral costs. Retrenchment typically represents a problematical exercise in blame avoidance (see Weaver 1986). Thus, despite the impressive discussion on the need of structural pension reforms in the graying Europe, few radical reforms have actually been implemented (see section 2.1.2). Interestingly some of the most far-reaching retrenchment measures have been introduced as a response to imminent social security budgetary crisis, as in the case of the 1992 Dini reform in Italy (see chapter 7 for a detailed description) and of the 1983 US Social Security Amendment pursued by President Reagan (see Pierson 1996). Even in these instances, however, despite the urgency of taking restrictive policy measures and the availability of a credible blame avoidance strategy, policy-makers refrained from acting unilaterally and sought a large consensus among the political forces and in the social arena. For instance, the Reagan 1983 reform plan followed the advices of a bipartisan commission, whereas the Italian government ruling in 1992 was careful to conduct lengthy discussion with the unions and all the parties. The demand for a consensus-building strategy—commonly associated during the extension of the welfare state to weak coalition governments and hence typically to proportional systems (see Lijphard 1999)—emerges from the need to limit possible electoral backslashes. Strong governments enjoying broad support in the Parliament face a trade-off when deciding over welfare state policies. Their political strength would allow them to carry retrenching measures through the Parliament (see Pierson and Weaver 1993), yet they would also be more clearly accountable to the electorate for their policy decisions (see Persson and Tabellini 2000).

The 1986 UK pension reform (the 1986 Social Security Act) constitutes a unique example of use of a strong, concentrated power—by the Conservative government of Mrs Thatcher—to retrenching the public provision of the system, while increasing the private market involvement. Several scholars (see Pierson 1994) suggest that the government was willing to impose this retrenching policy for ideological reasons—the "Thatcherite"—but electoral concerns were clearly present. Certainly the deep crisis experienced in that period by the Labour Party limited the probability of an electoral defeat for the Tories. Moreover the pension reform belonged to a broader political strategy aimed at enlarging the proprietary base of the society through privatization, which, according to Jessop et al. (1988), was also expected to produce large electoral returns among the middle class. Indeed, the Conservative Party retained its majority in the following two elections after the reform (see Bonoli 2000).

In some countries—such as Italy in 1992 and 1995 and France in 1993—the retrenchment policies were presented as necessary measures to meet European Union requirements despite representing an indirect response to the impact of aging on social security. This use of external constraints was part of blame avoidance strategy. Nevertheless, long transition periods were still designed to reduce the share of the welfare state constituency, which was negatively affected by the reform, and hence to comply with electoral constraints (Pierson 1996). This divide-and-rule strategy (see Boeri et al. 2006) was particularly effective in splitting the electorate between a large group of—politically powerful—winner (or, at least, nonlosers) from the reform, composed of retirees and elderly workers (those already relatively close to retirement age), and a smaller group of less powerful, at least in the political and social arena, losers, formed of young workers (see the analysis of reforms in France, Germany, and Italy at chapters 5 to 7). The specific retrenchment measures proposed in the different reforms—albeit all aimed at curbing the growth in social security spending—depended in part on the type of constituency created by the initial design of the system (see Myles and Quadagno 1997; Ferrera 1996). In fact more redistributive systems—as in United Kingdom and United States—have typically become even more redistributive, whereas the more

Bismarckian system—as in France, Germany, and Italy—has further eliminated redistributive elements.

In this book, I endorse the relevance of the electoral considerations during a potential retrenching phase of the welfare states induced by the aging process. The next chapter will in fact present a model of "vested interests," which builds on the premises of the individual rationality and characterizes the preferences over social security for all individuals (as described in section 3.2)—rather than portraying interests over social security along party lines, social groups, or union movements. The natural divide over these pension issues is generational; depending on their age, individuals face distinctive future paths of contributions and benefits and different survivor probabilities. In a graying society this age partition becomes particular relevant, since it allows to capture the direct impact of the variation of the age structure on the political process of social security determination.

In the theoretical framework of the book, the centrality of the electoral considerations is recognized by the use of a voting model to aggregate the individuals' preferences over social security. A simple majority voting model—and its widely used median voter's application—represents a tractable, yet powerful instrument to describe the political decision process over social security. This simple framework clearly abstracts from several aspects of the political process, for instance, the roles played by the unions, the left parties, and other veto points in the determination of welfare state policies. Yet, as discussed above (see also Piersson 1996), in a retrenchment phase of the welfare state induced by population aging, the crucial concerns of the policy-makers are electoral, since the long-standing existence of large welfare states has contributed to create a strong constituency effect. In this scenario the median voter framework seems particularly effective, since it easily accounts for the effect of aging on the age structure of the electorate—and hence of the welfare state constituency—and ultimately for the political process[6] of aggregation of the individual preferences into a social security policy.

4 Assessing the Political Sustainability of Social Security Systems: A Theoretical Framework

The aim of this book is to provide a quantitative assessment of the political sustainability of social security in six graying societies—France, Germany, Italy, Spain, the United Kingdom, and the United States. In this chapter, I introduce the theoretical framework for the analysis of the economic and political decisions. A comprehensive economic environment includes most of the economic factors featured in the recent political economy literature on social security (see section 3.2.1), which may lead social security to enhance some individuals' well-being. The formal model, with a detailed description of the individuals' utility function and budget constraints, the production function, and the market-clearing conditions is presented at section 4.1.

The individuals' preferences over social security induced by these —typically redistributive—economic elements are then aggregated through a simple majority voting process. At every election voters determine the size of the system by choosing the social security contribution rate.[1] Since preferences are single peaked, the well-known median voter's theorem applies, and the equilibrium outcome corresponds to the most preferred outcome for this pivotal voter. Section 4.2.2 provides a formal definition of the political system.

This political institution emphasizes the democratic role of the electorate in shaping economic policy. Incumbent politicians seeking reelection—or political candidates drafting their electoral platform—will only adopt social security policies that are supported by the electorate. Throughout the book the *political sustainability* of social security will hence identify the existence of a majority of voters backing the system in all its features, such as the contribution rate, retirement age, the benefit calculation criterion, and indexation. An advantage of this electoral approach is to provide a political environment that allows for a clear assessment of the effect of the demographic dynamics—through the

aging of the electorate—on the political determination of social security policies. Yet the role of veto players—such as unions or single parties in coalition governments—may also be important, and this will be
addressed in the following chapters whenever relevant. Section 4.2 discusses this electoral approach and addresses other modeling issues related to the political system, such as the dimensionality of the policy
space and the dynamic nature of this voting game when elections are
repeatedly held.

A relevant question is whether this notion of political sustainability
is consistent with the existence of the current social security systems.
Does a majority of voters in each country effectively support social security? Data from the Euro-barometer survey conduced by Eurostat
suggest a positive answer. Figure 4.1 displays the individuals' reac-
tions in some EU countries to the statement that "current pension
levels should be maintained even if this means raising taxes or contributions." Three out of four interviewed individuals agree with the
proposition above—thereby suggesting that an increase in social secu-

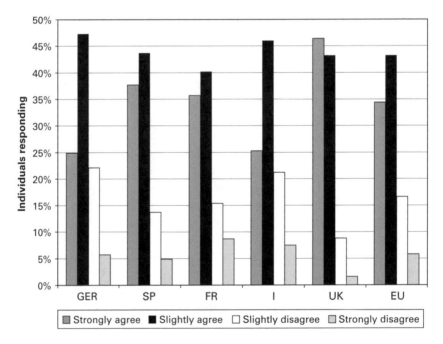

Figure 4.1
Individual preferences over social security in Europe, showing support for maintaining
current pension levels even if this means raising taxes or contributions (Source: EC 2003)

rity spending may represent the electoral path of least resistance to coping with the aging process.

The methodology used in this book to provide a quantitative evaluation of how political constraints may shape social security systems under population aging operates in two stages. First, the theoretical political economy model presented in the first two sections of this chapter is calibrated to match the main economic, demographic, and political characteristics and the crucial features of the social security system, for each country in our sample around the year 2000. This characterization allows the model to replicate each economy in its initial steady state, which is assumed to be at the turn of the century. In particular, in every country, individuals take economic and political decisions, and the social security contribution rate—determined through the political process—is calibrated to correspond to the actual average equilibrium contribution rate during the nineties,[2] while the resulting economic aggregates have to be consistent with the long-term features of each economy.

The simulations of the impact of the electoral constraints on the political determination of social security under aging are then obtained by feeding this calibrated model with the forecasted values of demographic, economic, and political variables for the year 2050. This methodology thus assumes that in fifty years each economy will have reached a new steady state in which the demographic process has stabilized and the social security systems have been modified to cope with these new demographic and economic elements. The social security contribution rate estimated by the model in this new steady state under different policy scenarios represents the political equilibrium outcome of the voting game in 2050; in other words, the most preferred social security contribution rate for the year 2050 median voter. The simulations' results at chapters 5 to 10 present a comparison between the initial steady state in 2000 and this future steady state in 2050.

4.1 The Economic Environment

The economic environment consists of an overlapping generation general equilibrium model, which is singularly calibrated to the main demographic and economic features of each country in exam. The economy is populated by several overlapping generations of workers and retirees, who may differ within cohorts by education types. At any time t, individuals face a probability of surviving until the next period,

$(\pi_t^{i,q})_{i=1,\ldots,G}^{q=1,\ldots,Q}$, which depends on their age i and type q, where Q is the total number of education types and G is the last possible period of any agent's life. The subscripts indicate calendar date, and the superscripts refer respectively to the agent's birth period and education level.[3] Agents who reach the Gth period of their life face certain death, $\pi_t^{G,q} = 0$, regardless of their type q. The demographic structure of the model can be synthesized by a population profile, which combines these survival probabilities with the population growth rate, n_t. The profile summarizes the fraction of population in each cohort and group type, $\mu_t^{i,q}$, with $\sum_{i=1}^{G} \sum_{q=1}^{Q} \mu_t^{i,q} = 1$ for all t.

Agents work during the first J^q periods of their life and then retire. Two possible specifications of the model are provided for the individual labor supply decisions. In the first case, labor supply is exogenous: labor is supplied inelastically, and retirement age is mandatory, although it may differ across types. In the second specification, which is meant to capture possible labor market distortions,[4] individuals decide how many hours to work in any given week. In this labor supply decision, they trade off the utility from leisure against the opportunity cost of the free time. At a fixed retirement age, which may possibly vary across types, individuals are forced to retire and to enjoy leisure.

4.1.1 Preferences

Agents value consumption or consumption and leisure—depending on the specification of the model—according to the following expected utility function:

$$\sum_{j=0}^{G} \beta^j \left[\prod_{i=0}^{j} \pi_t^{i,q} \right] U(c_{t+j}^{t,q}, l_{t+j}^{t,q}) \qquad \forall j = 0, \ldots, G; \ \forall q = 1, \ldots, Q, \qquad (4.1)$$

where $c_{t+j}^{t,q}$ and $l_{t+j}^{t,q}$ denote respectively consumption and leisure at time $t + j$ for an individual born at time t with education level q, $\pi_t^{i,q}$ is the age specific individual probability of surviving until the next period, and β is the subjective time discount rate.

The utility function is further specified by assuming that agents have a constant degree of risk aversion. In the model with exogenous labor supply, the period utility function becomes

$$U(c_{t+j}^{t,q}) = \frac{(c_{t+j}^{t,q})^{1-\rho}}{1 - \rho}, \qquad (4.2)$$

where ρ indicates the coefficient of relative risk aversion. In the model with endogenous labor supply, in which workers may decide to change their working hours depending on the fiscal burden on labor income, the utility function is

$$U(c_{t+j}^{t,q}) = \frac{[(c_{t+j}^{t,q})^{\alpha}(l_{t+j}^{t,q})^{1-\alpha}]^{1-\rho}}{1-\rho} \qquad (4.3)$$

where α represents the relative importance of consumption with respect to leisure.

This economic environment shares a common feature with all life-cycle economic models: every agent—depending on her expected lifetime horizon and income—decides how much to consume and save in every period in an attempt to smooth consumption over time, despite the possible fluctuations in the annual income. In taking these decisions, agents face the following sequence of budget constraints:

$$c_{t+j}^{t,q} + a_{t+j+1}^{t,q} = a_{t+j}^{t,q}R_{t+j} + y_{t+j}^{t,q} + H_{t+j}^{t,q} \qquad \forall j = 0,\ldots,G; \ \forall q = 1,\ldots,Q, \tag{4.4}$$

where $a_{t+j+1}^{t,q}$ and $y_{t+j}^{t,q}$ represent respectively the end-of-period asset holding and disposable income at time $t + j$, and R_{t+j} is the interest factor on private financial assets. Since some individuals fail to survive until the next period, their involuntary bequest, which amounts to $H_{t+j}^{t,q} = (1 - \pi_{t+j-1}^{q})a_{t+j}^{t,q}R_{t+j}/\pi_{t+j-1}^{q}$, has to be redistributed. A common assumption in the literature is to assume that this bequest, consisting of the assets of those who do not survive, is shared among all living individuals with the same characteristics. Effectively this amounts to assuming that individuals enter a one-year annuity contract to distribute the assets of the deceased. Alternatively, asset holdings may be redistributed in a lump-sum fashion among survivors of all ages and types or only to young individuals.[5]

Within each age cohort, agents may differ by level of education and, accordingly, by income, working history, retirement age, longevity and degree of political participation. Individuals also vary in their working ability. More educated agents tend to be more productive, and in any given period, middle-aged workers are typically more productive than young and elderly workers. The disposable labor income respectively for workers and retirees is summarized as follows:

$$y_{t+j}^{t,q} = \varepsilon_{t+j}^{j,q} h_{t+j}^{t,q} w_{t+j} (1 - \tau_{t+j}) \qquad \forall j = s^q, \ldots, J^q - 1;$$

$$\forall q = 1, \ldots, Q; \qquad \qquad (4.5)$$

$$y_{t+j}^{t,q} = P_{t+j}^{j,q} \qquad \forall j = J^q, \ldots, G; \; \forall q = 1, \ldots, Q;$$

where w_{t+j} indicates wage per labor efficiency unit, $\varepsilon_{t+j}^{j,q}$ is a measure of labor efficiency, which may depend on the worker's age and education level, s^q is the initial age at which agents in the education class q begin their working career and τ_{t+j} and $P_{t+j}^{j,q}$ represent respectively the contribution rate to social security and the (annuity) pension benefit received by a type q retiree aged j. The number of working hours that are supplied at time $t + j$ by a type q agent born at time t, $h_{t+j}^{t,q}$, is constant in the exogenous labor supply model, whereas in the endogenous labor supply specification it is endogenously determined by each individual worker in her labor-leisure decision, $h_{t+j}^{t,q} = 1 - l_{t+j}^{t,q}$.

Clearly, all this diversity across individuals will induce different economic choices by the agents with respect to labor supply and savings, as well as different individual preferences over social security policies.

4.1.2 Technology

The production side of the economy is characterized by a constant returns to scale aggregate production function, which transforms the productive inputs—labor and capital—into the production of a final good. The economy enjoys an exogenous technical progress that enhances labor productivity. The aggregate production function can be represented as follows:

$$Q_t = f[\eta_t(1 + \lambda)^t, k_t] = b k_t^{\theta} (\eta_t(1 + \lambda)^t)^{1-\theta}, \qquad (4.6)$$

where λ is the growth rate of labor productivity—a crucial variable for the profitability of unfunded social security systems—η is a measure of the per capita unit of labor measured in efficiency units, k denotes the per capita stock of capital, b is a total factor productivity index, and θ is the factor share of capital.

In the model with exogenous labor supply, in which social security imposes no economic distortion on the labor market, the labor supply in efficiency units is simply determined by the product of the (exogenous) average number of hours worked and the average labor efficiency units in the economy:

$$\eta_t = h \sum_{q=1}^{Q} \sum_{i=1}^{J^q} \varepsilon_t^{i,q} \mu_t^{i,q}, \tag{4.7}$$

where $h_t = h_t^{t-i,q} \; \forall q$ and $\forall i$.

In the endogenous labor supply model, instead, the number of hours worked by each individual is endogenous, and thus the aggregate labor supply becomes

$$\eta_t = \sum_{q=1}^{Q} \sum_{i=1}^{J^q} (1 - l_t^{t-i,q}) \varepsilon_t^{i,q} \mu_t^{i,q} \tag{4.8}$$

The aggregate capital stock is obtained by aggregating the individual net savings over education classes and generations:

$$k_t = \sum_{q=1}^{Q} \sum_{i=1}^{G} \frac{\mu_t^{i,q} a_t^{t-i,q}}{1+n} \tag{4.9}$$

Agents maximize their expected utility—subject to their individual budget constraints—with respect to the consumption flow and—in the model with endogenous labor supply—to their labor supply; while firms maximize profits with respect to their choice of the factors of production—capital and labor—given the technological constraint. The optimizing conditions for agents and firms and equilibrium conditions in the factor markets determine the usual expression for hourly wage, w_t, and rate of return on capital, r_t:

$$w_t = f_1[\eta_t(1+\lambda)^t, k_t],$$
$$R_t = 1 + r_t = f_2[\eta_t(1+\lambda)^t, k_t] + 1 - \delta, \tag{4.10}$$

where δ is the parameter of the physical depreciation rate in the economy and subscripts for the function f denote the partial derivatives with respect to the relevant variable—respectively the marginal product of labor and the marginal product of capital.

4.1.3   Social Security Systems
In pure unfunded social security systems, in every period total contributions equal total benefits. Since every agent at any time t contributes a fraction τ_t of her labor income, total contributions depend on the tax rate τ_t, and on the retirement age J^q according to the following equation:

$$T_t(\tau_t, J^q) = \tau_t \sum_{q=1}^{Q} \sum_{j=s^q}^{J^q-1} \mu_t^{j,q} \varepsilon_t^{t-j,q} h_t^{t-j,q} w_t^j. \tag{4.11}$$

Everywhere pension benefits represent an annuity paid to the retirees. Under budget balance the total amount of pensions paid out to retirees is equal to the aggregate contributions of the current workers:

$$T_t(\tau_t, J^q) = \sum_{q=1}^{Q} \sum_{j=J^q}^{G} P_t^{j,q} \mu_t^{j,q}. \tag{4.12}$$

As detailed at chapter 2, social security systems differ across countries along several institutional features, such as (1) statutory and effective retirement age, (2) pension benefit calculation, and (3) pension indexation criterion. For instance, in Italy, prior to the reforms, and in Germany, pension benefits are indexed to aggregate productivity (real wage) growth, λ, and hence evolve according to $P_{t+1}^{j,q} = P_t^{j,q}(1 + \lambda_t)$. However, if pension benefits are only indexed to inflation, they remain constant in real terms: $P_{t+1}^{j,q} = P_t^{j,q}$.

4.1.4 Economic Equilibrium

In this model economy, an equilibrium requires all agents to take their economic decisions between savings and consumption—in the second specification of the model, also between labor and leisure—in order to maximize their well-being given their budget (and time) constraints. Analogously, firms have to determine their demand of the factors of production (labor and capital) so as to maximize profits, given the technological constraints. Finally, factor prices are endogenously determined to clear all markets. Notice that since the determination of the social security contribution rates occurs in the political arena, the economic equilibrium is obtained for a given sequence of these contribution rates. The following definition of equilibrium may be skipped by the nontechnical readers.

Formally, for a given sequence of social security contribution rates, labor productivity and population growth rates, and retirement ages, $(\tau_t, n_t, \lambda_t, J_t^q)_{t=0,...,\infty}^{q=1,...,Q}$ a competitive economic equilibrium is characterized by a sequence of allocations and prices, $(c_{t+j}^{t,q}, l_{t+j}^{t,q}, w_t, R_t)$ $\forall t = 0, \ldots, \infty, \forall j = 0, \ldots, G,$ and $\forall q = 1, \ldots, Q,$ such that in every period the following conditions are satisfied:

• The consumer problem is solved for each type $\forall q = 1, \ldots, Q$, and generation $\forall j = 0, \ldots, G$. Hence every type-q agent aged j maximizes the expected utility at equation (4.1)—further described at equations (4.2) and (4.3), depending on the specification of the model—with respect to $(c_{t+j}^{t,q}, l_{t+j}^{t,q})$ and given the sequence of budget constraints at equation (4.4).

• Firms maximize their profits, and the conditions at equation (4.10) are satisfied.

• Labor, capital, and goods markets clear, and thus respectively equation (4.8), equation (4.9), and the following expression are satisfied:

$$\sum_{q=1}^{Q} \sum_{i=1}^{G} (a_t^{t-i+1,q} + c_t^{t-i+1,q}) \mu_t^{i,q}$$

$$= f[\eta_t (1 + \lambda)^t, k_t] + (1 - \delta) \sum_{q=1}^{Q} \sum_{i=1}^{G} \mu_{t-1}^{i,q} a_{t-1}^{t-i,q}. \tag{4.13}$$

It is convenient at this point to define the expected utility in a competitive equilibrium for a type-q agent aged i at time t, which will be used in the formal definition of the political game in section 4.2.2. For a given sequence of social security contribution rates, labor productivity and population growth rates, and retirement ages, $(\tau_t, n_t, \lambda_t, J_t^q)_{t=0,\ldots,\infty}^{q=1,\ldots,Q}$, the remaining expected utility in a competitive equilibrium for a type-q agent aged i at time t, is

$$v_t^{t-i,q}(\{\tau_t, n_t, \lambda_t, J_t^q\}_{t=0,\ldots,\infty}^{q=1,\ldots,Q}) = \sum_{j=0}^{G-i} \beta^j \left[\prod_{x=i-1}^{j+i-1} \frac{\pi^{x,q}}{\pi^{i-1,q}} \right] U(c_{t+j}^{t,q}, l_{t+j}^{t,q}), \tag{4.14}$$

where $U(c_{t+j}^{t,q}, l_{t+j}^{t,q})$ is defined according to equation (4.2) in the first specification of the model (with exogenous labor supply) and to equation (4.3) otherwise; and $(c_{t+j}^{t,q}, l_{t+j}^{t,q}, w_t, R_t) \, \forall t = 0, \ldots, \infty, \forall j = 0, \ldots, G$, and $\forall q = 1, \ldots, Q$ is a competitive equilibrium for a given $(\tau_t, n_t, \lambda_t, J_t^q)_{t=0,\ldots,\infty}^{q=1,\ldots,Q}$.

4.2 The Political System

In the political environment every individual expresses her preferences over the size of the system—specifically over the social security contribution rate—given the different institutional settings prevailing in each system, such as retirement age,[6] eligibility criteria, indexation, and benefit rule. The individuals' preferences over the level of social security typically depend on their characteristics,[7] such as age and educational attainments, and on the main features of the system. Since a PAYG social security system imposes a cost on the young—the contribution—and provides a transfer—the pension benefit—to the elderly, retirees will generally support the system. Workers are instead willing to incur in current and future costs only if they expect to be sufficiently compensated by future pension benefits. More specifically, every agent determines her most preferred social security contribution rate by evaluating two factors: (1) the implicit return provided by the social security in comparison to the returns available on the capital market from assets of comparable risk, and (2) the effects on wage and rate of returns induced by a social security system through changes in the stock of capital. This theoretical framework thus embeds all the economic determinants discussed in the chapter 3: the latter factor relates to the crowding out effect, while the former captures the within cohort redistributive element and the "partial time horizon" motive. This last element represents a crucial factor of sustainability. Past contributions to the system do not affect the agents' decisions, since they could not be re-appropriated by the agents, were the system to be abandoned, and thus represent a sunk cost. Therefore middle-aged and elderly individuals are more supportive of social security systems, as they will mostly enjoy pension benefits in their remaining time horizon. Figure 4.2 describes an individual's residual time horizon when taking her political decision over the contribution rate.

This book shares Pierson's (1996) view that social security issues—especially in graying societies, in which retrenchment policies are widely debated—raise large electoral concerns among policy-makers. I

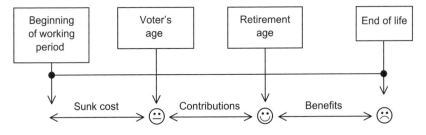

Figure 4.2
Voter's time horizon

hence consider a simple majority voting model to aggregate individual preferences. Since preferences over social security are single peaked, the equilibrium outcome of the voting game coincides with the most preferred social security contribution rate by the median voter. The political sustainability of a social security system is therefore identified with the existence of a political majority willing to support the pension system in all its provisions, and this majority is summarized by the median voter. Analogously, the future political sustainability of social security under population aging will require some features of these systems—such as retirement age, contribution rate, or their generosity—to be modified in order to retain the support of a majority of voters.

4.2.1   Political System: Some Modeling Issues

Social security policies clearly involve a complex decision process that can only be partially described by a simple majority voting model. The brief discussion in chapter 3 outlined the existence of several economic and political aspects that may account for the different paths of expansion and, possibly, of retrenchment of the welfare state. The corporatist view—that emphasizes the role played by unions, left parties and lobbies in the social security policy-making—and the institutional approach—that highlights the importance of veto power and political accountability as shaped by the political and electoral institutions—have largely contributed to explain the rapid increase in social spending and the diversity across OECD countries. Yet, as suggested by Pierson (1996), once established, welfare states build their own political constituencies—thereby creating large electoral concerns among policymakers dealing with social security issues. Simple majority voting represents the minimal political environment where to analyze these electoral concerns. This modeling choice abstracts from corporatist or institutional considerations, whose role in a retrenching phase of the system does not seem crucial (see section 3.3), but it has the advantage of providing a coherent and transparent analysis of the impact of the demographic dynamics on the political process. Aging leads to an older electorate, and thus to more political demand for social security.

Another important modeling decision is to assume that elections over social security contributions—as in a direct democracy—take place every period. Who will favor social security in these repeated elections? Despite the aging process and—in some countries—the low retirement age or the elderly high participation rate[8] at elections, retirees do not constitute anywhere—at least yet—a majority of the voters. Political sustainability thus requires some workers to vote in favor of social security. Yet, why should workers be willing to support a system that entails a sure current cost—the contribution—but only uncertain future benefits, since the system may be abandoned in any future election, and hence before they reach retirement age? Would agents not be better off by waiting a few years and by supporting the system only after their retirement?

In a repeated voting environment, an implicit social contract among successive generations of voters may emerge that induces some workers to support the system. As discussed in the previous chapter (see section 3.2.2), the compliance with this social norm—and hence the support to social security—by some current young or middle-aged workers is entirely based on self interest. Today's voters agree to transfer resources to current retirees because they expect to be rewarded for their actions with a sufficiently large transfer in their old age. If current voters fail to comply with the contract—thus choosing not to pay any social security to current old—they will receive no transfers in their old age.

This strategic approach to voting over social security issues is known to generate a high degree of indeterminacy, as many sequences of contributions rates can be sustained as a political equilibrium of the voting game (see Galasso and Profeta 2002). For instance, if workers expect their current voting behavior to carry no consequences for future elections, their dominant voting strategy will be to set a contribution rate equal to zero, and hence no social security system will ever be introduced. However, since the aim of the calibration analysis is to provide for each country a quantitative assessment of the impact of aging on social security by comparing the economic and political equilibria at two distant points in time, in the year 2000 and in the year 2050, I choose to concentrate on stationary voting strategy profiles. These voting strategies are consistent with a steady state analysis and induce an equilibrium with social security, in which the contribution rate maximizes the remaining life time expected utility of the median voter (for a formal definition, see section 4.2.2).

Throughout most of the book the political sustainability of social security is defined with respect to the size of the system, in particular, to the contribution rate. While funding may represent the most characterizing feature[9] of the system, a positive theory of the impact of aging on the determination of social security should ideally predict also the effects of aging on all other features, such as degree of redistributiveness, benefit calculation formula, pension indexation, and retirement age. The aggregation of individual preferences on all these elements through a political institution, such as simple majority voting, represents a difficult task. In fact in elections with a multidimensional policy space, where several issues have to be determined contemporaneously, a political equilibrium in a simple majority voting may fail to exist, since Condorcet cycles typically arise. The heart of the problem lays in that different voting majorities may exist that support alternative bundles of policies—each one representing a full characterization of the social security system. Voters are constantly induced to switch from one majority to another by the temptation of getting closer to their most preferred configuration of the system. Unfortunately, this process of majority building may be endless; and hence a political equilibrium may not arise (see Ordershook 1986 for an extensive discussion of these issues).

The conventional economic wisdom and most of the simulation analysis of the following chapters, however, suggest that modifying one feature of the current social security system—the effective retirement age—may represent the most efficient response to aging. In an attempt to extend the predictive power of this political economy model beyond the effects of aging on the size of social security, and thus to assess the political feasibility of postponing retirement, I present in section 11.3 the simulations of a political equilibrium that jointly determines contribution rate and retirement age.

To overcome the possible lack of a political equilibrium, the simple majority voting model formally described in the next section is changed into a bi-dimensional voting environment in which individuals vote over these two policies. This voting framework supports the notion of structure induced equilibrium, introduced by Shepsle (1979). The idea behind this notion of equilibrium is that some institutional restrictions need to be imposed to convert a simple majority bi-dimensional election into a simultaneous issue-by-issue voting game, in which an equilibrium exists. These restrictions consist of assigning the entire electorate—or its representatives, in Shepsle's (1979) original formulation—to two committees, one with jurisdiction over the social security contribution rate, and one over the retirement age, which separately—but simultaneously—decide over the two issues at stake.

This separation between the two issues prevents the voters to shift among different voting majorities, and is thus crucial for a (structure-induced) equilibrium to arise (for more details, see Shepsle 1979).

Since elections still take place every period, and hence a strategic voting component may emerge, the equilibrium concept for these repeated elections is the SPSIE (subgame perfect structure induced equilibrium) developed by Conde-Ruiz and Galasso (2005). This notion of equilibrium applies the idea of subgame perfection to the concept of structure-induced equilibrium, in the context of a bi-dimensional voting game (a formal description of this voting model is in the appendix). The next section provides a formal description of the political environment, and may be skipped by the nontechnical readers.

4.2.2 A Formal Definition of the Political Game

Social security contribution rates represent the equilibrium outcome of a voting game played by successive generations of voters, with elections taking place every period. Players in this voting game are all agents alive at every election. They are forward-looking in their voting behavior, as they take into consideration the consequences of their decisions on future elections.

At time t, for each type q and generation i, a representative player is defined as the type-q generational player i. Hence at every election there are $G \times Q$ players whose political mass will differ depending on the size of the education groups and of the cohorts and also possibly because of different participation rates at elections. The relative weight of the vote of a type-q generational player i at time t is equal to $\psi_t^{i,q}$, with $\sum_{q=i}^{Q} \sum_{i=1}^{G} \psi_t^{i,q} = 1 \ \forall t$. This aggregation through generational players restores the strategic aspects of this pension game, which may be lost if one considers an infinite number of agents, each one having zero mass.

Every individual's action space is the set of social security contribution rates, $[0, 1]$; an action for a type-q generational player i at time t is a contribution rate, $\alpha_t^{i,q} \in [0, 1]$, and hence the action profile at time t is the vector of actions played at time t by all generational players: $\alpha_t = \{\alpha_t^{1,1}, \ldots, \alpha_t^{1,Q}, \alpha_t^{2,1}, \ldots, \alpha_t^{2,Q}, \ldots, \alpha_t^{G,1}, \ldots, \alpha_t^{G,Q}\}$.

In this majority voting system the political outcome is the one preferred by a majority of voters. If individuals' preferences are single peaked over the political outcome, the realized contribution rate at time t, τ_t, is the median of the distribution of actions played by all players at time t. Given $Q + 2$ sequences $(n_t, \lambda_t, J_t^q)_{t=0,\ldots,\infty}^{q=i,\ldots,Q}$ and a sequence of profiles of actions and corresponding outcomes, $(\alpha_0, \ldots, \alpha_t,$ $\alpha_{t+1}, \ldots)$ and $(\tau_0, \ldots, \tau_t, \tau_{t+1}, \ldots)$, the expected payoff for a type-q generational player i at time t is given by her expected utility, as defined at equation (4.14), $v_t^{t-i,q}(\{\tau_t, n_t, \lambda_t, J_t^q\}_{t=0,\ldots,\infty}^{q=1,\ldots,Q})$.

The history of the game at time t describes the sequence of social security contribution rates up to time $t - 1$: $H_t = (\tau_0, \tau_1, \ldots, \tau_{t-1})$. Hence, a strategy for a type-q player of age i at time t is a mapping: $\sigma_t^{i,q}$: $H_t \to [0,1]$. The collection of strategies adopted at time t by all generational players is summarized by $\sigma_t = \{\sigma_t^{1,1}, \ldots, \sigma_t^{1,Q}, \sigma_t^{2,1}, \ldots, \sigma_t^{2,Q}, \ldots,$ $\sigma_t^{G,1}, \ldots, \sigma_t^{G,Q}\}$, while $\sigma_t^{-(i,q)}$ denotes the collection σ_t without the element $\sigma_t^{i,q}$. Given the realized sequence of social security tax rates resulting from the sequence of strategies $(\sigma_0, \ldots, \sigma_t, \ldots, \sigma_{t+G-i+1})$ and $Q + 2$ sequences $(n_t, \lambda_t, J_t^q)_{t=0,\ldots,\infty}^{q=1,\ldots,Q}$, the consumption and leisure in a competitive equilibrium of a type-q generational player i at time t are $c_t^{t-i,q}(\sigma_0, \ldots, \sigma_t, \ldots, \sigma_{t+G-i+1}, \{n_t, \lambda_t, J_t^q\}_{t=0,\ldots,\infty}^{q=1,\ldots,Q})$ and $l_t^{t-i,q}(\sigma_0, \ldots, \sigma_t, \ldots,$ $\sigma_{t+G-i+1}, \{n_t, \lambda_t, J_t^q\}_{t=0,\ldots,\infty}^{q=1,\ldots,Q})$ respectively. Finally, define $\Theta = (\sigma_0, \ldots,$ $\sigma_t^{i,q}, \sigma_t^{-(i,q)}, \ldots, \sigma_{t+G-i+1}, \{n_t, \lambda_t, J_t^q\}_{t=0,\ldots,\infty}^{q=1,\ldots,Q})$. Then a type-$q$ generational player i at time t maximizes

$$V_t^{t-i,q}(\Theta) = \sum_{j=0}^{G-i} \beta^j \left[\prod_{x=i-1}^{j+i-1} \frac{\pi^{x,q}}{\pi^{i-1,q}} \right] U(c_{t+j}^{t,q}(\Theta), l_{t+j}^{t,q}(\Theta)) \qquad (4.15)$$

with respect to $\sigma_t^{i,q}$, where $U(c_{t+j}^{t,q}, l_{t+j}^{t,q})$ is defined according to equation (4.2) or (4.3), depending on the specification of the model.

Consistently with the steady state analysis performed throughout the book, I concentrate on a stationary strategy profile that will lead to the formal definition of a politically sustainable social security contribution rate. Consider a positive contribution rate $\hat{\tau} > 0$, at time t a family of histories with social security $\hat{\tau}$ is defined as $H_t(\hat{\tau}) = (\tau_0 = 0, \ldots, \tau_{j-1} = 0, \tau_j = \hat{\tau}, \tau_{j+1} = \hat{\tau}, \ldots, \tau_{t-1} = \hat{\tau})$ $\forall j \in [0, t-1]$. Hence this family of histories identifies situations in which either no social security system has ever been introduced, $\tau_j = 0$ $\forall j \in [0, t-1]$, or social security with a contribution rate of $\hat{\tau} > 0$ has been introduced at some point, and has always prevailed since then.

A stationary social security strategy profile $\hat{\sigma}_t^{i,q}$ $\forall t = 0, \ldots, \infty$, $\forall j = 0, \ldots, G$, and $\forall q = 1, \ldots, Q$ requires generational players with intermediate age (from l to u) and low education types (below q^u) to vote $\hat{\tau}$ if these histories prevailed; or otherwise, it demands all types of generational players in their working age to dismantle the system, $\tau = 0$:

- $\hat{\sigma}_t^{i,q}(H_t) = \hat{\tau}$ for $i \in [l, u]$ and $q < q^u$ if $H_t = H_t(\hat{\tau})$;
- $\hat{\sigma}_t^{i,q}(H_t) = 0$ for $i \in [1, J^q]$ and $\forall q$ if $H_t \neq H_t(\hat{\tau})$.

This stationary social security strategy profile $\hat{\sigma}_t^{i,q}$ is a subgame perfect Nash equilibrium of the voting game if—for given sequences of population and labor productivity growth rates and of retirement ages for all Q education groups, $(n_t, \lambda_t, J_t^q)_{t=0,\ldots,\infty}^{q=1,\ldots,Q}$, and for a given capital stock, k—individual optimality conditions are satisfied $\forall t = 0, \ldots, \infty$, $\forall j = 0, \ldots, G$ and $\forall q = 1, \ldots, Q$, that is,

$$V_t^{t-i,q}(\hat{\sigma}_0, \ldots, \hat{\sigma}_t^{i,q}, \hat{\sigma}_t^{-(i,q)}, \ldots, \hat{\sigma}_{t+G-i+1})$$

$$\geq V_t^{t-i,q}(\hat{\sigma}_0, \ldots, \sigma_t^{i,q}, \hat{\sigma}_t^{-(i,q)}, \ldots, \hat{\sigma}_{t+G-i+1});$$

if $\sum_{q=1}^{q^u} \sum_{i=l}^{u} \psi_t^{i,q} \geq 1/2$ and $\sum_{q=1}^{Q} \sum_{i=1}^{J^q} \psi_t^{i,q} \geq 1/2 \ \forall t$, that is, at least a majority of the voters follows the strategy, and if the capital stock associated to the equilibrium contribution rate, $k(\hat{\tau})$ from equation (4.9), is equal to the given initial capital stock, that is, $k = k(\hat{\tau})$.

Since several positive tax rates $\hat{\tau} > 0$ could be sustained by this strategy profile, consistently with the median voter theorem, I choose to concentrate on the constant sequence among the subgame perfect equilibrium contribution rates that maximizes the utility of the median voter. Formally, for given sequences of population and labor productivity growth rates and of retirement ages for all Q education groups, $(n_t, \lambda_t, J_t^q)_{t=0,\ldots,\infty}^{q=1,\ldots,Q}$, the politically sustainable social security contribution rate is the outcome of the stationary social security strategy profile $\hat{\sigma}_t^{i,q}$ that maximizes the median voter's indirect utility.

4.3   Methodology and Calibration

To evaluate quantitatively how the policy-makers' response to electoral concerns may affect social security systems in graying societies, I use a two-stage methodology consisting of the calibration of the model and of its simulation. In its initial steady state, the model is calibrated to capture the main economic, demographic, and political aspects, and the institutional elements of the different social security systems in France, Germany, Italy, Spain, the United Kingdom, and the United States, around the year 2000. According to this strategy (see Cooley and Prescott 1995) the calibration exercise considers each country as a closed economy and pins down the values of the key parameters of the theoretical model. To simulate how political constraints will shape social security under aging, the model is then fed with the forecasted values of demographic, economic and political variables for the year 2050, and the social security contribution rates, which arise as a political equilibrium, are calculated under different policy scenarios.

In the calibrated model every period corresponds to one year. Agents are born at age 18 and may live up to age 95 $(G = 77)$, according to age specific probability of survival. For each country, these probabilities are averages by gender of 1999 official estimates. For Italy, Spain, the United Kingdom, and the United States, surviving probabilities by education level are also computed according to the following procedure: official survival probabilities are assigned to agents in the intermediate education group; survival probabilities of agents in the low education group are obtained by increasing the mortality rate by 5 percent at every age; while the survival probabilities of the agents in the third group—the high education level—are obtained by reducing it by 5 percent. Given these surviving probabilities, the population growth rate used in the calibration for the year 2000 is calculated to match the elderly dependency ratios reported in chapter 2. All these estimated parameters are displayed at table 4.1.

For the calibration of the labor market, the crucial variables are the average employment rate and the labor efficiency by age and—in some cases—by education. In the first specification of the model (with exogenous labor supply), the average amount of time dedicated to productive activities equals the average employment rate. The labor efficiency units by age and education correspond to the labor income

Table 4.1
Estimated parameters of the model

	France	Germany	Italy	Spain	United Kingdom	United States
Population growth	1.04%	0.62%	0.7%	0.8%	0.5%	1.35%
Average employment	65.4%	71.4%	45.6%	43.5%	64.7%	60%
Median voter's age	43	46	44	44	45	47
Capital share	31%	34%	38%	34.7%	30%	36%
Capital–output ratio	2.21	2.32	3.18	2.37	1.81	2.43
Productivity growth	1.6%	1.8%	1.92%	2.2%	2.6%	1.94%

Sources: See data appendix.
Note: Estimates for all parameters but capital–output ratios refer to averages for the 1990s.

lifetime profile, and these are obtained by using country-specific microeconomic data on labor income by age—and education. In the second
specification (with endogenous labor supply model), the *endogenous*
amount of time dedicated to productive activities by age is calibrated
to the average employment rate by age. The labor efficiency index by
age (and education) is obtained from microeconomic data by combining wage income and employment rate by age. Another crucial labor
market variable is the retirement age, which is set at the median effective retirement age for each country (see chapter 2). All these parameters' values are reported at table 4.1.

The calibration of the production side is standard. For the constant
return to scale production function at equation (4.6) the value of the
average capital share is taken from national accounts, while the exogenous productivity growth is given by the average per-capita GDP
growth rate during the nineties. Depreciation rate is set equal to an
average value of 5 percent for all countries. The long-term characteristics of each economy are described by its capital–output ratio (see
Cooley and Prescott 1995), which can be obtained from several publications (see the data appendix).

The crucial feature of each social security system is taken to be the
equilibrium—rather than the legal—social security contribution rate,
which in each period equates total contributions to total pension benefits. In the calibration, this equilibrium social security contribution is
computed for the nineties; for countries running a budget deficit (or
surplus), the transfer from the general taxation is thus imputed to the
contribution rate.

For each country, the model is calibrated to match the capital–
output ratio and the equilibrium social security contribution rate in the
initial scenario, that is, in 2000. The contribution rate is chosen by the
median voter. If agents only differ by age, the political system is easily
parameterized to the median voter's age; whereas if individuals differ
also by education, the median voter has to be identified in terms of
age and education class. For computation of the median voter, electoral
participation rate by age—and, when relevant, by education classes—
are also considered. These restrictions on the capital–output ratio and
on the equilibrium contribution rate (as chosen by the median voter)
jointly pin down two parameters of utility function: the subjective time
discount rate and the coefficient of relative risk aversion, which are
reported at table 4.2. In the specification of the model with endogenous
labor supply, the restriction that the average amount of time dedicated

Table 4.2
Calibrated parameters of the model

Model parameter	France	Germany	Italy	Spain	United Kingdom	United States
Exogenous labor supply						
CRRA	4.0	2.41	2.67	1.86	3.65	4.17
SDF	1.08	1.01	1.07	1.00	1.04	1.08
Endogenous labor supply						
CRRA	6.62	3.18	2.42	2.42	4.84	9.95
SDF	1.16	1.04	1.06	1.01	1.08	1.35
CE	0.71	0.82	0.61	0.61	0.75	0.80

Notes: CRRA, coefficient of relative risk aversion (ρ in equations 4.2 and 4.3), SDF, subjective discount factor (β in equation 4.1), and CE preference for consumption elasticity (α in equation 4.3). The former two parameters are jointly calibrated to match the capital–output ratio and the equilibrium social security contribution rate; the latter parameter to match the average employment rate.

Table 4.3
Forecasted parameters of the model for 2050

	France	Germany	Italy	Spain	United Kingdom	United States
Population growth	−0.05%	−1.14%	−1.5%	−1.69%	−1.0%	0.25%
Median voter's age	56	55	57	57	53	53
Productivity growth	1.8%	1.8%	1.8%	1.8%	1.7%	1.94%

Sources: See data appendix.

to labor has to equal the average employment rate allows to calibrate also the relative importance of the leisure in the utility function, that is, α at equation (4.3).

In the second step, corresponding to the simulation exercise, I retain the calibrated parameters and feed the model with forecasted values of economic, demographic, and political variables for the year 2050. In particular, to simulate the size of the aging population, I use the official 2050 surviving probabilities for France and the United States, while for Germany, Italy, Spain, and the United Kingdom, I compute the surviving probabilities by reducing the 1999 official mortality rate by 10 percent. The population growth rate used in the simulation for 2050 is also calculated to match—given the corresponding surviving probability—the expected elderly dependency ratios (see chapter 2). The forecasted demographic dynamics modifies the age of the median voter (in the specification with no heterogeneity within cohort) as described in chapter 2. The 2050 simulations are provided for several retirement ages; while the forecasts for the exogenous productivity growth are taken from EC projections. All these forecasted parameters are reported at table 4.3.

With this new set of parameters, the model simulates—in a new steady state—the political sustainability of the social security system—that is, the social security contribution rate chosen by the median voter in the year 2050 for different retirement ages. The simulations results in the following chapters compare the initial steady state equilibrium—as calibrated for the year 2000—with the political equilibrium emerging in the 2050 steady state under different policy scenarios.

5 The Future of the Social Security System in France

The public provision of retirement income in France is characterized by the coexistence of basic statutory pensions and supplementary schemes based on industrywide agreements. The first pillar, instituted in 1945 as an unfunded scheme, was intended to cover all workers and is composed of several programs related to the worker's type. The largest scheme is the *régime général*, which covers employees in the private sectors, while other programs exist for farmers, self-employed, and employees in the public sector.

Supplementary programs also unfunded, administrated by the unions[1] and the management under the supervision of the state, form the second pillar. The two largest complementary schemes are AGIRC (*Association Générale des Institutions de Retraite des Cadres*), which was instituted in 1947 in favor of executives and managerial staff, and ARRCO (*Association pour le Régime de Retraite Complémentaire de Salariés*) which was launched in 1961 to cover all salaried workers. Currently this unfunded second pillar covers all workers in the private sector, as its affiliation became mandatory in 1972.

This complex system of public provision of retirement income based on two unfunded pension schemes grants, on average, around 80 percent of the income of a French retiree (see Legendre and Pelé 2001). Unsurprisingly, the financial burden of the pension system is large: in 2000, it amounted to 12.1 percent of GDP. Under the challenge of an aging population, France underwent a period of reforms in the nineties (see section 5.1), aimed at reducing the fractionalization of a system, which was based on a plethora of private and public schemes with distinct rules and conditions, in an attempt to improve its efficiency and to reduce its cost.

Unlike in many other countries, pension spending does not entirely dominate the French welfare state. As displayed at figure 5.1, in 2000

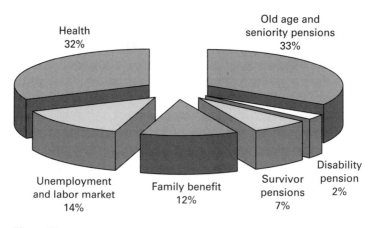

Figure 5.1
Welfare expenditure decomposition in 2000 (Source: OECD)

old age and seniority pensions amounted to 33 percent of total welfare spending, while survivor and disability pensions added 9 percent. Health care expenditure—an item largely targeted to elderly and children—represented an additional 32 percent of the welfare spending, but unemployment and labor expenditure (14 percent) and family benefits (12 percent) were also sizable.

Another crucial feature of the French pension system rests with the widespread use of early retirement options by the elderly workers. Among French workers this common practice has caused the participation rate for males aged 55 to 64 years to drop from 80.3 percent in the sixties to only 41.1 percent in 2000. As suggested by Blanchet and Pelé (1999), the main reason for this retirement behavior is the introduction, in the early seventies, of several types of generous early retirement provisions—such as early retirement programs, disability, and unemployment pensions—that failed to incorporate adequate reductions in the early retirees' pension benefits. The cost of early retirement in terms of forgone potential income, as estimated by Herbertsson and Orszag (2003), is expected to rise from 6.2 percent of GDP in 1980—when the average across OECD countries was 5.3 percent—to 15.1 percent of GDP in 2010, vis-à-vis an OECD average of 9.1 percent.

This extensive use of early retirement provisions—the median effective retirement age among male workers in 2000 was only 58 years—coupled with the aging process has been largely responsible for the substantial increase in the French pension spending, which is expected to raise to almost 16 percent by 2050, according to the official EC-OECD estimates (see table 2.3). Since the aging process in France has been characterized by significant longevity gains (see section 5.2), the combined effect of early retirement and aging has led to large increases in the average length of the retirement period, which—according to estimates by Colin, Legros, and Mahieu (2000)—has reached 18.7 years for workers in the private sector and 23.9 years for those in the public sector.[2]

The main focus of this chapter is to evaluate the long-run political sustainability of the French pension system under population aging, using the political economic model described at chapter 4. The demographic process, examined in detail at section 5.2, largely depends on the French population increased longevity. The corresponding rise in the dependency ratio—the share of elderly per worker—is further augmented by the early retirement pattern observed among French workers. Section 5.3 discusses the simulations results on the political future of the French system. While the aging process reduces the profitability of the pension system—since fewer contributors have to finance a growing number of retirees—longevity gains amplify the political weight of the elderly voters and modify the identity of the crucial political player—the median voter. The simulations suggest that this tighter political constraint will induce more social security, a higher contribution rate, and more generous pension benefits. The politics of aging will thus lead to an increase in the total resources dedicated to the pension system also in per-capita terms since the replacement rates are projected to rise. These simulations results are in line with the experience of the French pension reforms of the 1990s, which aimed at reducing the generosity of the system, along lengthy transition phases, but are not expected to be sufficient to decrease (or even to maintain) the total size of the system (see table 2.3)—thereby suggesting that future contribution rates will have to increase. According to the estimates at section 5.3, only a large rise in the effective retirement age—particularly beneficial due to the current low level in France—may counterbalance the political pressure for a large system induced by the aging process and limit the growth in pension spending. The long-term political feasibility of this reform measure, in a country currently featuring an extremely low effective retirement age, is addressed in section 11.3.

5.1   The Current Social Security System: An Overview

Retirement income provisions have long been present in France, mainly as fully funded occupational plans. As the war inflation swiped out most of these assets, a general PAYG old-age pension scheme was created in 1945. This general scheme was intended to cover all private workers, yet those workers enrolled in preexisting schemes at favorable conditions prevented a complete enlargement of the general system. As a result the French system has been characterized by a plethora of private and public schemes, each featuring distinct rules and conditions.

After the introduction in 1945 of a general PAYG pension system (*régime général*), two complementary schemes were created: AGIRC (*Association Générale des Institutions de Retraite des Cadres*) in 1947 and ARRCO (*Association pour le Régime de Retraite Complémentaire de Salariés*) in 1961. The former scheme was targeted to executives and managerial staff only, while the latter covers all salaried workers. The peculiarity of these complementary schemes, with respect to the occupational plans featured in several other countries, is in their PAYG financing method. Moreover these schemes were entirely run by the unions and the management, until some modifications were introduced in 1995. By 1972 the affiliation to a complementary scheme for private sector workers became mandatory.

In 1974 a first attempt to homogenize the existing schemes for the different types of workers—such as private and public sector employees, farmers, and self-employed—took place, with the adoption of a system of inter-regime compensation from schemes with the more favorable demographic profiles—namely the *régime général*—toward others schemes, such as the miners' and farmers'.

In the following years the generosity of the French system increased, as more early retirement options became available. In 1983, for instance, the retirement age required to qualify for a full pension was reduced from 65 to 60 years, although it was made contingent on the number of years of contributions. Early retirement was also available through pre-retirement schemes targeted to workers in specific sectors and unemployment insurance for old workers (see Blanchet and Pelé 1999).

By the end of the eighties the rise in pension spending, accompanied by a reduction in the labor market participation rate of elderly workers, stimulated a large debate on the need to reform the French pension system. The government, through the General Planning Agency, actively participated to this debate with the publication of a White Book on pensions (*Livre blanc sur les retraites*). This report contained projections of the social security contribution rates needed to finance pension spending up to 2040 and suggested some reform measures to reduce the financial unbalance of the system (see Blanchet and Legros 2002). Yet only years later some of the proposals in the *Livre blanc* were actually adopted.

5.1.1 Recent Reforms

Having secured a large majority to his right-to-center coalition at the 1993 general elections, which determined the *cohabitation* with the socialist President of the Republic, François Mitterrand, the Prime Minister Edouard Balladur launched a plan to reform the pension system, along the suggestions of the *Livre blanc*. The main reform measures aimed at containing the expected increase in pension spending, by limiting the generosity of the system. Eligibility was restricted, as the contribution period to obtain a full pension was increased from thirty-seven years and six months to forty years, over a ten-year transition period. Generosity was on average reduced, since the time period for computing the reference wage in the pension benefit formula was extended from the best ten to the best twenty-five years, in this case along a fifteen-year phase-in period. Pension benefits indexation shifted from earnings to inflation.

The choice of rather long transition periods allowed mature cohorts of workers and retirees to largely escape these pension cutbacks, which instead fell strongly on the younger generations (see Natali and Rhodes 2004a). According to calculations by the Institut de Recherches Economique et Sociales (see Math 2002), in fact per-capita pension spending over GDP for individuals aged 65 years or more is actually expected to increase from 72 percent in 2000 to 74 percent in 2010; and to drop to 69.1 percent only in 2020, and to 57.5 percent in 2040. These calculations and other evidence in Natali and Rhodes (2004a) tend to suggest that in 1994 individuals in their forties—hence corresponding to the French median voter, who was presumably 45 years old—were only marginally affected, if at all, by the reform. Bonoli (2000) and Béland (2001) highlight instead the role of the unions. They argue that Balladur adopted a nonconfrontational style and accompanied these unpopular measures with some concessions to the unions, in an effort to create a large consensus for reforming the system and to avoid overt protests among the most radical labor sectors. In particular, an attempt was made to eliminate noncontributory elements from the pensions system, by establishing a *Fonds de solidarité vieillesse* (FSV), from which noncontributory benefits—such as part of the pensions for individuals with insufficient contributions and contribution credits to the unemployed—were financed. The government committed an earmarked tax to this fund. Another crucial move was to restrict the reform measures to private workers only—that is, to the *régime général*—while leaving the position of almost 5.5 million, highly unionized, state employees untouched (see Bonoli 2000).

Two years later a reform of the public employees' pension system was launched by the Juppé conservative government, but had to be largely withdrawn, as a consequence of three weeks of massive strikes. During his 1995 political campaign the conservative Jacque Chirac had denied the need for any additional reform, while emphasizing the role of economic growth in solving the financial distress of the French pension system. In fact after his election to president, minimum pensions were immediately increased by 2.8 percent. Yet the conservative Prime Minister Juppé—appointed by President Chirac—pushed to extend the Balladur reforms' measures to the public sector in order to achieve equity between private and public workers and to improve the financial sustainability of the entire pension system. The Juppé Plan included also the introduction of a 0.5 percent tax on all revenues, intended to reduce the outstanding social security debt, and a modification of the French Constitution granting the Parliament the right to approve the social security budget. Backed by a large majority in the Parliament and under the external constraint of having to comply with strict economic criteria for entering the European Monetary Union, Juppé was determined to confront the unions in an attempt to reduce their control over the pension system. Three long weeks of massive strikes followed, which literally blocked the nation. Juppé was forced to abandon his plan to reform the public sector pensions, although other measures, including the increased control of the government over the system, were adopted.

According to Bonoli (2000), the failure of the Juppé's reform plan was mainly due to his confrontational style and to the strong opposition by the public employees' unions, which enjoyed a much larger representation than in the private sector. Yet the 1995 reform plan had also a different impact on the workers' well-being than the 1993 reform (see Natali and Rhodes 2004a). For instance, in 1993, the increase in the contribution period to 40 years had no impact on a large majority of the workers in the private sector (62 percent), who featured a contribution period of more than 40 years. However, in 1995, the application of this measure to the public sector instead affected a large majority of workers, since the average contribution period among public employees did not even reach 31 years. As in the case of the Berlusconi reform attempt in Italy (see chapter 7), the 1995 Juppé failure to reform the system may hence be attributed to an ill-designed plan, which was unable to properly divide (and rule) the electorate in winners and losers. This interpretation is thus in line with the prediction of the median voter's model described at chapters 3 and 4.

The worsening of the financial situation—with the EC warning France on its budget deficit being about to exceed 3 percent of GDP—triggered a new pension reform in 2003, aimed again at reducing the generosity of the pensions, in particular for public employees. Despite its large majority in the Parliament, the Raffarin's conservative government privileged the social dialogue, engaging in lengthy negotiations with all social partners, and was finally able to pass the reform during the summer of 2003.

The novelty in the "Fillon reform"—named after the Social Affairs Minister François Fillon—was the introduction of tax-deductible, voluntary individual pension plans (*plans d'épargne individuel pour la retraite*), which were intended to provide the workers with fiscally advantageous saving instruments for retirement income. The crucial measures to retrench the system included—for the public employees—the progressive increase of the minimum contribution period from 37.5 to 40 years (by 2008) and the institution between 2006 and 2015 of an annual deduction for early retirement equal to 5 basis points per year; and—for all workers—the rise of the minimum contribution period to 41 years by 2012 and to 42 years by 2020. This projected increase in the contribution period was made contingent on the actual realization of the expected longevity gains for a 60 years old. Yet some reform measures went in the direction of increasing pension spending, in an attempt to secure the support of the biggest union, CFDT (Confédération Française Démocratique des Travailleurs). In fact the minimum retirement age remained at 60 years and early retirement plans were introduced, in the private sector, for employees aged 56 years, with 40 years of contributions who began to work when 14 to 16 years old. Still in the private sector, the annual early retirement deduction was reduced from 10 to 5 percent by 2013 for workers with less than 40 years of contributions. The overall effect of these measures—as estimated by Buffeteau and Godefroy (2005)—is to modify the future retirement age among French workers. In the public sector the Fillon reform is expected to postpone retirement age by 1.6 years for the 1945–54 cohorts and by 2.2 years for workers born between 1955 and 1974, while more moderate changes are estimated in the private sector. As a consequence of this new retirement behavior, Buffeteau and Godefroy (2005) forecast an increase in the average pension benefit for the 1945–54 cohorts in the public (and private) sector, while the generosity will drop for younger workers (born in 1965 to 1974) in the public sector. Hence, as argued by Natali and Rhodes (2004a) as well, the Fillon reform was designed according to a divide-and-conquer strategy aimed at protecting mature workers close to retirement and the most militant unionists, such as the metro and railway workers. Additionally this reform recurred heavily on the future postponement of the retirement age—a measure whose political feasibility is addressed in chapter 11. The simulations' results in section 5.3 will pursue further this median voter approach to predict whether new divide and rule strategies will arise in the future to guarantee a reduction of the French social security system, or instead some of these reforms' measures will actually be overturned by the political push of an older electorate.

5.1.2 The French System at the Turn of the Century

The French system of retirement income provision is highly fragmented; yet through its different schemes, it provides around 80 percent of the individuals' retirement income. The four main categories of workers belong to different programs: waged employees in the sectors of commerce and industry are under the *régime général* (which covers 65 percent of the total insured individuals); while separate schemes cover public sector employees (20 percent), self-employed (12 percent), and farmers (3 percent). Within the public sector, separate schemes exist for civil servants, local government employees, miners, rail workers, electricity employees, and gas employees; self-employed workers are separated into craftsmen, self-employed in industry or commerce, and liberal professions.

The French PAYG social security system has been designed along few key principles. Since entitlements are acquired through employment, the system tends to protect the breadwinner, rather than providing an enlarged safety net (see Esping-Andersen 1999). Benefits are primarily financed by contributions. Since the link between pension benefits and contributions has always been tight, the system entails little direct redistribution across individuals of different income groups. Another important specificity of the French system is the coexistence of a basic PAYG statutory pension and of PAYG supplementary schemes based on industrywide agreements. The former compulsory social insurance scheme provides pension benefits which depend on individual earnings and on the duration of the insurance affiliation. The *régime général* and the farm workers' social insurance scheme belong to this pillar. The latter compulsory supplementary pension insurance scheme covers all the employees already in the general pension scheme or in the scheme for employees in agricultural sector. Although there exists a multiplicity of programs under this second pillar, the two main schemes are ARRCO (association for supplementary retirement scheme for salaried workers) and AGIRC (general association of pension institutions for managerial staff). A third pillar composed of not compulsory—typically funded—supplementary pension schemes is instead not widely developed.

Eligibility to the first pillar—the *régime général* for private sector employees—is conditional on the workers having reached a minimum legal retirement age of 60 years and on having paid at least one quarter worth of contribution.[3] *Régime général* pensions depend on three factors: (1) a reference wage, which measures the average earnings of the worker, (2) a replacement rate, which varies according to the number of years of contribution and to the worker's retirement age; and (3) the number of quarters of contribution to the system.

The reference wage is equal to the average annual wage below the social security ceiling, calculated over a reference period. In 2002, this reference period[4] was equal to the best 19 years of wages (for an insured born in 1942). In this calculation, wages are adjusted using the growth rate of average wages until 1987, and the consumer prices index thereafter. The replacement rate ranges between a minimum of 25 percent and a maximum of 50 percent. It is separately computed according to the number of years of contribution and the worker's retirement age; the larger between the two values is then applied. The maximum replacement rate may hence be achieved by an individual retiring at age 65, regardless of the years of contributions; by an individual retiring at age 60 or more, who has accumulated 160 quarters (i.e., 40 years) of contributions; or in other instances related to disability or special credits for children. A reduction of 5 basis points to the replacement rate applies for every year of retirement prior to 65 years, while a 1.25 basis points reduction is used for every quarter needed to achieve 160 quarters of contributions. Regardless of the contribution period, the minimum replacement rate of 25 percent is always achieved when retiring at 60 years old.

These two factors—the reference wage and the replacement rate—are then multiplied by the ratio between the number of quarters of contribution—up to 150—and 150, in order to obtain the individual's *régime general* pension benefit. In 2002 pension benefits were capped at €14,112, while there was a minimum pension equal to €6,307.62 per year granted to any person eligible for a pension with the maximum replacement rate. All pension benefits are linked to the consumer price index.

Eligibility to the two main complementary schemes—ARRCO and AGIRC—depends on the workers' type, with the former program covering all private salaried workers, and the latter only executives and managerial workers (*cadres*). Hence the *cadres*—managers and professional staffs—pay contributions to and receive pension benefits from both schemes. The legal retirement age for these two programs is 65 years; however, early retirement is possible as soon as a worker turns 55, with no reductions of the pension benefit, if the conditions to retire with the maximum replacement rate in *régime general* are satisfied.

Both ARRCO and AGIRC follow a point system to calculate the pension benefits, as the German pension system (see chapter 6). Annual contributions by the workers are divided by the cost of acquiring a point—the reference wage—to find the annual points, which are then collected in individual accounts, along with any additional points obtained for periods of inability to earn, such as sickness and unemployment. Upon retirement, pension benefits are calculated as the product between the number of points in the workers' individual accounts and the current value of a point. For ARRCO, the value of a point at retirement in 2002 was €1.053, while the reference wage to obtain a point was equal to €11.8949. The basis for calculating ARRCO pension benefits is given by the wage below the social security ceiling for manager and professional staff (*cadres*) and below three times the social security ceiling for other employees. For AGIRC, in 2002, the value of a point at retirement was €0.3737, the reference wage was €4.1494, while the basis for calculating the points under AGIRC—and hence the AGIRC pension benefits for the *cadres*—was the wage above the social security ceiling. All pension benefits awarded under these two complementary schemes are linked to the consumer price index.

The financing of this complex pension system is guaranteed by a series of contribution rates on different portions of the workers' labor earnings, paid by employees and employers. In particular, for the *régime general* the contribution rate is equal to 1.6 percent on the entire salary—due by the employers—plus 14.75 percent of the wage below the social security ceiling—of which 8.2 percent due by the employers and 6.55 percent by the employees. The financing of ARRCO is ensured by a contribution rate of 6 percent—of which 3.6 percent is due by the employers and 2.4 percent by the employees—on the wage below the social security ceiling, for managers and professional staffs, and below three times the social security ceiling, for the other employees. To this contribution rate a temporary 1.5 percent has been added in an attempt to achieve the financial balance of the system. Above the social security ceiling (or the three times the ceiling for the non-*cadres*) the contribution rate depends on the year of birth of the firm at which the worker is employed, and this is set to reach 20 percent. The contribution rate for financing AGIRC is equal to 16 percent—plus a temporary 4 percent aimed at achieving the financial balance of the system. Between the ceiling and four times the ceiling, 12.5 percent is due by the employers and 7.5 percent by the employees, whereas between four and eight times the ceiling, the sharing is contracted upon by the two parts.

5.2 Demographic Elements

Aging in France is largely due to a strong increase in longevity. In 1960, life expectancy at birth amounted to 73.6 years for females and 67 years for males, hence comparing favorably with other European countries. Already in 1980, longevity had reached 78.4 years for females and 70.2 years for males, while increasing respectively to 82.8 and 74.8 years in 2000.

The reduction in fertility has instead been less pronounced in France than in other European countries. The fertility rate—the number of children per every woman between 18 and 45 years—dropped from 2.7 in the sixties and 2.5 in the seventies to 1.78 in the nineties. Moreover fertility has recovered to almost 1.9 in the year 2000, and is expected to remain above 1.8 in 2050—the highest value, together with the United Kingdom, among the six countries analyzed.

Due mainly to a further rise in the longevity at birth, which in the year 2050 is expected to reach 87 years for females—the highest in the

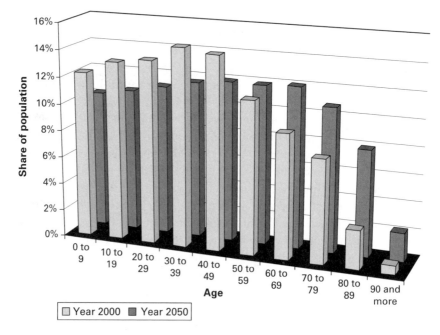

Figure 5.2
Aging in France: Population by age group in 2000 and 2050 (Source: Eurostat)

sample—and 80 years for males, EC estimates for the next fifty years indicate that in France the aging process will continue. The forecasted large reductions in the mortality rate at old age will modify the population profile by age as described at figure 5.2 for the years 2000 and 2050. The aging process increases the relative weight of the older generations: in 2000, individuals in their thirties and forties represented the two largest generations in the French population; in the year 2050, instead, people in their sixties (and fifties) will constitute the most numerous generation. Interestingly the very elderly individuals—those older than 80 years old—will increase from 2000 to 2050 by a factor of four.

A measure of the relevance of the aging process for the future of the France unfunded social security system is provided by the old age dependency ratio, which relates the share of elderly individuals—aged 65 years or more—to the potentially active individuals—aged 18 to 64 years. Table 2.5 suggests that the old age dependency ratio is expected to rise from almost 26 percent in 2000 to almost 49 percent in 2050. In other words, while in the year 2000 there were four individuals of working age for every elderly person, in the year 2050 there will only be two. Moreover, if the French early retirement behavior continues in the future, the impact of aging on the pension system will be magnified. In fact, when pension dependency ratios are considered—they are calculated by splitting workers and retirees according to the effective median retirement age in 2000—the picture is gloomier. As shown in table 2.5, in the year 2000, the ratio of retirees to workers was two to five, yet, if the effective retirement age remains at 58 years in 2050, it will increase to three to four.

The aging process—and in particular the increase in longevity—is also expected to modify the political representation of individuals in the different age groups. A synthetic measure of this phenomenon is given by the variation in the median age among the voters. In the year 2000 the median age among French voters was equal to 47 years, thus being the highest in the countries in the sample with the United States, which however display a large asymmetry in the participation rate at elections among age groups. Figure 2.3 shows that the median age among the voters is expected—according to EC demographic forecasts—to increase to 56 years by 2050. The aging of the voters, jointly with the early retirement behavior among French workers, will combine to magnify the political relevance of pension spending.

5.3   Political Constraints and the Future of Social Security

In 2000 France featured a large public intervention in the provision of retirement income, mainly through the *régime general* and the complementary schemes (ARRCO and AGIRC). The heated debate over the future of the French social security system focused on two crucial elements: the demographic process of population aging, which tends to expand pension spending by increasing the mass of retirees, and the popular early retirement practice among French workers, which could potentially exacerbate the demographic dynamics by enlarging the proportion of retirees.

Despite the reforms of the 1990s, official EC projections anticipate the French pension spending to rise to 15.9 percent of GDP in 2050. The changes in the benefit formulas introduced by the reforms of the 1990s (see section 5.1) are estimated to reduce pension spending by 3.4 percent of GDP; yet, the impact of the aging process on pension spending is expected to dominate (see table 2.3). The major drawback of these projections is that they fail to recognize that future modifications may

Table 5.1
Direct impact of aging: Simulation results

Year	Median voter's age	Effective retirement age	Social security contribution rate	Replacement rate
2000	47	58	22.4%	49.2%
2050	—	58	22.4%	30.0%
2050	47	58	32.4%	43.4%
2050	56	58	40.8%	54.6%
2050	56	59	39.0%	56.4%
2050	56	60	37.3%	58.4%
2050	56	61	35.6%	60.5%
2050	56	62	34.0%	62.9%
2050	56	63	32.5%	65.7%
2050	56	64	31.1%	68.8%
2050	56	65	29.7%	72.2%

Note: The first line describes the year 2000 scenario, and the second line shows the impact on the replacement rate of the expected aging for 2050 under a constant social security contribution rate. The third line displays the simulations for the social security contribution rate under the 2050 economic and demographic scenario, but with the year 2000 median voter's age. All other lines report the simulations for the social security contribution rates—carried out using the model in chapter 4, with exogenous labor supply—under the 2050 economic, demographic, and political (median voter's age) scenario for different retirement ages.

occur to the rules of the pension system—even to those implemented during the recent reforms—possibly as a political response to aging.

The simulations in this section take a different approach, by evaluating the political constraints that aging will impose on the French pension system. The initial situation featured by the French *régime général* and complementary schemes in the year 2000 is compared with the political equilibrium which is predicted to arise in 2050, under the expected demographic, economic and political scenario.

The principal features of the French system in the year 2000 are reported at the first line of table 5.1. Since in the calibrated model voters only differ with respect to their age, the median voter's age coincides with the median age among the voters, which in 2000 was equal to 47 years (see section 5.2). The social security contribution rate used in the simulations for the year 2000 represents an average of the different statutory values faced by an average worker in the private sector. This equilibrium contribution rate equalizes total contributions to total pension benefits, and is set equal to 22.4 percent, which—in the model—commands an overall replacement rate of almost 50 percent.

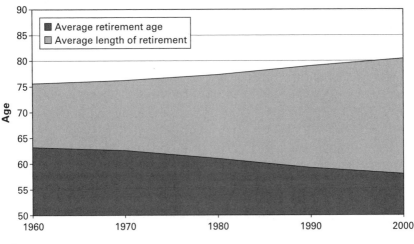

Figure 5.3
Longevity and retirement (Sources: Latulippe 1996 and OECD)

A peculiar characteristic of the French economy—often blamed for the large rise in pension spending—is the low participation rate among male workers aged 55 or older (see Blanchet and Pelé 1999). In fact, as shown in figure 5.3, the average retirement age has dropped since the sixties, while the average longevity has risen, thereby inducing a substantial expansion of the average length of retirement from more than 12 years in 1960 to more than 22 years in 2000. In the simulations the retirement age for the year 2000 was set at 58 years—the average effective retirement age among male workers in the private sector.

As discussed in chapters 3 and 4, population aging has been a factor in changes to individual preferences for social security. The profitability of the pension system is expected to be reduced by the increase in the dependency ratio, yet, the elderly voters—in particular, those closer to retirement age who favor a large pension system—become more influential in the electoral arena.

The simulations results displayed at table 5.1 illustrate the relevance of this political pressure: pension spending, as measured by the social security contribution rate, is projected to rise, and the generosity of the system—as calculated by the replacement rate at retirement—is expected to increase despite the large increase in the share of retirees.

The economic effect of aging—through the higher dependency ratio—on the French PAYG pension system for the year 2050 is captured at lines 2 and 3 in table 5.1. If the social security contribution rate were to remain constant at 22.4 percent, the replacement rate in 2050 would fall from almost 50 to 30 percent, due to the increase in the dependency ratio. Yet, if a 47-year-old median voter were to choose her most preferred contribution rate under the 2050 demographic scenario, she would indeed rise the contribution rate to 32.4 percent, to obtain a replacement rate of 43.4 percent. In this case the economic effect would turn out to be positive, since the reduction in the average return from the PAYG pension system—due to the aging process—is compensated by the large increase in the individual longevity. In other words, the average profitability of the system is reduced, but agents live longer, so they benefit more from the pension annuity.

The estimated impact of the political constraints on the future development of the French pension system is reported in the remaining part of table 5.1. For the 2050 projected demographic and economic features, political equilibria associated to a 56-year-old median voter are calculated under different retirement ages. If the average worker retires at age 58, as in the year 2000, the social security contribution rate is predicted to jump to 40.8 percent, with a replacement rate of almost 55 percent. The drop in the generosity of the pension benefits—despite the increase in the share of retirees to workers—is clearly due to the higher contribution rate. Every worker contributes more, and although there are fewer workers and more retirees, pensions increase.

Individuals' consumption decisions are largely affected by these modifications in the size of the French pension system. The estimated consumption patterns by age in the year 2000 and the projected profiles for 2050 are shown in figure 5.4 for two different situations. In the aging only scenario of figure 5.4, the 2050 forecasted demographic and economic variables are used, but the contribution rate and retirement age are fixed at their year 2000 levels. In the modified system case, retirement age and contribution rate are also updated, respectively to 65 years and to 29.7 percent (corresponding to the last line of table 5.1).

With no modification to the social security system, and a decrease in the rate of returns, consumption while young becomes more desirable, so aging induces a large shift toward more consumption in youth and less in old age. Yet the increase in the social security contribution rate, from 22.4 to 29.7 percent, and the large increase in the retirement age, from 58 to 65 years, partially tilt the profile back toward more old age consumption.

In line with the results of the other country studies, the insight derived from the simulations at table 5.1 is that the only effective way

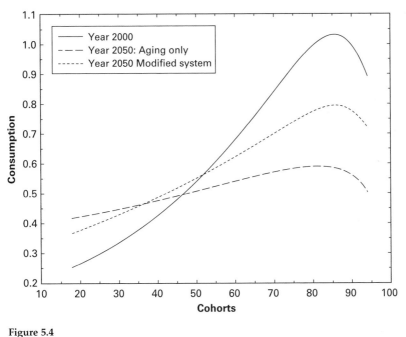

Figure 5.4
Consumption profiles by age in 2000 and 2050

to limit the growth of French pension spending is for the elderly to
postpone retirement. If retirement age can be postponed from 58 to 64
or 65 years, the social security contribution rates—as chosen by a 56-
year-old median voter in 2050—would still increase, but less, and the
generosity of the system, as captured by the replacement rate, would
also rise. Postponing retirement age hence mitigates the effect of the
political constraints on the future behavior of the pension system, by
increasing the contribution period for the median voter, while reducing the (long) average length of retirement (see figure 5.3). Faced with
a less favorable decision, the median voter will be motivated to accept
a lower raise in contribution rate. Furthermore, since postponing retirement increases the share of workers vis-à-vis the retirees, population
aging becomes less of a problem. The simulations results at section
11.3 suggest that raising the retirement age is politically feasible, even
up to 67 years (see table 11.4).

The second set of simulations, displayed at table 5.2, includes possible distortions in the labor market caused by the social security system.
In this setting, workers may react to an increase in the contribution rate

Table 5.2
Model with labor market distortions: Simulation results

Year	Median voter's age	Effective retirement age	Social security contribution rate	Replacement rate
2000	47	58	22.4%	51.8%
2050	—	58	22.4%	29.5%
2050	47	58	30.6%	41.0%
2050	56	58	39.0%	53.6%
2050	56	59	37.1%	54.5%
2050	56	60	35.3%	55.5%
2050	56	61	33.6%	56.6%
2050	56	62	31.9%	57.7%
2050	56	63	30.2%	58.8%
2050	56	64	28.7%	60.2%
2050	56	65	27.2%	61.6%

Note: The first line describes the year 2000 scenario, and the second line shows the impact on the replacement rate of the expected aging for 2050 under a constant social security contribution rate. The third line displays the simulations for the social security contribution rate under the 2050 economic and demographic scenario, but with the year 2000 median voter's age. All other lines report the simulations for the social security contribution rates—carried out using the model at chapter 4, with endogenous labor supply—under the 2050 economic, demographic, and political (median voter's age) scenario for different retirement ages.

by reducing their working hours. In the case of labor market distortions, the political impact on both the contribution rate and the replacement rate is smaller. As expected, the distortionary effect of the contributions on the labor supply leads to a reduction in pension spending. However, when labor decisions are endogenous, a second effect arises. As population aging rises, so do the stock of capital and wages; hence labor income is higher, which partially counterbalances the distortionary effect of taxation.

The main features of the French social security system in 2000, as well as the magnitude of the economic effect of aging for the year 2050, reported in the first two lines of table 5.2, are in accordance with the case of no tax distortions (see table 5.1). The differences occur in the projected political equilibria for 2050, since the social security contribution rates are smaller than in the previous case by almost 2 percent. For a retirement age of 58 years—the 2000 level—a 56-year-old median voter will tend to choose a social security contribution rate equal to 39 percent, with an associate replacement rate of 53.6 percent. This result accords well with the policy measures implied by the simulations in table 5.1. Postponing retirement age appears to be the most, effective way to limit the expansion of the system under population aging.

From the simulations there can be inferred the political strength of the aging population. Control of pension spending both in economic and political terms can only be accomplished by an increase in the retirement age. Indeed, this measure is the most appropriate to consider for France where the average effective retirement age as of 2000 has been 58 years. These results also throw into question the sustainability of the reform measures introduced over the last fifteen years. Will an older electorate accept the implementation of these retrenching measures? These simulations suggest that the contribution rates will probably not decrease, while the pension's generosity—as measured by the replacement rates—most certainly will. Yet a positive message emerges from the simulations at chapter 11: the most effective way to limit the growth in pension spending—postponing retirement—as was pursued in the most recent reforms will be politically sustainable at least in the long run.

The Future of the Social
Security System in
Germany

The German public pension system is organized as a monolithic scheme of retirement income provision. Established at the end of the nineteenth century as a fully funded scheme, the public pension system has evolved over time, switching to PAYG at the end of WWII, while constantly expanding its coverage among German workers. At the beginning of the nineties, the system represented the most relevant—often unique—source of retirement income: almost 85 percent of the people aged 55 and older received a substantial public pension benefit, amounting to more than 83 percent of their income for low-income retirees (those positioned in the first three income quintiles), to 75 percent for the retirees in the fourth quintile, and to more than 50 percent even for the richest elderly (those in the fifth quintile). This monolithic structure is mainly due to the Bismarckian[1] nature of the German public pension system, which features little, if any, redistribution within individuals of the same generation.[2] Since its origin the system is designed as a form of retirement insurance rather than as a pure social security system. Individuals contribute to the system during their working years, and at retirement receive a pension annuity, which is tightly linked to the level of their previous wages and thus guarantees them a similar standard of living as enjoyed during their working years.

In 2000, pension spending—consisting of old age, seniority, disability, and survivors pensions, according to the OECD classification—was equal to 11.8 percent of GDP, thus amounting to 43 percent of the total welfare expenditure. An additional 34 percent (see figure 6.1) was devoted to public health care, another welfare program largely targeted to the elderly.

The large operational scale of the German pension system, as can partially be attributed to its intrinsic nature of retirement insurance

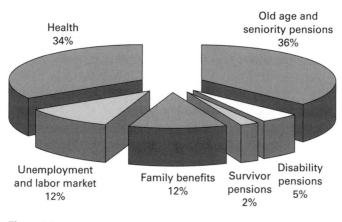

Figure 6.1
Welfare expenditure decomposition in 2000 (Source: OECD)

scheme, was further increased during the seventies. Several generous early retirement programs were introduced that substantially reduced the workers' effective retirement age. Since life expectancy has constantly increased among the elderly, the early retirement behavior among German workers has contributed to extend the average length of retirement. Over the years Germans have come to live longer but to retire earlier.

During the nineties and at the beginning of twenty-first century, this expansion phase was replaced by an effort to containing the increasing cost of the German system. Several reforms aimed at reducing the generosity of the pension's benefits, at tightening the eligibility criteria for disability and unemployment pensions, and at increasing the effective retirement age took place. Although most retrenching policies will be entirely phased in only after long transition periods, some innovative measures that attempt to share the burden of aging among several generations of current and future workers have recently been implemented. A detailed description of these policies is provided in the next section, while an evaluation of the impact on the long-term financial sustainability of the German system is presented in section 6.3.

The main objective of this chapter is to evaluate the future political sustainability of the German pension system. The driving force in this analysis is the expected process of population aging, which is examined in section 6.2. As for other countries, the effect of the aging process on the pension system, captured by the increase in the dependency ratio, is magnified by the early retirement behavior among German workers. The ratio of retirees to workers is in fact higher than its demographic counterpart—the old age dependency ratio. The simulations presented in section 6.3 show how political constraints may shape the future size of the public pension system, under population aging. They suggest that despite the recent reforms the aging process will tight the political constraints and lead to a larger size of the social security system, as measured by the contribution rate, although the generosity of the pensions will actually drop. As for other countries, postponing retirement represents the only effective measure in limiting the political pressure for a large system. In this sense the simulations on the political feasibility of this measure, as presented at chapter 11, are encouraging.

6.1   The Current Social Security System: An Overview

Germany features one of the oldest social security systems in the world. It was established by Chancellor Otto von Bismarck in the late nineteenth century in an attempt to increase popular support vis-à-vis the upsurge of the socialist movement. Interestingly the pension scheme was fully funded—although contributions were typically invested in government bonds—and was mainly intended as an insurance against old age poverty among workers, since individuals would only become eligible for pension benefits after turning 70 years old—and this was at a time when the average life expectancy at birth did not even reach 70 years.

In 1957, after the real value of the funded systems' assets had largely been eroded by the war inflation, the system shifted to PAYG in an attempt to collect the resources needed to provide old age pensions to the current retirees. This new arrangement covered only manual and white-collar workers.

A major reform of the German system, which largely raised the standards of generosity for the system, occurred in 1972. Replacement rates at retirement were increased, hence leading to higher pension benefits for new retirees, while pensions were indexed to nominal wage growth, thereby expanding also the future cost of the stock of existing pensions. Eligibility criteria were relaxed. Retirement age was reduced from 65 to 63 years for individuals with 35 years of contributions, and to 60 years—through unemployment and disability insurance—for workers who had been unemployed for 52 weeks and for individuals with 35 years of contributions, who were unable to work for physical inability or labor market reasons.

This reform had dramatic effects on the retirement behavior of the Germans: the number of regular disability pensions plummeted, but there was a surge in flexible retirement at age 63, in unemployment pensions at age 60 and in old age disability pensions after age 60 (see Börsch-Supan and Schnabel 1999). Although this composition changed somewhat over the following two decades, as new early retirement programs were introduced for workers in particular sectors—such as steel, automobiles, metal, and chemical—the broad picture remained unchanged and the share of individuals retiring at age 65 continued to drop.

6.1.1 Recent Reforms

After two decades of growing pension expenditure, due partly to demographic dynamics but also partly to the 1972 reform, which relaxed eligibility criteria and increased the generosity of the system, a new reform was passed in November 1989. The reform measures aimed at containing the expansion of the system, and their actual implementation only began in 1992. They included a shift in the indexation of pension benefits from gross to net wages,[3] and perhaps more important, they reduced early retirement pensions. This was achieved by adjusting benefits to the effective retirement age rather than to the years of contributions as prior to the reform, although less than the criterion of actuarial fairness would have required (for each year before age 65, pension benefits were reduced by 3.6 percent, see Börsch-Supan and Schnabel 1999). Yet these early retirement penalties were introduced along a lengthy transition period. The pivotal age for calculating the reductions was assumed to be 65 years in 2004, but their full implementation was scheduled to occur only after 2011. Moreover special pre-retirement pathways out of the labor market still remained. Perhaps due to this long phase-in period, which effectively allowed workers in their mid-forties and older to be only marginally, if at all, affected by these measures, the reform enjoyed a large consensus among the political forces. It was backed by all political parties but the Green.

However, the financial imbalance of the system survived these retrenching measures, and new attempts to reform followed in the late nineties. In 1997, a reform proposal—known as the 1999 reform, since the policy measures were scheduled to be implemented from 1999—was put forward by the Christian-Democratic government led by Helmut Kohl. This reform aimed at decreasing the fiscal burden of the system on the future generations and contemplated a gradual reduction in the average pension replacement rate from 70 to 64 percent. In particular, the proposal envisaged an increase in the amount of federal subsidies to the pension system (financed by a 1 percent rise of the VAT rate), the application of early retirement penalties to disability pensions, and the introduction of a demographic factor to index pension benefits to gains in average longevity.

This last measure met the fierce opposition by the Social Democratic Party and the unions. The use of a demographic factor was anticipated to reduce pension benefits to all current generations—including the current retirees; furthermore a large share of the overall burden of the reform would have fallen on workers in their fifties or younger (see Borgmann et al. 2001). In 1998 the reform was revoked, as Gerhard Schroeder—the leader of a newly elected Social Democratic government—kept his electoral campaign promises to drop the plan. However, temporary changes in the pension indexation were introduced, with benefits being indexed to inflation, rather than to net wages, and an ecological tax on fossil fuel was imposed in order to stabilize the proportion of financing from general federal revenues.

Few years later, Schroeder presented his own reform plan, known as the Riester reform, which was implemented in 2001, under the Pension Reform Act. The key novelty of this reform package was the introduction of highly subsidized personal pension plans, in an attempt to shift part of the burden of providing retirement income from the monolithic public pension system towards more private provision. Two additional measures of the Riester reform regarded the contribution rate, which was legislated to remain below 20 percent until 2020 (and below 22 percent until 2030), and the net average replacement rate, which was scheduled to decrease from 70 to 67–68 percent by 2030. The plan also required government intervention, possibly through an increase in federal subsides to the pension system, if the net replacement rate dropped below 67 percent. Other measures were also introduced, which redefined the concept of "disability," while the generosity of the survivors' pensions was reduced.

The Riester reform's plan regarding contribution rate and net average replacement rate proved to be highly controversial. Several scholars pointed out that the double goal of limiting the rise in the contribution rates while keeping the replacement rate above 67 percent could not be achieved without resorting to massive federal subsidies (see Börsch-Supan and Wilke 2004). Yet, in the political arena, the Riester reform met little resistance. It was not endorsed only by the left wing of the Social Democratic Party and, initially, by the unions (see Natali and Rhodes 2004b). Retrenchment was in fact rather mild, if compared to the 1999 reform, and accompanied by compensative measures, such as tax incentives for private funds.

It soon became evident that the 2001 Riester reform was not able to reach this double target, and that further political decisions had to be taken either to privilege the cost containment target or to maintain the generosity of the benefits. A Commission for Sustainability in Financing the German Social Insurance Systems led by Bert Rürup was instituted already in November 2002 within the context of the wider Agenda 2010 reform project, promoted by the Social Democratic Chancellor Schroeder, to improve the poor performance of the German economy. Two main measures were recommended by the commission (see Rürup 2002 and Börsch-Supan and Wilke 2004 for a detailed description of the reform proposal): a gradual increase in the normal retirement age from 65 to 67 years, to be achieved by 2035, and a change in the benefit indexation formula. The latter feature consists of indexing pension benefits to a "sustainability factor," which depends on the relative share of contributors to retirees (the actual pension dependency ratio[4]). This mechanism allows to spread the cost of aging over several generations, by combining per-capita cost containment with an overall increase in the size of the system. According to this "sustainability factor," in fact, the expected drop in the ratio of workers to retirees would partially reduce the pensions' benefits, while an additional increase in the social security contribution rate would still be needed to balance the system. Analogously a relative increase in the share of workers to retirees—achieved, for instance, by increasing the effective retirement age—would lead to higher pensions and lower contributions. This mechanism, which has drawn large interest among the scholars, was finally approved by the Bundestag in March 2004, while a decision on the other measure—consisting of a gradual increase in the retirement age—was postponed to 2008.

This political result was somewhat surprising: using survey data, Börsch-Supan et al. (2004) show that the initial proposal by the Rürup Commission would only be supported by 45 percent of the respondents, or 47 percent if marginal modifications were introduced. Yet the approval rate would rise to 55 percent among individuals, who were more informed about the working of the German social security system and the details of the reform. It appears that these more informed supporters of the Rürup reform valued more highly the cost containment measures—aimed at keeping the contribution rate under control—and the proposed administrative changes to occupational and private pensions, which increased the convenience of recurring to the second and third pillar.[5] The long-run political sustainability of these reforms' measures will be analyzed in section 6.3, with simulations on the social security contribution rates in 2050. Section 11.3 addresses the political feasibility of postponing retirement.

6.1.2   The German System at the Turn of the Century

Since the 1972 reform, the German public pension system has had four types of pension benefits: old age pensions, disability pensions (converted to old age benefits when the recipient turns 65 years old), survivor pensions, and unemployment pensions. Eligibility requirements vary according to the pension type but typically depend on the worker's age and years of contributions. Old age pensions are awarded to persons aged 65 with at least 5 years of contributions. Disability pensions require an individual to be at least 60 years old, to have 35 years of contributions and a loss of 50 percent in earning capability. Interestingly, before the 2001 Riester reform, this loss of earning capability could also be due to labor market reasons. Also, prior to the Riester reform, unemployment pensions were available to individuals of at least 60 years of age and with 15 years of contributions, who had been unemployed for 18 to 36 months. The requirements for this pension benefit have been tighten up.

A distinguishing feature of the German pension system—largely due to the 1972 reform—is the existence of several ways to an early exit from the labor market for workers who have not reached 65 years of age. Disability and unemployment pensions have widely been used to accommodate the early exit of middle-aged and elderly workers, yet the 1972 reform opened a bigger window to retirement by introducing an official general early retirement scheme.[6] Men aged 63 years and with 35 years of contributions and women aged 60 years with 180 months of contribution were eligible for an old age pension with no direct adjustment of retirement benefits. In 1992 a more actuarially fair formula for early retirement pensions was introduced. Thus early retirement has remained a critical feature of the German pension system, with the median effective retirement age in 2000 being equal to 61 years.

In the German system, pension benefits are strictly related to the workers' earnings and years of contributions, according to a pension formula that highlights the Bismarckian, nonredistributive nature of the system. Pension benefits depend on four factors: (1) the earning points, which measure the relative level of earnings of the worker, (2) the years of services, (3) an adjustment factor, which varies according to the pension type and to the worker's retirement age, and (4) the current relative pension value, which links the current average pension to the average wage through an indexation criterion.

The earning points measure the position of the worker's earning relative to an average salary, which is determined annually by the government (in 2001, it was equal to €27,960). They are easily obtained by dividing the worker's earnings by this average salary, so that the average earner obtains one earning point, while workers who earned half as much as the average earner receives half a point, and so on. The years of services represent the years of contributions made by the worker to the system plus any additional allowance credited for non contributory periods. The adjustment factors are used to provide weights for two different features: the type of pension and the worker's retirement age. A value of one is given to the old age pension of an individual retiring at age 65 with complete requirements. Early retirement, that is, before age 65, is penalized with a reduction in the adjustment factor of 3.8 basis points per year. Other modifications take place depending on the pension type; for instance, the adjustment factor is equal to 2/3 for disability pensions, to 0.6 for widow's survivor pensions and to 0.1 for orphans.

The fourth element in the pension benefit formula is the current relative pension value, which provides a link between pension benefits and workers' earnings. This factor has received the most attention among recent reforms, since it is key to limiting the growth in pension spending. If the current pension value is indexed to gross wages, as it was until 1992, or the net wage, from 1992 to 1998, the retirees share the benefits created by the economic growth. Indexation to inflation, as after 1999, instead reduces the relative purchasing power of the retirees, but contributes to decrease the level of pension spending. With the 2004 Rürup reform, the current relative pension value has been indexed to a demographic factor—the pension dependency ratio—that captures the relative share of recipients (the retirees) to contributors (the workers).

The financing of the generous German public pension system is guaranteed by two sources. Contributions to the system by the insured workers and their employees cover around 75 percent of the total pension spending, and the remaining part is financed through federal subsidies. As in most PAYG system, in Germany a payroll tax is levied on labor income, which is equally shared by employers and employees. The total statutory social security contribution rate was equal to 19.5 percent in 2002, and is imposed on the salary below a certain ceiling. Interestingly, while the contribution rate has not dramatically increased in the last decades—it was equal to 17 percent in 1970—the upper earnings ceiling has been anchored to the average wage, rather than to the inflation, thereby increasing the share of earning over which individuals have to pay contributions. Federal subsidies represent roughly 25 percent of the social security budget. They are linked to net wages and are set to finance a security reserve of at least a fifth of one month's worth of pension benefits.

6.2   Demographic Issues

Population aging—together with the increase in the generosity of the pension system during the 1970s—has typically been blamed for the expansion of the German social security spending after WWII. The slow, yet persistent process of aging in Germany is largely due to a sensible reduction in the fertility rate, from 2.4 children per woman between 18 and 45 years in the sixties and 2 in the seventies to 1.45 in the eighties and nineties. Notably this drop in fertility from the postwar levels is expected to be permanent: EC projections for the year 2050 forecast a fertility rate of 1.5.

Germany has also experienced a substantial increase in longevity. In 1960, life expectancy at birth was equal to 72.4 years for females and 66.9 years for males, hence in line with the other European countries. Already in 1980, longevity had increased to 76.1 years for females and 69.6 years for males; while it was equal respectively to 80.8 and 74.7 years in 2000. Coupled with the reduction in fertility, this increase in longevity, which is mainly due to large reductions in the mortality rates at old ages, has originated the aging process.

EC estimates for the next fifty years indicate that population aging will continue to rise in Germany. The estimates show the fertility rate

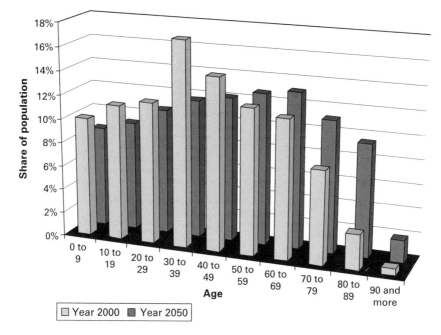

Figure 6.2
Aging in Germany: Population by age group in 2000 and 2050 (Source: Eurostat)

to remain around 1.5 children per woman, and further reductions in old age mortality. The population profile by age for the year 2000 and the forecasted profile for the year 2050 are depicted at figure 6.2. Population aging is identified by the shift to the right in the relative weights of the different generations. Note that in 2000, individuals in their thirties constituted by far the largest generation in the population; by the year 2050, the largest group will be individuals in their sixties, followed closely by those in their fifties.

The impact of population aging on the functioning of the German unfunded social security system is captured by the variation in the old age dependency ratio, which measures the ratio of old individuals—aged 65 years or more—to potentially active individuals—aged 18 to 64 years. As shown at table 2.5, this old-age dependency ratio is expected to double: while in 2000 there were four individuals in working age for every elderly person, in 2050 there will only be two. If the German retirement behavior is allowed to continue into the future, the demographic effect on the pension system will be greatly amplified. In 2050, the pension dependency ratio reported in table 2.5, which is calculated by splitting workers and retirees according to the effective median retirement age (61 years), was equal to 36 percent, amounting to three workers per retiree. If the effective retirement age is left at 61 years, in 2050 the pension dependency ratio will be equal to 67.7 percent, corresponding to three workers for every two retirees.

The large impact of population aging on the political representation of the different age groups could be summarized by the changes in the median age among the voters. In the year 2000 the median age among German voters was equal to 44 years. As shown in figure 2.3, according to EC demographic forecasts, the median age among the voters is expected to increase to 55 years in 2040 and to remain at this level in 2050. The aging of the median voter will certainly make a difference for pension expenditures on the agenda of the German policy-maker.

6.3 The Future of the German System

The flurry of pension reforms during the nineties and at the start of the twenty-first century indicates the widespread concern of Germans about the future of their public pension system. A recent survey by Boeri et al. (2002) shows that 85 percent of the Germans interviewed expect to see the system in crisis in the next ten to fifteen years.

This section addresses the sustainability of the public pension system in the future, under the challenge posed by the expected demographic dynamics of an aging society. First, I discuss the expected financial sustainability of the system modeled by the 2001 Riester and 2004 Rürup reforms and the generous early retirement provisions. I then evaluate the long-term political sustainability of the system under population aging in terms of how future political constituencies could shape social security in Germany.

6.3.1 Financial Sustainability

At the beginning of this century, the European Commission, jointly with the OECD and the country member's governments, elaborated a set of official projections on the future public pension spending in each country member. These estimates were based on the current social security rules and included also those reform measures, which had already been approved, but whose implementation was to occur along a transition period. According to these 2002 EC estimates (see table 2.3), old age pension expenditure in Germany will expand from 11.8 percent of GDP in 2000 to 16.8 percent in 2050. Aging accounts for a

6.4 percent rise in pension spending over GDP because of the increasing number of retirees and hence of pension benefits. The modifications in the benefit formula introduced by the reforms implemented until 2002 are instead expected to decrease pension spending by 2.7 percent. An additional reduction of 0.7 percent should come from an increase in the employment rate among the elderly, while changes in the eligibility criteria should account for a 2.1 percent rise in spending.

Since these EC calculations, additional studies on the long run implication of the 2001 Riester reform have become available. Börsch-Supan and Wilke (2004) estimate that—to keep the replacement rate above 67 percent—social security contribution rates will have to go beyond the targeted levels, reaching 20 percent by 2015, 22 percent by 2024, and almost 26 percent in 2040. According to Jackson (2003), despite substantial transfers of resources from general taxation, contribution rates will increase to 26 percent in 2030 and 28 percent in 2040, hence leading the total payroll cost of public pension financing from 27 percent in 2002 to 37 percent in 2030 and to 40 percent in 2040. Future levels of old age spending over GDP may thus be larger than official projections suggest.

In March 2004 additional reform measures, originally proposed by the Rürup Commission, were approved, thus making the EC official estimates obsolete. The crucial aspect of the implemented reform consists of linking the pension benefits to the pension dependency ratio through a "sustainability factor." An increase in the pension dependency ratio reduces the pension replacement rate, and should hence limit the rise in pension spending. The extent to which this expected reduction in pension generosity is socially acceptable—and hence politically feasible—depends also on the contemporaneous development of occupational and private pension plans. According to Jackson and Howe (2003)'s calculations, in absence of alternative sources of revenues, a reduction of 10 percent in public benefits would push 5.7 percent of the elderly below the poverty line, thereby creating deep social concerns.

The two key measures proposed by the Rürup Commission—the indexation of the pension benefits to the dependency ratio, as implemented in the 2004 reform, and the gradual increase in the retirement age from 65 to 67, whose discussion has been postponed to 2008—demonstrate the crucial role of the retirement behavior on pension spending. After the 1972 reform, when several early pathways from the labor market became available to middle-age workers, the average

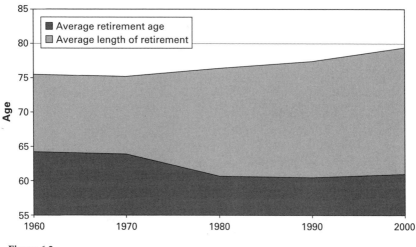

Figure 6.3
Longevity and retirement (Sources: Latulippe 1996 and OECD)

effective retirement age in Germany dropped, while individual's longevity continued to rise. As displayed in figure 6.3, the combined effect
of these two phenomena has led to a large increase in the average
length of retirement. Individuals live longer but retire earlier, thereby
enjoying their pension annuities for longer years and increasing the
total amount of pension benefits to be financed by workers.

6.3.2 Political Sustainability

The debate over the Riester and Rürup reforms drew attention to
the trade-off between retaining the generosity of the German social
security system under population aging and containing the hike in the
contribution rate needed to finance the system. A political economy
analysis by Sinn and Uebelmesser (2002) supported the latter option,
and argued in favor of retrenching the German social security system
by switching to a fully funded scheme by 2016. According to their calculations, in 2000 the age threshold for individuals to be indifferent between remaining in the current PAYG pension system and switching
to a fully funded scheme was equal to 48 years. Since the median
age among the voters was only 46, this reform option was politically
feasible. Because of the expected demographic dynamics, however,
the median age among the voters is expected to grow faster than
this age threshold: these two ages are forecasted to coincide at 50
years in 2015—when the window of opportunity to reform will thus

disappear—whereas in 2025 the median age among the voters will be 53 years, while the indifferent individual will have 51 years.

The analysis on the future political sustainability of the German system carried out in this section takes a different route. A quantitative evaluation of how aging will affect the German system is provided, by comparing the demographic, economic, and political situation in the year 2000 with the political equilibria estimated to arise in 2050. Aging has two crucial economic and political effects on a social security system (see chapters 3 and 4): its profitability is reduced, because of the rise in the dependency ratio, while the political influence of the elderly voters increases. The overall assessment from the simulation results displayed at table 6.1 suggests that the political aspect dominates. The size of the system, as measured by the social security contribution rate, is forecasted to increase. Yet its generosity—calculated by the replacement rate—is expected to decrease, due to the large rise in the dependency ratio.

The main characteristics of the system in the year 2000 are summarized at the first line in table 6.1. The median voter's age corresponds to the median age among the voters, as presented in section 6.2, since voters are assumed to differ only along one dimension—their age,

Table 6.1
Direct impact of aging: Simulation results

Year	Median voter's age	Effective retirement age	Social security contribution rate	Replacement rate
2000	46	61	23.8%	68.3%
2050	—	61	23.8%	35.0%
2050	46	61	15.0%	22.1%
2050	55	61	37.7%	55.4%
2050	55	62	36.3%	60.4%
2050	55	63	35.0%	66.4%
2050	55	64	33.7%	73.3%
2050	55	65	32.6%	81.2%

Note: The first line describes the year 2000 scenario, and the second line shows the impact on the replacement rate of the expected aging for 2050 under a constant social security contribution rate. The third line displays the simulations for the social security contribution rate under the 2050 economic and demographic scenario, but with the year 2000 median voter's age. All other lines report the simulations for the social security contribution rates—carried out using the model at chapter 4, with exogenous labor supply—under the 2050 economic, demographic, and political (median voter's age) scenario for different retirement ages.

while the effective retirement age is equal to its 2000 average level. The social security contribution rate differs from its statutory value, as federal subsidies are factored in to obtain the equilibrium contribution rate—that is, the rate that equalizes total contributions to total pension benefits. Its average value in the nineties was equal to 23.8 percent which—in the model—induces an average replacement rate of 68.3 percent.

Table 6.1 (see lines 2 and 3) evaluates also the relative magnitude of the economic effect associated with the aging process for the year 2050. If the social security contribution rate remains at 23.8 percent, in 2050 the generosity of the system will drop dramatically as the replacement rate falls from 68.3 to 35 percent because of the large hike in the dependency ratio. Moreover, if the median voter is 46 years old (as in the year 2000), under the new demographic scenario that voter's most preferred contribution rate drops to 15 percent, because of the lower profitability of the system, and the replacement rate drops to 22.1 percent.

The remaining part of table 6.1 describes the political equilibria associated with a 55-year-old median voter for the 2050 forecasted demographic and economic features, under different retirement ages. With the retirement age at its 2000 level (61 years), the equilibrium social security contribution rate is expected to jump to 37.7 percent, while the replacement rate drops to 55.4 percent. Despite a higher contribution rate pensions are less generous than in 2000, since fewer workers contribute and more retirees are entitled to a pension.

Such radical changes to the German pension system would clearly modify the individuals' economic decision over saving and consumption. Figure 6.4 displays the individuals' estimated level of consumption by age for the year 2000 and the forecasted profiles of the lifetime consumption for 2050 under two different scenarios. The first case—labeled "aging only" in figure 6.4—corresponds to the 2050 forecasted demographic and economic scenario, but with contribution rate and retirement age at their 2000 level; while in the second case—labeled "modified system"—the contribution rate associated with the simulated political equilibrium and a retirement age of 65 years apply (see table 6.1). Two interesting features emerge. Aging shifts down the average consumption profile because of the lower lifetime wealth,[7] but it increases the consumption of the young because of the reduction in the rate of returns, which makes consumption in youth more convenient. Nevertheless, an increase in the contribution rate from 23.8 to 32.6 percent and in the retirement age from 61 to 65 years partially

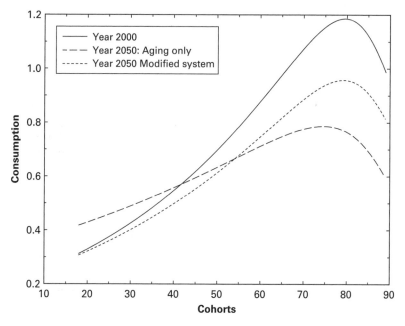

Figure 6.4
Consumption profile by age in 2000 and 2050 (Source: Galasso and Profeta 2004)

counterbalances the effect of aging. If compared to the case of aging
with an unchanged social security system ("aging only" in figure 6.4),
the consumption profile ("modified system") in fact tilts toward more
old age consumption. This result follows from the decision by an older
median voter of reshaping the pension system to increase consumption
in old age.

The simulations in table 6.1 convey an important insight for economic policy: an increase in the retirement age reduces social security
contribution rates and leads to more generous pensions. For an effective retirement age of 65 years, the contribution rate is equal to 32.6
percent and the replacement rate is above 81 percent. Postponing retirement limits the hike in the contribution rate by moderating the political effect. As the working life widens and the retirement period
shrinks (see figure 4.2), the returns from the pension system decrease,
and the median voter prefers a lower contribution rate. Also the generosity of the system may increase—despite the drop in the contribution
rate—because postponing retirement reduces the ratio of retirees to
workers, thereby counterbalancing the population aging problem.

Table 6.2
Model with labor market distortions: Simulation results

Year	Median voter's age	Effective retirement age	Social security contribution rate	Replacement rate
2000	46	61	23.8%	67.6%
2050	—	61	23.8%	35.2%
2050	46	61	14.9%	24.6%
2050	55	61	35.7%	50.0%
2050	55	62	34.0%	51.5%
2050	55	63	32.4%	52.9%
2050	55	64	30.8%	54.3%
2050	55	65	29.2%	55.4%

Note: The first line describes the year 2000 scenario, and the second line shows the impact on the replacement rate of the expected aging for 2050 under a constant social security contribution rate. The third line displays the simulations for the social security contribution rate under the 2050 economic and demographic scenario, but with the year 2000 median voter's age. All other lines report the simulations for the social security contribution rates—carried out using the model at chapter 4, with endogenous labor supply—under the 2050 economic, demographic, and political (median voter's age) scenario for different retirement ages.

The evidence suggests that the political power of an older electorate will increase the tax burden on workers. A second set of simulations considers an economic environment with labor market distortions due to workers who respond to the high contribution rates by reducing their labor supply[8]—and hence the tax base. The results at table 6.2 show that the political aspect still dominates but less than in the previous scenario because labor market distortions shave off some of the hike in the contribution rate.

The main features of the German pension system in 2000 and the relative importance of the economic impact of aging for the year 2050—summarized at the first three lines in table 6.2—are in line with the scenario with no tax distortions (see table 6.1). Some differences do, however, emerge in the forecasted political equilibria for 2050, as the distortionary effect of taxation increases the cost—in terms of forgone income—of increasing the social security contribution rate. With an effective retirement age of 61 years and a 55-year-old median voter, the equilibrium social security contribution rate is estimated at 35.7 percent, slightly lower than in the case with no deadweight loss of taxation; while the replacement rate drops[9] even further to 50 percent.

The results of table 6.2 confirm the insights emerging from the previous simulations, and suggest a policy measure for the future. Postponing retirement age limits the expansion of the system under population aging. It leads to lower social security contribution rates than otherwise decided by an older median voter and at the same time increases the generosity of the system.

This policy measure seems particularly appropriate for Germany, where the average effective retirement age in 2000 was only 61 years. The Riester and Rürup reforms faced the need to contain the cost of the system while retaining its generosity. The most natural policy to reach both targets is to postpone retirement. A higher retirement age could additionally offset the increases in pension spending expected of a powerful older electorate. However, during the 2004 Rürup reform, the decision to gradually increase the official retirement age from 65 to 67 years was postponed to 2008. Whether this policy option will become more palatable in the future remains to be seen.

7   Political Sustainability and
       Reforms in Italy

Italy has one of most generous social security systems in the world. In 2000 pension spending amounted to 14.2 percent of GDP. Italy's pension system constitutes also the largest program of the Italian welfare state. As shown in figure 7.1, old age and seniority pensions accounted for 46 percent of total welfare expenditures in 2000; when survivor and disability pensions are also included, this share reaches 61 percent. This large transfer of resources to the retirees is complemented by a large expenditure on health care mainly devoted to the elderly.

The Italian PAYG social security system covers the entire workforce by means of three pension schemes: for private employees, the so-called *Fondo pensione lavoratori dipendenti* (FPLD) administered by the National Institute for Social Security (INPS); for public employees, a special program administered by the National Institute for the Social Security of the Public Employees (INPDAP); and for the self-employed, a program also administered by INPS. Pension benefits represent the main source of income for a large majority of elderly individuals because occupation plans and private pension funds have not been fully developed despite the fiscal incentives introduced by the reforms of the nineties. In 1999, only 30 percent of all workers had contributed some (usually small) amounts to complementary pension schemes. An additional institution of the Italian social security system is the *trattamento di fine rapporto* (TFR), which provides deferred wages to the workers typically upon retirement.

A specific characteristic of the Italian social security system—at least until the reforms of the nineties—was the existence of generous seniority pensions awarded to workers, who had accumulated a sufficient number of contribution years, regardless of their age. The large amount of generous seniority or early retirement pensions and the

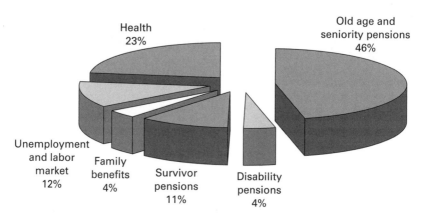

Figure 7.1
Welfare expenditure decomposition in 2000 (Source: OECD)

extensive use of disability pensions for redistributive purposes have typically been implicated as determinants of the drastic fall in the employment rates among elderly workers during the eighties and nineties (e.g., see Brugiavini 1999).

These peculiar features of the Italian social security system and the dramatic population aging of the last two decades account for the upward trend in pension expenditure, driven by an increase both in the number of individuals entitled to a pension and in the generosity of the pension benefits. Faced with the expectations of further aging, the Italian system was largely re-designed during the nineties—with the Amato reform in 1992, the Dini reform in 1995, and the Prodi reform in 1997—and in 2004, with the introduction of several retrenchment measures aimed at coping with the immediate financial distress of the government budget and also at eliminating the long-run financial unbalances of the public pension system. The main reform measures were the switch from a defined benefits to a notional defined contributions system (Dini reform), a sharp reduction in the incentives to retire early (Dini), an increase in the statutory retirement age (Amato and the 2004 reform), and the indexation of pension benefits to price inflation rather than to wage growth (Amato). Although several scholars have prized the innovative structure of the system introduced by the 1995 Dini reform, some criticisms have emerged about its long transition period—with a complete phase-in of the new regime expected only by 2040—but also about the long-run sustainability of the new regime,[1] under the political pressure of a graying electorate.

This chapter addresses the long-term political sustainability of the Italian social security system under the expected process of population aging. To fully evaluate the phased-in system that emerged from the Amato and Dini reforms, the analysis concentrates on the year 2050. The main modifications in the economic and political scenarios are particularly sizable in the case of Italy. The old age dependency ratio is forecasted to reach almost 65 percent in 2050, and this demographic effect is further magnified by the early retirement behavior among Italian workers. The average profitability of the social security system will hence take a large drop. The median age among voters will reach 57 years in 2050.

The simulations presented in section 7.3 assess the political constraints that will shape the size of the social security system under future population aging. From the simulations we appraise the effectiveness of the measures introduced by the Amato and Dini reforms in limiting the Italian social security expenditures in the long run. The lengthy transition period envisaged by these reforms is examined from a political economy perspective to provide a rational for its long duration. By allowing for a slow phasing-in, the Dini government was able to isolate the middle-aged workers from the cost of the reform and hence to receive the support of the unions and of a majority of the Parliament.[2] The results of the simulations, discussed in section 7.4, suggest that despite the structural reforms of the nineties population aging process will lead to a larger social security system, as measured by the contribution rate, although the generosity of the pension will decline. The only effective way to ease the political pressure on a large system is to increase the retirement age, as recommended in the Amato and Dini reforms and more recently in the 2004 reform. The analysis on the political feasibility of postponing retirement presented in chapter 11 further supports this view.

The next section describes the Amato and Dini reforms and provides a brief historical overview of the private employees' scheme of the Italian social security system, which is the object of the simulations at sections 7.3. The large aging population in Italy and the consequences for political representation by age groups are discussed in section 7.2.

7.1 An Overview of the Italian Social Security System

The compulsory pension scheme for private employees was introduced in Italy in 1919. The system was funded by payroll taxes and revenues were invested, typically, in government bonds but also in equities and in the real estate. Upon retirement, individuals received old age pensions that depended on the capitalized contributions. In the aftermath of World War II, however, the postwar inflation eroded the real value of the pension system's assets, and the system became PAYG. To bail out the elderly from losing their savings, workers' contributions were no longer invested in assets, but instead used to provide pension benefits to the current elderly. The transition toward a PAYG system was completed in the early 1950s, with the institution of a guaranteed minimum pension (see Franco 2002).

Until the mid-eighties, a sequence of (sometimes overlapping) reform measures consistently increased pension expenditure by extending coverage to self-employed and work-disabled individuals, by relaxing eligibility criteria and raising pension benefits' generosity. Pension spending soon became an instrument of social assistance and redistribution, via early retirement or seniority pensions, noncontributive (or "social") pensions and disability benefits. The early retirement provision, introduced in 1965 in the private sector (but already in 1956 for public employees), modified the eligibility criterion, as the entitlement to a pension became contingent only on having reached a minimum contributory period—independently of the worker's age. These seniority pensions have become a popular early pathway from the labor market since the late sixties, when labor market conditions deteriorated and elderly workers were forced to retire early, to avoid unemployment. Noncontributive pensions and disability benefits were widely used to provide income support to elderly people in the poorer regions. In particular, eligibility for disability benefits was often made contingent on inability to earn income rather than on actual physical disability (see Franco 2002). Only in the eighties were some restrictions on pension spending introduced by tightening eligibility criteria for disability benefits. Yet no cutbacks were applied to early retirement provisions, and generous seniority pensions remained available to middle-aged workers (see Brugiavini 1999).

As a result of the widespread use of these instruments, pension spending increased from less than 1 percent of GDP in 1951, to above 10 percent in the mid-eighties, and to almost 15 percent in 1992, in the eve of the Amato reform. The share of elderly individuals in the population, as measured by the fraction of individuals older than 60 years, also increased: from 12 percent in 1951 to 21 percent in the mid-eighties and to 25 percent in 1992. Until the eighties, however, the overall in-

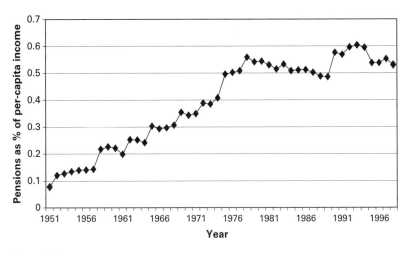

Figure 7.2
Pension expenditures per elderly person (Source: Ferrera 1985, OECD, and Eurostat)

crease in pension spending was mainly due to a rise in the pension spending per elderly person, which remained almost constant thereafter. Figure 7.2 displays this trend for the ratio of pension per elderly (individuals aged 60 or more) over per-capita income.

In 1992, before the Amato and Dini reforms, Italy featured an unfunded, defined benefit, social security system. For the private employees' scheme, a payroll tax (26.4 percent in 1991) was imposed on labor earning—a third paid by the employees and the remaining part by the employer. Since these contributions were typically not sufficient to cover all private employees' pensions, additional revenues were collected through general taxation. Under the FPLD scheme, male workers who contributed to the system for at least 15 years were entitled to an old-age pension benefit after turning 60 years old (55 for women). Regardless of their age, workers could, however, be entitled to a seniority pension[3] if they contributed for at least 35 years.

Under the FPLD scheme, pension benefits depended on the average wage received by the employee in the last five years prior to retirement and on the number of years of contribution. The pension's replacement rate was calculated by multiplying the number of years of contribution, up to a maximum of 40 years, by a "rate of return" (equal to 2 percent). A retiree with 40 years of contribution would thus receive 80 percent of the average wage in the five years prior to retirement. Interestingly, additional year of contribution after the fortieth year did not count towards increasing the replacement rate. This feature of the benefit formula and the existence of early retirement provisions created strong incentives to retire early, placing Italy among the countries with the lowest labor participation rate among the elderly (see Gruber and Wise 1999).

The Italian private employees' pension scheme also featured a minimum pension benefit level, for those retirees with entitlements to a pension below a certain threshold. Additional benefits were granted to the retiree's survivors, namely widows (but also widowers) and children, but there was no dependent wife benefit. "Social" pension and the disability benefits were still quite relevant, despite the tightening of the eligibility criteria. Finally, all pension benefits were indexed to nominal wages and taxed as regular income.

A peculiar provision in the Italian social security system, which complemented the unfunded pillar, was the TFR (*Trattamento di fine rapporto*), which essentially represented a form of deferred wage or severance payment. Every year, employers contributed a sizable share of the workers' labor earnings (7.41 percent in 1992) toward the TFR. These resources were indeed retained by the firm and used as internal funding. At the end of the labor contract or upon retirement, the firm liquidated to the worker the contributions made over the working years capitalized at a fixed 1.5 percent, plus 75 percent of the past inflation.[4]

7.1.1   A Season of Reforms

During the nineties, the Italian system was re-shaped by three major reforms: the Amato reform in 1992, the Dini reform in 1995, and the Prodi reform in 1997. The main objective of these reforms[5] was the progressive stabilization of the pension expenditure over the GDP, to be achieved by introducing less generous criteria for computing pension benefits and by restricting eligibility, in particular with respect to retirement age. All three reforms aimed at harmonizing the highly fragmented social security schemes and at providing incentives for the development of private pension funds to complement the public system.

In 1992 the Amato reform introduced a gradual tightening, over a ten years period, of the eligibility requirements. Retirement age was increased to 60 years for women and to 65 years for men, and the minimum contribution period for pension eligibility was extended to 20 years. The reference wage in the pension benefit formula moved from the average wage over the last five years prior to retirement to the average wage over the entire work carrier,[6] with past earnings capitalized at the cost of living index plus 1 percent per year. Perhaps the single most effective measure of the Amato reform in containing pension spending was the shift of the pension benefit indexation from nominal wages to prices (with the possibility for the government of further intervention through the Budgetary Law in case of financial distress). All the main measures are summarized in table 7.1.

In 1995 the Dini reform completely redesigned the architecture of the Italian social security system. The defined benefit nature of the scheme was abandoned in favor of a notional defined contribution scheme. Seniority pensions were eliminated—over a long transition period—and additional norms were introduced to complete the harmonization process across regimes and to provide fiscal incentives for individuals to invest in the private pension funds.

With the shift to a notionally defined contribution scheme, the Italian social security system remained unfunded. Current retirees' pensions were still being financed by current workers' contributions, but individuals' pension benefits became directly linked to their lifetime contributions to the system. Naturally this contributive aspect is only figurative. The system works *as if* every worker has a personal fund where the contributions—corresponding to 33 percent of a worker's annual earnings—are accrued during his or her working career. These contributions are capitalized at an interest rate, which is computed as a five-year moving average of the nominal GDP growth. At retirement, the accumulated asset value is transformed into an annuity through a conversion coefficient, which depends negatively on the expected longevity at retirement and positively on the retirement age. The application of this new computation method has been pro quota for workers with less than 18 years of contributions in 1995, while workers with higher seniority remain under the previous regime.

The Dini reform also largely revised the eligibility criteria. Seniority pensions, whose eligibility was exclusively based on reaching a minimum contribution period, were abolished. Under the private employees' scheme, the minimum number of years of contribution to be eligible for a pension was reduced to 5 years only, and only individuals aged between 57 and 65 years are entitled to a pension. These measures have partially reduced the incentives to retire early, since pension benefits depend on retirement age through an actuarial adjustment factor—ranging from 4.72 to 6.136 percent per year—which

Table 7.1
Main features of the phased-in systems for private employees

	Before Amato	Phased-in Amato reform	Phased-in Dini reform
Type	Defined benefit	Defined benefit	Notional defined contribution
Pension benefit formula	Reference wage multiplied by replacement rate	Reference wage multiplied by replacement rate	Conversion coefficient (depending on life expectancy and retirement age) applied to capitalized (at a five years moving average of the nominal GDP growth) carrier contributions (equal to 33% of the annual earnings)
Reference wage	Average wage in the last 5 years before retirement	Carrier average wage (capitalized at price index +1%)	—
Replacement rate	2% * Number of years of contributions	2% * Number of years of contributions	—
Normal retirement age	60 (men), 55 (women)	65 (men), 60 (women)	Above 56
Eligibility for old age pension	15 years of contributions and retirement age	20 years of contributions and retirement age	5 years of contributions and retirement age
Eligibility for seniority pensions	35 years of contributions	35 years of contributions	Not available
Benefit indexation	Nominal wages	Prices	Prices

is included in the pension benefit's conversion coefficient. All these measures are summarized in table 7.1.

In 1997, the Prodi reform extended the share of the workforce covered by the Dini reform to the public employees, and reduced the length of the transition period (see Giarda 1998). Finally, in 2004, the Berlusconi government further modified the system by introducing tax incentives to postpone retirement and by increasing the minimum retirement age. The implementation of the latter measure was postponed to 2008, effectively granting an exception to the workers already excluded from the Amato and Dini reforms.

Two main features of the reform process of the nineties have been criticized in the literature: the lengthy transitions and the financial sustainability of the phased in system. A common opinion among scholars—see Franco (2002) and references therein—is that the transition from the pre-1992 to the new regime has been and will continue to be excessively slow and gradual. The decision of guaranteeing the old claims to those workers who had more than 15 years of contributions in 1992 (and more than 18 years in 1995) will induce only a slow improvement in the financial unbalance of the social security budget, and will clearly violate a notion of intergenerational equity by postponing most of the burden of the transition onto the younger generations of workers.

However, doubts have also been cast on the long-run financial sustainability of the system in the new regime and on its ability to avoid crowding out the development of a complementary funded pillar. The critical element is represented by the conversion coefficients, translating the capitalized contributions into a pension annuity for every individual, which were meant to achieve an age-neutral pension system, by eliminating the incentives to retire early. Calculations by Barbi (2002) and Brugiavini and Peracchi (2001) suggest instead that once the system is entirely phased in, it will still provide an incentive to retire early. Spending reductions due to eligibility restrictions may thus fail to be as large as expected.[7]

Indeed, the Dini reform entitled future governments to modify these conversion coefficients every ten years "on the basis of current demographic forecasts and of the comparison between the actual dynamics of the GDP growth rate and the growth rate of wage income that is subject to contribution to the system." However, the risk is that the large discretionary power of the governments in this revision process might be used by political accountable policy-makers to respond to political pressures from the elderly (see Peracchi and Rossi 1998; Giarda 1998; Gronchi and Aprile 1998). This issue will be addressed in sections 7.3 and 7.4.

7.2   Aging in Italy

The demographic dynamics of the last two decades has largely re-shaped the age profile of the Italian population. As in many industrial-ized countries, the dramatic aging of the population has been due to the combined effect of a large reduction in fertility rate and a steady increase in life expectancy. In Italy the fertility rate—measuring the number of children per woman between 18 and 45 years—has dropped from 2.4 in the sixties—the years of the Italian baby boom—and in the seventies to 1.2 in the eighties and nineties. Meanwhile longevity has increased as life expectancy at birth rose from 77.4 year for females and 70.6 year for male in 1980 to respectively 80 and 73.5 years in 1990, and 82 and 75.5 in 2000. This increase in longevity has been mainly achieved through substantial reductions in old age mortality, thereby producing an increase in the share of very elderly individuals—aged 80 years or more—in the population.

Estimates by the Italian National Institute of Statistics (ISTAT) for the next 50 years suggest that aging population problem will be large. Although the fertility rate may recover and stabilize around 1.5 children per woman, reductions in mortality rates are expected to be made. Figure 7.3 shows the population profile by age in the year 2000 and the forecasted profile for the year 2050. One characteristic is imme-diately apparent: in the year 2000, individuals in their thirties—the Italian baby boomers—represented the single largest generation in the population; in the year 2050, the most numerous generation will then be composed of individuals in their seventies. Although these persons born in the 1960s and 1970s are expected to enjoy large increases in life expectancy, fewer children are being born to enlarge the base of the Italian population pyramid.

This impressive size of the aging population will have big conse-quences for the functioning of the current unfunded social security system. The old age dependency ratio, which measures the ratio of individuals aged 65 years and more to potentially active individuals aged 18 to 64 years, will spike from almost 28 percent in 2000 to almost 67 percent in 2048 (see figure 7.4). This means that whereas in the year 2000 there were almost four individuals in working age for every el-

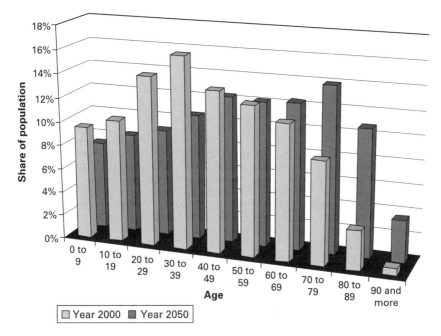

Figure 7.3
Aging in Italy: Population by age group in 2000 and 2050 (Source: Eurostat)

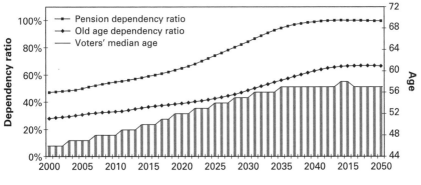

Figure 7.4
Demographic dynamics (Source: ISTAT)

derly person aged 65 years and more, in the year 2050 there will only be three workers for every two elderly.

Additionally there is the concern that the current early retirement behavior of the Italian workers will continue into the future, so this demographic effect could even be magnified. Currently, because of the low labor force participation rates of middle-aged workers, the age threshold between active and nonactive individuals is well below 65 years, which is the divide used in the calculation of the old age dependency ratio. The pension dependency ratio shown in figure 7.4 in fact separates workers from retirees according to the effective median retirement age in 1995, which was equal to 58 years. In the year 2000 this pension dependency ratio was equal to 44 percent, amounting to approximately two workers for every retiree. Were the effective retirement age to remain at 58 years, the pension dependency ratio would reach 100 percent by the year 2043: If that were allowed to happen, there would be contribution of only one worker for every retiree receiving a pension.

In the year 2050 individuals in their seventies—presumably retirees—will constitute the largest population group in Italy. Their number is expected to be almost 14 percent of the adult population. Again, the political strength of numbers suggests that these elderly will be able to protect their pension benefits. A synthetic indicator of the relative importance of the elderly among the electorate is the median age of voters. In 1992, before the Amato reform, this median age was 44 years, and it increased to 46 years in 2000. Figure 7.4 shows the expected rise of the median age among the voters based on ISTAT demographic forecasts: the median age will peak at 58 years in the years 2043 to 2044, and will slightly decrease to 57 years in the year 2050.

7.3   Political Sustainability of the Reforms

The two most criticized features of the Italian reforms of the nineties discussed in section 7.1—the use of the long transition period and a conversion coefficient that delegates to future policy-makers the determination of the effective generosity of the pension system—may be explained by political considerations. The long transition period was used by politicians to build the necessary consensus among the electorate and allowed several generations of elderly workers to escape the new, more restrictive rules. This feature was further decisive in persuading the unions not to oppose the social security reform package.

The failure of the 1994 Berlusconi reform proposal, which did not include a long transition period, demonstrated the need for consensus building on the social security issues and the power of unions in opposing legislation relating Italian worker benefits. The next fifty years will intensify the need for such political consensus among the more numerous elderly. The demographics imply that politicians will choose to adjust the conversion coefficient to increase the system's generosity in order to please an older electorate, rather than follow to the letter the Dini law to preserve actuarial fairness as longevity increases. An evaluation of how political constraints may shape the Italian social security system in the long run is the object of section 7.3.3.

7.3.1 Reforms and Transition Periods

During the nineties there were three important attempts to reform the private employees' scheme of the Italian social security system: the Amato reform in 1992, the reform project presented by the Berlusconi government in September 1994, and the Dini reform in 1995. The Amato and Dini reforms permitted long transition periods. These reforms succeeded only after the agreement of the unions—and the approval in the Parliament. Some of the measures of these reforms have begun to be implemented, but the complete phasing in will occur only around 2040. In 1994 the Berlusconi proposal was fiercely opposed by the unions, so it failed to be approved. Soon after the Berlusconi government proposed its package of reforms, it had to resign. A new government—led by a former minister in the Berlusconi government, Lamberto Dini—was appointed.

As reviewed in section 3.2, the political support in favor of the reform proposal calls for a clear evaluation of the effects of the reform package on the economic well-being of workers and retirees. The expected economic value of the system to retirees is quantified by their net pension wealth, which is defined as the discounted value of all future pension benefits that an individual is entitled to under the current legislation minus the discounted value of all future contributions to the system. Thus changes in the net pension wealth of an individual due to the reform package are used as the measure of the costs of the reform to this individual.

Beltrametti (1995, 1996) compared the variations in the individual net pension wealth due to the Amato and Dini reforms and the plausible changes that would be due to the 1994 Berlusconi reform. Table 7.2

Table 7.2
Economic effects of the reforms on individuals' net pension wealth by age group

	Amato reform			Berlusconi proposal			Dini reform	
	Before	After	Δ	Before	After	Δ	After	Δ
15–19	28	−31	−59	−48	−52	−4	−56	−8
20–24	152	−50	−202	−101	−116	−15	−128	−27
25–29	276	−43	−319	−112	−131	−19	−145	−33
30–34	347	46	−301	−20	−56	−36	−63	−43
35–39	415	198	−217	139	71	−68	99	−40
40–44	504	282	−222	227	174	−53	227	0
45–49	497	349	−148	306	251	−55	306	0
50–54	533	441	−92	402	338	−64	402	0
55–59	394	360	−34	339	238	−101	339	0
60–64	183	177	−6	168	160	−8	168	0
65+	79	76	−3	74	74	0	74	0
Workers	3,407	1,802	−1,605	1,375	997	−378	1,225	−151
Retirees	2,660	2,527	−133	2,710	2,710	0	2,710	0

Source: D'Amato and Galasso (2002).
Note: In billion of Italian liras in 1992. The net pension wealth is defined as the difference between discounted current and future pension's benefits and social security contributions.

shows these calculations and emphasizes the different impacts on individuals by age group.

The 1992 Amato reform stands out for its effective retrenchment effort. The net pension wealth of the workers decreased by 52.9 percent, and even the retirees had to bear part of the cost—their net pension wealth was reduced by 5 percent. These reform measures were adopted in a period of large financial imbalances of the pension scheme, and aimed at guaranteeing the financial solvency of the system—and hence the payment of pension benefits to the eligible individuals—in the near future. The largest share of the cost was born by the young cohorts—as the net pension wealth of the individuals aged 30 years or less decreased by more than 100 percent, while the reduction for the workers and retirees aged 60 years or more was below 5 percent. The unequal cost sharing across generations was due to a long transition process that only partially affected middle-aged and elderly workers but entirely a cohorts of young workers.

The reform package of the Berlusconi government envisaged in 1994 large reductions in the individuals' net pension wealth, estimated to be around 27.5 percent for the workers; retirees were not to be affected. This reform project was intended to spread the cost more equally among workers of different age groups than the Amato reform. No long transition was planned, and middle-aged or elderly workers were expected to be penalized as severely as young cohorts.

The 1995 Dini reform was milder than the Berlusconi's project, with a reduction in the net pension wealth of the workers of only 11 percent, and it also featured a long transition period. This characteristic of the Dini reform became much criticized, but it was crucial to achieve this unequal division of costs across generations, with the under 40 years old individuals assuming the full cost of the reform.

The estimates by Beltrametti (1995, 1996) are consistent with the view that the political success of the Amato and Dini reforms—as opposed to the 1994 Berlusconi's attempt—was due to the decision of placing a larger share of the costs of the reforms on the young generations of workers. In fact, because the majority of the voting population in 1995 was older than 44 years, the Dini reforms was effectively backed by a majority of voters—workers and retirees—who did not bear any cost of the reform. A reform package presented only few months earlier by Berlusconi failed to enjoy the same political support because it proposed a reduction in the net pension wealth of workers older than 40 years. The long transition periods envisaged by the Amato and Dini reforms hence represented the key element for political support. Whether these reform measures will continue to receive political support from an aging electorate in the long run will be addressed in the next section.

7.3.2   The Phased-in System

By the year 2040, unless other modifications, such as the 2004 reform, occur—all the measures introduced by the 1995 Dini reform will finally be phased in. The system shaped by the Amato and Dini reforms will present substantial differences from the pre-Amato scheme, particularly in the benefits' calculation method and indexation. These changes were expected to allow the Italian pension system to cope with the dramatic increase of the aging population and to retain its financial balance. Social security spending is forecasted to slightly decrease in the year 2050 (see table 2.3) because the sizable aging population is expected to be offset by the reforms measures.

In the long run any political dissatisfaction with the phased-in system will have to be evaluated along two dimensions: age group and income, or educational level. With population aging, in the year 2050 the pivotal voter will be older and belong to an age group that would benefit from an increase in the generosity of the system. Yet the reforms will necessarily reflect, for individuals of the same age, the different earnings and working histories in the benefit calculation method. These differences are evident in table 7.1 where the pre-Amato pension scheme and the phased-in system following the Amato and Dini reforms are compared.

Before the 1992 Amato reform, pension benefits for an agent with education level q and retirement age J^q were computed as the product of three elements: the average wage in the last five years before retirement $(\overline{w}_{J^q}^q)$, the number of years during which the agent contributed to the system (N^q), and a coefficient α (equal to 2 percent), which converted the number of contribution years into a replacement ratio:

$$P_{t,J^q}^q = \alpha N^q \overline{w}_{J^q}^q. \tag{7.1}$$

Pension benefits were indexed to the growth rate of nominal wages.

In the phased-in system following the Amato and Dini reforms, pension benefits will be computed according to a notional defined contribution scheme. Agents contribute to the system a constant fraction of their labor income, $\tau_t w_t^q$, over their work life . This amount is then capitalized at an annual rate, g, which is related to the long-run return of the social security system—the growth rate of the economy. At retirement age the capitalized contributions are transformed into an annuity according to a conversion coefficient, γ, which depends on the actual retirement age and on other factors, such as the residual expected longevity at retirement. The pension benefit in the new phased-in scheme for an agent with education level q and retiring at time t with a retirement age J^q is hence described by the following expression:

$$P_{t,J_q}^q = \gamma \sum_{i=s^q}^{J^q-1} (1+g)^{J^q-i} w_{t-(J^q-i)}^{q,i} \tau_{t-(J^q-i)}, \tag{7.2}$$

where s^q represents the first period in the work life of an agent with education q. Following the Amato reform, pension benefits are indexed only to inflation.

As discussed in chapter 4, the simulations on the political sustainability of social security concentrate on the equilibrium contribution rate[8] that equates total contributions to total pension benefits. Hence the determination of the contribution rate indirectly pins down the conversion coefficients—denoted respectively by α, in the pre-reform regime, and by γ, in the post-reforms regime—that measure the average generosity of the system. Higher contribution rates increase the total contribution to the system and—through a rise in the conversion coefficients—total pension benefits to the retirees. However, how these resources are allocated to retirees of different ages and incomes (or education) depends on the benefits calculation criteria.

To examine the political issues in the debate over social security reforms due to population aging and the possible redistributive measures of the reforms, it is convenient to consider an economy populated by adult individuals who differ in age and education level. Individuals may live from 18 to 95 years, but face age-specific mortality rates. Within each age cohort, agents differ by education and, accordingly, by retirement age, working history, income, and degree of political participation.

Using the 1995 Bank of Italy Survey on Consumption and Wealth, I divide these individuals into three classes based on educational level, as shown in table 7.3. The low-level education group, with at most a primary education (five years of schooling), accounts for 35.6 percent of the sample of the Italian adult population in 1995; the medium-level education group, composed of individuals with secondary education, represents 31.2 percent of the sample, and the third most educated group, whose members have at least a high school diploma, has a relative weight of 33.2 percent.

Similarly the working history and earning profile by age for the median individual in each educational group can be constructed using 1995 Bank of Italy Survey data. Highly educated individuals have a median working history of 35 years, since they usually start working

Table 7.3
Population characteristics by educational level

Educational level	Share of adult population	Election participation rate	Years of contribution	Median retirement age
Low	35.6%	71.8%	30	57
Medium	31.2%	79.2%	35	56
High	33.2%	82.5%	35	58

Sources: Bank of Italy (1995) and Abacus (1999).
Note: Individuals with low education have a primary education or less; medium refers to secondary education and high to high school and university graduates.

at 23 and retire when 58 years old; their earning profile is steep. Agents in the intermediate group enter the labor market earlier, at age 19, and retire at 56 with an overall working history of 37 years. They also contribute only for 35 years because of small unemployment spells in their contributing history. The low-educated group has, in contrast, a median working history of 43 years—from age 15 to 57—but this group contributes to the system only for 30 years because its members frequently drop out of the official labor market. Low- and medium-educated individuals have flat earning profiles (see figure 7.5); they are typically less productive than the high-educated workers at any age.

Educational level is also a factor in individuals' political participation, as measured by their turnout rate at elections. According to Abacus poll data for the 1999 European Parliament election, high- and medium-educated individuals are more likely to vote than low-educated individuals, but no significant difference emerges in the political behavior by age. Further educational level and income heterogeneity may influence the longevity differentials because of the pro-

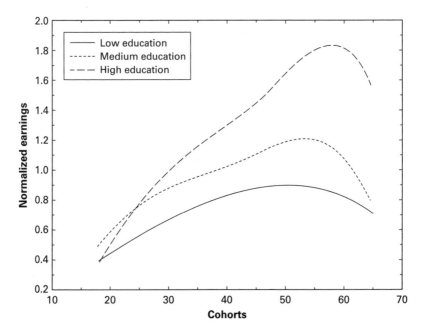

Figure 7.5
Earning profiles by age (Source: D'Amato and Galasso 2002)

tective effect of income on maintaining health (e.g., see Deaton and Paxson 1998, 2001; Smith 1999). To account for this element, the simulations described in the next section are carried out allowing for age-specific probabilities of longevity across education groups, with high- and low-educated persons showing respectively a 5 percent lower and higher mortality rate than medium-educated individuals.

7.3.3 Political Constraints

In the decade before the 1992 Amato reform, the average equilibrium contribution rate for the private employees' pension system (FPLD) was equal to 38 percent of the workers' labor income. Pension benefits were calculated according to the average wage in the last five years prior to retirement (see equation 7.1), and the real value of the existing pensions increased at the average productivity growth rate (almost 2 percent in the 1982–91 period).

However, population aging and the reforms of the 1990s will significantly change the demographic, economic, and political structure of the Italian economy, along with the basic structure of the social security system. In the year 2050, when the system introduced by the Amato and Dini reforms is entirely phased-in, the demographic pyramid (see figure 7.3) will have shifted toward the old age, and the dependency ratio will reach 67 percent. The effect of this shift will be a drastic drop in the profitability of the social security system, since obviously the relative share of contributors to the system—the workers—will decrease, while the proportion of recipients from the scheme—the retirees—will rise. Additionally the aging shift will determine the pivotal voter in the political process, whose median age among voters will be 57 years in 2050. The older pivotal voter will be apt to expand an old age transfer program despite its lower average profitability.

The simulations of the model in chapter 4 provide a quantitative evaluation of how these political constrains will shape the size and generosity of the Italian social security system. They address some crucial questions: which contribution rate will prevail in 2050, given the rules set in by the Amato-Dini reforms? How does this contribution rate depend on the effective retirement age? And what size would the unfunded pillar have reached in absence of reforms?

Table 7.4 presents the simulations results. The first line—corresponding to the year 1992—summarizes the scenario prior to the reforms. An equilibrium contribution rate of 38 percent commands

Table 7.4
Simulation results

Year	Regime	Median retirement age by educational level			Equi-librium contri-bution rate	Replacement rate by educational level		
		Low	Medium	High		Low	Medium	High
1992	Pre-reforms	57	56	58	38.0%	59%	69%	69%
2050	Pre-reforms	57	56	58	61.0%	43%	50%	50%
2050	Amato-Dini	58	58	58	61.1%	69%	77%	61%
2050	Amato-Dini	59	59	59	59.9%	73%	81%	64%
2050	Amato-Dini	60	60	60	57.5%	76%	84%	65%
2050	Amato-Dini	61	61	61	55.3%	79%	87%	67%
2050	Amato-Dini	62	62	62	53.2%	83%	92%	69%
2050	Amato-Dini	63	63	63	51.3%	87%	98%	72%
2050	Amato-Dini	64	64	64	50.0%	92%	106%	77%
2050	Amato-Dini	65	65	65	48.9%	99%	116%	82%

Source: D'Amato and Galasso (2002).
Note: The first line described the year 1992 pre-reforms scenario, and the second line displays the simulations for the year 2050, if the Amato and Dini reforms had not occurred. All remaining lines show the simulations for the social security contribution rate under the 2050 economic, demographic, and political scenario with the phased-in Dini reform for different retirement ages.

a replacement rate of almost 60 percent for the low-educated individuals, who contributed for 30 years, and of almost 70 percent for the medium- and high-educated individuals, who had 35 years of contributions. These percentages are in line with a conversion coefficient of 2 percent per year of contribution.

For the year 2050 demographic and economic scenario, this political economy model suggests that in the absence of reforms, and with retirement ages at their 1992 levels—respectively, 57 years for low educated, 56 for the intermediate education group, and 58 for highly educated—the equilibrium contribution rate would jump to 61 percent, while the initial replacement rate would fall to 43 percent for first group and to 50 percent for the others.

The future effective retirement age is crucial for simulations that assess if the Amato and Dini reforms measure will succeed in limiting the hike in social security expenditure. If all individuals retire at age 58, in 2050 the equilibrium contribution rate would be 61.1 percent, and the reforms would have failed to delimit the expansion of the system. However, as shown in table 7.4, postponing retirement age to 62

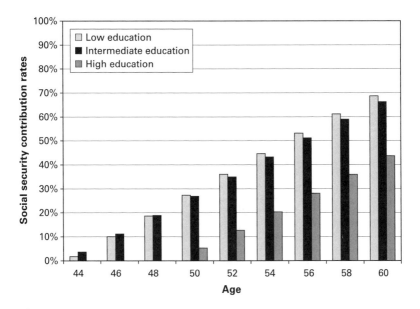

Figure 7.6
Most preferred contribution rates by age and education level in 2050 (Source: D'Amato and Galasso 2002)

or to 65 years would contain the rise in the contribution rate to 53.2 percent or to 48.9 percent, while the corresponding reduction in the dependency ratio would lead to a higher replacement rate. These results suggest that the adoption of a notional defined contribution formula will not have a large impact on the contribution rate, unless the retirement age is significantly increased.

These reforms have also modified how the system treats individuals of the same age, but with different earnings profile—and hence education. A priori, a shift from a defined benefit to a notional defined contribution scheme should reduce the degree of redistribution in the system, as individual pension benefits become more tightly related to individual contributions. Figure 7.6 displays the most preferred contribution rate by individuals in different cohorts and education classes, under the 2050 demographic and economic scenario with the phased-in system in place and a retirement age of 65 years. For any given age, agents in the low-education group always prefer a larger contribution rate than more educated individuals, since the benefit formula of the new notional defined contribution scheme (see equation 7.2) penalizes careers with steep labor income profiles (see also Peracchi and Rossi

1998), such as those typically featured by highly educated workers (see figure 7.6). This redistributive element may also be appreciated by observing the variations in the replacement rates by education level: low- and medium-educated individuals enjoy larger increases in the replacement rate than highly educated individuals.

The last reform measure to be examined is the shift of pension indexation from wage growth to inflation, which occurred with the Amato reform in 1992. Contrary to a common opinion that price indexation, rather than wage indexation, may lead to a reduction in pension spending—and therefore in the contribution rate—the simulations carried out for the 2050 scenario under the two alternative pension regimes (see the second and third lines of table 7.4) suggest that the contribution rate is almost unaffected, while the replacement rate at retirement increases. The intuition is straightforward. Since in the case of price indexation the value of the pension annuity decreases—relative to the average wage in the economy—during the retirement period, in their voting decisions, individuals will try to preserve the relative values of their pension benefits, by asking for higher replacement rates at retirement. As a result total pension spending may fail to decrease, as the lower pension benefits paid out to old retirees are compensated by the higher pension benefits awarded to more recent retirees.

7.4 An Evaluation of the Reforms in a Graying Society

Faced with a dramatic aging process and the tight external constraints provided by the EU Maastricht requirements, the Italian reforms of the nineties aimed mainly at limiting the forecasted expansion in pension spending, while designing a more equitable and less fragmented system. During the slow phase-in period, however, the treatment of successive generations of workers will be arbitrarily different, thereby creating concern about the distributive equity of the system. This much criticized feature of the reforms is that they adhere to the political constraints imposed by voters and unions. The Dini reform—and to some extent also the Amato reform—met these political requirements with a divide-and-rule strategy, which partitioned the electorate between a minority of losers from the reform and a majority of individuals whose economic well-being was basically unaffected. The long transition period is the result of this political decision. The pension reform project presented by the Berlusconi government in 1994, which did not comply with these political criteria, instead met with fierce opposition of the unions and had to be withdrawn.

Some doubts may also be cast on the long run sustainability of the phased-in system. In fact, although official EC-OECD projections forecast a reduction in pension spending in the year 2050—see table 2.3—long-term political risks still remain.[9] The main source of concern rests with the possible manipulation of the conversion coefficient in the notional defined contribution formula, which transforms the capitalized contributions into a pension annuity at retirement. While the Dini reform set this coefficient according to actuarial criterion and envisaged its periodical revisions to account for longevity gains, future policymakers may choose to modify the coefficient to increase (or to maintain) the pensions' generosity, and hence the contribution rate, as the electorate ages. Simulations—based on the political economy model described at chapter 4—of the Italian economic, demographic, and political scenario for the year 2050 validate these concerns. Population aging greatly increases the political power of the elderly, as the median age among the voters increases from 44 years in 1992 to 57 in 2050. Despite the Amato and Dini reforms, public spending for pension provision is expected to grow even higher, since the equilibrium contribution rate is estimated to increase from 38 percent in 1992 to at least 48.9 percent in 2050. Contrary to the conventional view, two of the main provisions introduced by the Amato and Dini reforms have had little impact in reducing the political pressure generated by population aging. The adoption of a notional defined contributions formula has mainly intragenerational effects, by transferring resources from agents with a steep income profile to agents with a flat profile, while the price indexation has virtually no consequence on the overall size of the system. This is because voters anticipate the future relative reduction of pension benefits vis-à-vis the average wage in the economy, and vote for a larger replacement rate at retirement.

The only effective reform measure to limit the political pressure on pension spending is a rise in the effective retirement age. According to these simulations, an increase of the median retirement age for all education groups from 58 to 65 years would induce a reduction in the equilibrium contribution rate of more than twelve points, from 61.1 to 48.9 percent, as shown in table 7.4. The intuition is straightforward. For every worker, an increase in the retirement age expands the remaining social security contributions' period, while reducing the average residual length of retirement. In this respect an increase in the retirement age amounts to making an individual younger, as she is moved farther away from retirement, and hence reduces the individual profitability of the system. Moreover, postponing retirement reduces the ratio of retirees to workers—the pension dependency ratio—and thus increases the profitability of the system. The simulations in the previous section suggest that the former effect strictly dominates, leading to a reduction in the equilibrium contribution rate. Simulations on the political feasibility of this measure at chapter 11 confirm the importance of postponing retirement, particularly for Italy.

The economic, demographic, and political scenario used for the simulations incorporates most of the features related to the aging process, as forecasted for the year 2050. Additional characteristics unrelated to aging, which were not included in the simulations of table 7.4, however, may still be relevant to the magnitude of the shift in political pressure, such as variations in the economic growth rate and in the educational structure of the population. Contrary to conventional wisdom, simulations carried out within the context of a political economy model suggest that higher economic growth can lead to more social security spending. As is often argued in the public debate, by increasing the overall tax base, higher growth allows the underlying pension obligations to be met without increasing the contribution rate. A higher growth rate can therefore boost the average profitability of an unfunded system. Political economy models internalize this latter effect, which induces voters to increase the overall pension spending.

Expected changes in the educational structure of the population would lead to less gloomy conclusions about the political effects of the aging process on social security. An increase in the overall educational level, with most individuals shifting respectively from the low- to medium-educated group, and from the medium- to the highly educated group, would reduce the size of the intragenerational redistributive effect and lower the equilibrium contribution rates.

8

Political Sustainability and
the Silent Reform in Spain

Social security provides the overwhelming majority of the retirement income of the elderly Spaniards. Initially established in 1919 as a fully funded system for private sector's employees (*Retiro Obrero Obligatorio*), the Spanish system became PAYG in the thirties under the dictatorship. Since then, successive reforms have converted this public provision of retirement income into a highly fragmented system with two main institutions: the *Régimen General*, covering most private employees, and the *Regímenes Especiales*, targeted mainly to self-employed and agricultural workers.

Because of the system's extended coverage among workers and its generosity, in 2000 public pension expenditure in Spain amounted to 9.4 percent of GDP, slightly below the spending of continental European countries, such as France and Germany (see table 2.3). Public pensions represent the main program in the Spanish welfare state: in 2000 old age pensions accounted for 42 percent of total welfare expenditure, which becomes 54 percent, when survivor and disability pensions are also included (see figure 8.1). Among the other programs, health care constituted 31 percent of total welfare spending, whereas unemployment insurance and family benefits added respectively 12 percent and 2 percent.

Most of the concerns about the financial sustainability of the Spanish system that emerged during the eighties and nineties were related to the dramatic demographic process of population aging that Spain has been experiencing. Due to a large drop in fertility and a steady increase in longevity, the Spanish population is rapidly graying. In 2000 Spain featured one of the largest proportion of elderly to adult individuals among OECD countries, and the process is expected to continue (see table 2.5), thereby creating additional pressure on the financial sustainability of the system. In fact EC and OECD official estimates, reported

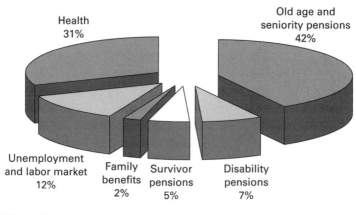

Figure 8.1
Welfare expenditure decomposition in 2000 (Source: OECD)

at table 2.5, predict pension spending to reach 17.4 percent of GDP in 2050.

Despite these projections Spain has so far failed to implement a comprehensive reform of its social security system. A serious attempt was carried out in 1995, as the government established a committee—composed of economists, public officers and unions' representatives—with the double task of analyzing the financial prospects of the system and of presenting adequate policy responses. Yet, although the suggestions put forward by this committee were agreed upon by virtually all political forces in the so-called *Pacto de Toledo*, little reforming effort followed.

Some scholars have recently hinted that in Spain a silent reform is currently underway (e.g., see Boldrin, Jimenez, and Sanchez 2000; Jimeno 2002; Alonso and Herce 2003; Conde-Ruiz and Alonso 2004). The reform seems to consist of changes to some crucial parameters of the system—namely to the minimum and maximum pensions and to the floor and ceiling on the contribution base. In the aggregate they may achieve substantial changes to the redistributiveness and overall generosity of the system, which may be difficult to detect by the public at large. An example of a "silent" reform measure would be the decision to adjust the maximum pension level to the inflation rate, rather than to the wage dynamics. In a period of economic growth, this small modification would induce a rise in the number of retirees whose pensions are capped by this maximum level—thereby reducing pension spending.

The task set up for this chapter is to provide an evaluation of the long-run political sustainability of the Spanish social security system under aging and to assess the relevance of this silent reform. The impact of the silent reform on the political sustainability of the system may come from an increase in the degree of redistribution of the system, which would typically strengthen the support for social security among low-income agents, while increasing the opposition among high-earners.

The effect of the aging process on the future political sustainability of the social security system is particularly relevant in Spain. Aging reduces the long-term profitability of the social security system, by increasing the ratio of the elderly individuals to the active population; but it also modifies the identity of the pivotal voter, who becomes older and hence more inclined to favor social security. The latter effect of aging is crucial in Spain, where the median voter's age will increase from 44 years in 2000 to 57 years in 2050.

The next section provides a brief history of the Spanish social security system and a description of its main features. A treatment of the dramatic aging process and of its impact on the political representation by age is in section 8.2. The last section of this chapter describes the Spanish social security system in great detail, with a special emphasis on the minimum and maximum pensions, and characterizes the crucial features of the silent reform. Finally, the simulation results, discussed at section 8.3.3, indicate that population aging process will raise a large political demand for more pensions, leading to higher contribution rates despite the silent reform currently underway.

8.1 An Overview of the Spanish Social Security System

A first pension scheme providing some form of retirement income to public employees was established already in 1900 together with the institution of an insurance against on-the-job injuries. In 1919, a more coherent system was introduced for workers in the private sector with the *Retiro Obrero Obligatorio*. This scheme required employees and employers to contribute a fraction of the workers' labor income to a common pension fund, whose assets were then to be used to finance the workers' pension benefits. Despite being funded, the *Retiro Obrero Obligatorio* was a defined benefit system in which pension benefits were awarded according to the individuals' age and years of contributions and some form of within-cohort redistribution took place. In

1926, the level of coverage of the public employees was extended with the institution of a new system—the *Régimen de Clases Pasivas*.

A major change in the early Spanish social security system occurred in the thirties. Under the dictatorship, the financing method of the *Retiro Obrero Obligatorio* shifted from fully funded to PAYG, and the new system was named Old Age Insurance. Later, several special regimes (*régimenes especiales*) were established to tailor the system to the requests of particular workers or professions. In the early sixties these special regimes were modified: their number was increased, and a wedge between the workers' actual wage income and the social security contribution base was introduced.

Only in 1978, after the Pactos de la Moncloa, a serious attempt was made to harmonize the Spanish social security system. A unique body, the National Institute for Social Security (Instituto Nacional de la Seguridad Social), was made responsible for the administration of the entire system; the social security treatment of workers belonging to different categories was standardized, and one social security contribution rate was applied to all workers. Furthermore the difference between the actual wage and the social security contribution base was eliminated, and contributions were paid on the entire labor earnings between a floor and a ceiling.

In 1985 the Socialist Party launched a series of reforms, though they were opposed by the unions. The reforms served to rationalize the fragmented Spanish system, while at the same time reducing its generosity. First, eligibility to disability pensions was restricted. Second, eligibility criteria for old age pensions were tightened, and the number of years of contributions to obtain an old age pension was increased from 10 to 15. Third, pension benefits were, on average, reduced by raising from 2 to 8 the number of years over which the reference wage for pension benefits is computed. Fourth, fragmentation was reduced, by combining together some special regimes or by incorporating them into the general regime (*Régimen General de la Seguridad Social*).

Despite these mild changes, a large debate emerged at the beginning of the nineties on how to improve the long-term perspective of the system. In 1994 a special committee—composed of scholars, economists, public officers, and unions' representatives—was instituted by the Parliament to analyze the long-term financial sustainability of the system and to propose some reform measures. According to the committee's final report (the *Pacto de Toledo*), any discussion regarding the social security reform measures ought to be excluded from political campaigns in order to isolate this policy issue from upcoming elections. The report, which was backed by almost the entire political spectrum, contained some suggestions to improve the future perspective of the system. They included more effort to make the different special regimes conform to the general system. Further a reserve fund was established to be used for financing the retirement of the baby-boom generation, along the lines of the US trust fund (see chapter 10). Other suggestions included a tightening of the link between contributions and pension benefits, but accompanied by an increase in the redistributiveness of some social security programs, and finally, postponement of the retirement age and the development of occupational funds and private pension plans. Some of these changes were made in the 1997 reform, which also introduced a gradual increase, from 8 to 15 of years, of the time period over which the average wage for the pension benefit calculation is computed.

8.1.1   A Description of the System

At the beginning of the twenty-first century, the Spanish social security system was composed of two major schemes[1]—the general regime (*Régimen General de la Seguridad Social*), covering most private employees, and the special regimes (*Regímenes Especiales de la Seguridad Social*), covering mainly self-employed and workers in the agricultural sector. In 2002, 71.8 percent of the workers in the private sector was enrolled in the *Régimen General* and only 28.2 percent in the other special regimes, although these *Regímenes Especiales* awarded almost 40 percent of the total pensions to the current retirees. Complementary private schemes—namely occupational plans and private pension funds—were instead less developed, although they are becoming more popular among young workers. According to Herce (2002), a third of the individuals covered by social security was also enrolled in a private plan in 2001, and their average contribution represents less than a quarter of the average social security contribution.

These public schemes provide four types of benefits: old age pensions, disability pensions, survivors' pensions, and family benefits. In 2002, old age pensions amounted to almost 60 percent of the total pensions, but to almost 70 percent of total pension spending, followed by survivors' pensions (30 percent of the total number, but 20 percent of spending).

In the Spanish system, eligibility to an old age pension depends on the number of years of contribution and on the retirement age. Since the 1985 reform, an individual is entitled to a pension, if she contributed to the system for at least 15 years, two of which in the last eight years prior to retirement, if she has reached 65 years of age and has retired from any occupation. Early retirement pensions are available to 60-year-old individuals, but pension benefits are reduced by 7 to 8 basis points per year of retirement prior to 65 years.

Eligible individuals receive an old age pension benefit equal to the product of a reference wage and a replacement rate. The reference wage is calculated as the weighted average of the wages coinciding with the social security contribution base over the fifteen years prior to retirement, with all wages, but those in the two years priors to retirement, indexed to the inflation. Interestingly this reference wage does not need to correspond to the actual wage because of the existence of a floor and a ceiling in the contribution base.

The replacement rate depends instead on the number of years of contributions. It is equal to 50 percent for the first 15 years of contributions and increases by 3 percent per year up to 25 years of contributions and then by 2 percent until 35 years. At 35 years of contributions the replacement rate has already reached its maximum (100 percent), and further years of contribution do not accrue additional benefits.

Since 1986 all types of pension benefits have been indexed to a government predetermined inflation rate, while they were previously linked to the nominal growth rate of the average wage. Differences between this predetermined rate and the actual inflation rate lead to modification in the pension benefits, which take place as soon as the inflation data become available.

The Spanish social security system features also a minimum and a maximum pension. The minimum pension is provided to those individuals who are entitled to an old age pension that does not reach a minimum threshold. This instrument guarantees a minimum retirement income to individuals who typically have low income or discontinuous working histories. The difference between the level of the contributory old age pension and the minimum pension is financed through general taxation. In the last decade the threshold for this minimum wage has increased in accordance with the nominal progression of the average wage. Moreover, unlike all other pension types, minimum pensions have often been raised by more than required by an indexation to the inflation rate.

The maximum pension instead restricts the pension of high-income individuals, whose benefits would be calculated above a certain threshold. Interestingly, after a large drop during the eighties, the level of the maximum pension has been kept constant in real terms in the last decades through the indexation to the inflation rate. The existence of a minimum and maximum pension and of a floor and a ceiling on the social security contribution base clearly introduce some element of intragenerational redistribution in the Spanish system. I will return to these elements in section 8.3.

The financing of the Spanish system is granted by the contributions paid by employers and employees. A proportional social security contribution tax rate is imposed on all labor earnings between a floor and a ceiling, with the exception of those related to extra hours. Both contribution base and contribution rate are established annually by the government. In 2002 the social security contribution rate was equal to 28.3 percent, of which 4.7 percent paid by the employee and the remaining 23.6 percent by the employer, down from 32.1 percent in 1982, when contributions were also used to finance health care expenditure. Notably the contribution base has also experienced an interesting trend featuring a constant reduction in the real value of the floor (the lower bound of the contribution base), whereas the ceiling has decreased in real terms only in the last decade.

8.2   Spain: An Aging Society

Spain is rapidly aging. Already in 2000 Italy and Spain had the largest old age dependency ratios among the six countries under analysis, but this demographic variable—measuring the ratio of elderly to adult individuals—is expected to rise in Spain and Italy more than anywhere else, as shown at table 2.5.

This dramatic aging process is mainly due to a large reduction in fertility and a steady increase in longevity. In Spain the fertility rate dropped from 2.8 children per woman aged 18 to 45 years in the sixties and seventies to 1.2 around the year 2000. Meanwhile longevity has largely increased. In fact life expectancy at birth has risen from 72.2 years for females and 67.4 years for males in 1960—a relatively low level if compared to other OECD countries—respectively to 78.6 and 72.5 years in 1980, and to 82.1 and 74.9 years in 2000, with the Spaniard females enjoying the largest longevity gain among the six countries under analysis. Interestingly most of these longevity gains have been achieved through substantial reductions in the mortality rates at old ages. For instance, life expectancy at age 65 has increased by

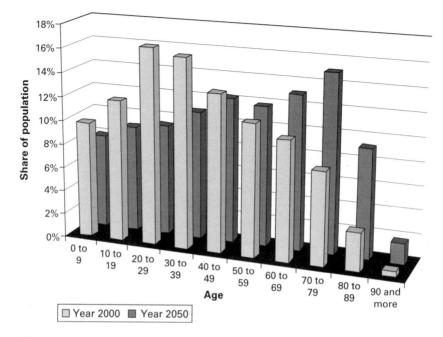

Figure 8.2
Aging in Spain: Population by age group in 2000 and 2050 (Source: Eurostat)

almost 1.5 years for males and 2.5 years for females between 1980 and 2000, as opposed to an increase by respectively 2.5 and 3.5 years for the life expectancy at birth over the same time period.

EC and OECD official demographic projections (see table 2.4) suggest that the Spanish population will indeed continue to age. Although the fertility rate is expected to recover slightly to around 1.5 children per woman, further reductions in the mortality rate will generate additional longevity gains. In 2050 life expectancy at birth is projected to reach 85 years for females and 79 years for males. The effect of these expected demographic changes is shown at figure 8.2, which displays the population profile by age in the year 2000, and the forecasted profile for the year 2050. Surprisingly, the two population profiles look almost symmetric. In fact, while in the year 2000, individuals in their twenties and thirties represented the largest generations in the population with the relative shares of the other generations constantly dropping with age; in the year 2050 the most numerous generation is expected to be composed by individuals in their seventies and the relative shares of the generations to increase almost constantly with age. In other words, the aging process is expected to induce a complete reversal of the Spanish population pyramid.

The relative magnitude of the impact of this impressive aging process on the functioning of the current unfunded social security systems may be captured by different indicators. Figure 2.2 shows the average length of retirement in the six countries under analysis. Longevity gains and the substantial drop in the retirement age have clearly widened the retirement period, thereby increasing the financial burden on these social security systems. This effect is particularly strong in Spain, where the average length of retirement has widened from 6.6 years in 1960 to reach 18.3 years in 2000.

Another measure of the effect of aging on the social security is given by the variation in the old age dependency ratio. Table 2.5 shows that the ratio of elderly individuals to the potentially active individuals is expected to jump from 26 percent in 2000 to 63.4 percent in 2050. Thus, while in the year 2000 there were almost four individuals in working age for every elderly person (aged 65 years or more), in the year 2050 there will only be three individual in working age for every two elderly. Moreover, if one accounts for the existence of early retirement institutions in the Spanish system, which reduce the labor force participation rates of middle-aged and elderly workers, the effect of aging on social security is magnified. The pension dependency ratio reported at table 2.5 suggests that in 2000 there were three workers per retiree, while in 2050 there will only be five workers for every four retirees.

However, if population ages, so does the electorate, thereby modifying the political strength of the different age groups. An older electorate will clearly emphasize the relevance of pension spending. In the year 2050 individuals aged 70 years or more will represent more than a quarter of the total voters and will presumably use their political power to protect their pension benefits. A synthetic measure of the political relevance of the elderly individuals is given by the median age among the voters. In 2000 this median age was equal to 44 years—the lowest among the six countries—but it is expected to reach 57 years in the year 2050.

8.3   Which Future for the Spanish System?

Aging in Spain is expected to put enormous pressure on the financial sustainability of the social security system, as pension expenditure is forecasted to reach 17.4 percent of GDP by 2050. Unlike in Italy—the other fast aging country whose social security system faces a tough challenge—no major reform has been implemented in Spain. A committee of experts established by the government in 1997 proposed several reform measures, backed by almost all political forces, yet little has been done since then.

Despite this seeming absence of reforming effort, a silent reform has been underway since the early nineties and has modified some crucial parameters of the Spanish system, such as the minimum and maximum pensions and the floor and ceiling in the contribution base. This silent reform could have far-reaching implications. For instance, if the threshold for the maximum pension is only adjusted to inflation, a long period of economic growth will largely increase the share of retirees whose pensions are capped by this maximum level, thereby making the system more redistributive.

This section examines the magnitude of this silent reform and the likely consequences for the future political sustainability of the Spanish social security system. First, a closer look is given to the Spanish system, with particular emphasis on the minimum and maximum pensions. These silent reform measures are then discussed, by examining the recent trends of the thresholds for the minimum and maximum pension and of the floor and ceiling in the contribution base. The last section provides an extensive analysis of the future political sustainability of the Spanish social security system, by concentrating on the aging process described at section 8.2 and on the redistributive effects of this silent reform.

8.3.1   A Closer Look at the System
An evaluation of the long-term prospects of the Spanish system has to include an analysis of two crucial elements of this scheme—the minimum and maximum pensions—which may introduce some redistribution among individuals of the same age but with different earnings and working histories, and hence influence their preferences over the pension system. Furthermore the silent reform described in the next section may intensify this redistributive feature through an increase in the share of individuals capped by the maximum pension.

The pension benefits calculation for the *Régimen General* depends on three elements: a reference wage—computed using the contribution base—the number of years of contribution and the retirement age. For an agent with education level (or income) q who retires at time t at age J_t^q the normal pension benefit, $P_{N,t}^q$, is computed as

$$P_{N,t}^q = \alpha \gamma \tilde{w}_t^q, \tag{8.1}$$

where $\tilde{w}_t^q$ is the reference wage for a type-q individual, α is the replacement rate and γ measures the reduction in the pension benefits in case of early retirement. The reference wage is calculated as an average of the social security contribution bases for a type-q individual over the fifteen years of contributions prior to retirement. Since these contribution bases—representing the fraction of the labor earnings subject to social security contributions—are bounded by a floor and a ceiling, they do not need to coincide with the individuals' actual wages. As shown in equation (8.2), the reference wage calculation includes 180 months of contribution bases, but it averages them out over 210 months, since in Spain annual pension benefits are divided in 14 payments while wages are paid out monthly. The reference wage is thus equal to

$$\tilde{w}_t^q = \frac{\sum_{i=1}^{24} b_{t-i}^q + \sum_{i=25}^{180} b_{t-i}^q (p_{t-25}/p_{t-i})}{210}, \tag{8.2}$$

where b_t^q is the contribution base at time t for a type-q individuals, and p_t represents the consumer price index at time t. As shown in (8.2), all past contribution bases are indexed to inflation except those in the two years prior to retirement.

The replacement rate α depends instead on the number of years of contributions N^q:

$$\alpha = \begin{cases} 0 & \text{for } N^q < 15, \\ 0.5 + 0.03(N - 15) & \text{for } 15 \leq N^q < 25, \\ 0.8 + 0.02(N - 25) & \text{for } 25 \leq N^q < 35, \\ 1 & \text{for } N^q \geq 35. \end{cases} \tag{8.3}$$

While no pension is awarded to individuals with less than 15 years of contributions, the replacement rate equals 50 percent at 15 years and increases by 3 percent for every year of contribution up to 25 years and by 2 percent thereafter, until reaching its maximum value of 100 percent after 35 years of contributions.

Finally, the coefficient γ relates the pension benefits to the retirement age, according to the following formula:

$$\gamma = \begin{cases} 0 & \text{for } J^q < 60, \\ 1 - \theta(65 - J^q) & \text{for } 60 \leq J^q < 65, \\ 1 & \text{for } J^q \geq 65, \end{cases} \tag{8.4}$$

where J^q represents the retirement age of a type-q individual and the discount parameter θ is equal to 8 percent for individuals with less than 40 years of contributions and to 7 percent for the others.

The Spanish system is also characterized by the existence of minimum and maximum pensions ($P_t^{\min}$ and $P_t^{\max}$). Minimum pensions are contributory pensions provided to individuals—typically low-earners with incomplete working history—who are eligible for an old age pension but remain below a threshold. These old age pension benefits are hence topped with resources coming from government general revenues in order to reach the minimum pension level. Maximum pensions provide instead a cap on the benefits of high-earnings retirees who would otherwise be entitled to an old age pension exceeding the upper threshold. Whether a type-q individual obtains the old age pension benefits as calculated in equation (8.1) or the minimum or maximum pension hence depends on these two thresholds. In particular, an agent with education level q receives a pension P_t^q equal to

$$P_t^q = \begin{cases} P_t^{\min} & \text{for } P_{N,t}^q < P_t^{\min}, \\ P_{N,t}^q & \text{for } P_t^{\min} \leq P_{N,t}^q < P_t^{\max}, \\ P_t^{\max} & \text{for } P_{N,t}^q \geq P_t^{\max}, \end{cases} \tag{8.5}$$

where $P_{N,t}^q$ is as defined in equation (8.1) and successive equations.

The existence of a minimum pension also introduces a powerful incentive to retire early. In fact, since the retirees receiving minimum pensions are typically low-earners with discontinuous working histories and long nonemployment spells (see Boldrin, Jimenez, and Peracchi 2000), an additional year in the labor force—and hence of contribution—is unlikely to raise the normal old age pension above the minimum pension. In other words, the change in these individuals' net social security wealth induced by an additional year of work may actually be negative, thereby providing a strong incentive to retire early. To appreciate the potential magnitude of this phenomenon is worth noticing that in 2002, 23 percent of all retirees received a minimum pension.

Employees and employers contribute to the social security system a fraction of the labor earnings—net of wages from extra hours—included between a floor, b_t^F, and a ceiling, b_t^C. In 2002, the social security contribution rate was equal to 28.3 percent. In each period, total contributions to the system hence depend on the social security contribution rate τ_t, on the contribution base's floor and ceiling b_t^F and b_t^C, and on the retirement age J^q. Total contributions to the system at time t are hence given by

$$T_t(\tau_t, b_t^F, b_t^C, J^q) = \tau_t \sum_{q=1}^{Q} \sum_{j=1}^{J^q-1} \mu_t^{j,q} b_t^{j,q}, \tag{8.6}$$

where $\mu_t^{j,q}$ represents the proportion of agents aged j and with education q in the population, Q is the number of education groups, and $b_t^{j,q}$, the effective contribution base of an agent aged j and with education q, is defined as

$$b_t^{j,q} = \begin{cases} 0 & \text{for } w_t^{j,q} < b_t^F, \\ w_t^{j,q} - b_t^F & \text{for } b_t^F \le w_t^{j,q} < b_t^C, \\ b_t^C - b_t^F & \text{for } w_t^{j,q} > b_t^C, \end{cases} \tag{8.7}$$

where $w_t^{j,q}$ represents the labor earnings—net of extra hours—of an agent aged j with education q at time t.

In a balanced budget social security system the total amount of pensions paid out to retirees equals the aggregate contributions paid by the current workers, except for the contributions to the minimum pensions, which are financed through general taxation. Thus the balanced budget constraint is equal to

$$T_t(\tau_t, b_t^F, b_t^C, J^q) = \sum_{q=1}^{Q} \sum_{j=J^q}^{G} \mu_t^{j,q} [P_t^q - \Gamma(P_t^{\min} - P_{N,t}^q)], \tag{8.8}$$

where P_t^q was defined in equation (8.5); G is the maximum longevity, which in the model is set equal to 95 years, and Γ is an indicator function that takes value 1 if $P_t^{\min} > P_{t,N}^q$ and 0 otherwise, to indicate that the financial coverage of the supplement to the minimum pensions is not financed through social security contributions.

The simulations on the political sustainability of the social security system presented in section 8.3.3 will concentrate on the equilibrium contribution rate, which—by satisfying equation (8.8)—determines the total amount of contributions to the system, T_t $(\tau_t, b_t^F, b_t^C, J^q)$ and the total amounts of pensions.

To capture possible redistributive effects of the social security system and to analyze the silent reform, the economic model (presented at chapter 4) emphasizes the differences in age and education (and income) level among individuals. Agents are assumed to live from 18 to at most 95 years, and to face age-specific mortality rates. Within each age cohort, individuals also differ by education level and, accordingly, by working history, income, and probability of survival. In particular, using the 2002 Spanish Active Population Survey (EPA, Encuesta de Poblacion Activa), agents are partitioned in three groups—with low, medium and high education—including respectively 31.8, 52.2, and 16 percent of the total population. Individuals typically differ in their working history and earning profile by age, according to their educational attainments. Using the 2002 EPA and the employment rate by education, the working history for each education group can be reconstructed. Agents with high education have a median working history of 37 years—they start working at 25 and retire at 62—and enjoy a steep earning profile. Agents in the intermediate group enter the labor market at 24 and retire at 60, thereby contributing for 36 years, while agents in the low education group have instead a median working history of 40 years, from 21 to 61, but only contribute to the system for 32 years, because of their highly discontinuous working carriers. These spells are accounted for by assuming that these agents work in the unofficial sector, hence non paying social security contribution, till age 28. The earning profiles of the latter two education groups are rather flat, particularly for the low-educated individuals.

8.3.2 The Silent Reform

Unlike many other European countries, which have been characterized by a flurry of social security reforms in the last decade, Spain has not experienced major changes in its retirement income system. Even the Pacto de Toledo—signed in 1995 by almost all political forces—despite promoting a large set of suggestions to enhance the efficiency and the financial sustainability of the social security system, did not create enough momentum for reforming.

Yet some scholars hint at a different interpretation of the evolution of the Spanish social security system since the late eighties and reconsider the effective relevance of the Pacto de Toledo (see Boldrin, Jimenez, and Sanchez 2000; Jimeno 2002; Alonso and Herce 2003; Conde-Ruiz and Alonso 2004). Substantial changes have occurred in the Spanish system, driven by the dynamics of some crucial parameters of the social security system, such as the minimum and maximum pensions and the floor and ceiling in the contribution base, whose importance for the financial sustainability of the system is often be overlooked. Yet adequate modifications of these parameters may induce major changes in the structure of the system, for instance, by modifying its degree of redistributiveness, by altering its overall generosity, and ultimately by affecting its future political sustainability.

Since the nineties these parameters have featured some marked trends. The threshold levels for the minimum and maximum pensions have only increased with the inflation—thereby retaining their real values, but reducing their purchasing power relatively to the average wage in the economy. The floor in the social security contribution base[2] has instead decreased even in real terms, hence provoking an enlargement of the social security tax base. The trend for the contribution base's ceiling is more difficult to describe, as the initial six ceilings (for different types of workers) have been merged into one. During this process most ceilings have either remained constant or increased in real terms, while the top ceiling has certainly dropped. Whether the tax base has shrunk or increased as a result of these modifications is difficult to assess.

This silent reform may only be effective in an environment characterized by economic growth. In a growing economy the lack of indexation of the maximum pension's threshold to the growth rate of the wages will cause several high-earners, whose wages have increased over time more than the inflation level, to have their pension benefits capped by the maximum pension level. For an increasing number of retirees, pension benefits will hence lose their tight link to previous wages (or contributions), and the system will hence become more redistributive.

To the extent that the ceiling in the contribution base has dropped too, these high-earners will pay lower total contributions as well. Whether these two opposing effects increase or decrease the overall degree of redistribution of the system depends on the relative magnitude of the changes in the maximum pension and in the contribution base's ceiling. Interestingly the Pacto de Toledo was an attempt to tie the social security contribution base to the growth rate of the economy, while leaving the maximum pensions connected to the inflation index—thereby introducing a strong redistributive element from high- to low-earners. Were the ceiling on the contribution base to remain indexed to the inflation, this silent reform would go in the direction of forcing high-earners to opt-out of the system, as it occurs—albeit on a voluntary basis—in the United Kingdom (see chapter 9), since they would contribute less, and receive lower pensions. The political implications of these silent reform measures—particularly the within-cohort redistributive aspect—are addressed in the next section.

8.3.3   Political Sustainability

The political economy model presented in chapter 4 allows an evaluation of the impact of the population aging and of the silent reform on the political sustainability of the Spanish system. Individual preferences over the size of the system are computed by analyzing the agents' economic well-being for different contribution rates under the expected demographic and economic scenario for the year 2050. The shift in the age distribution of the voters induced by the aging process is also considered.

The results of the simulations on the future political sustainability of the Spanish system are reported at table 8.1. In the first line, describing the system in the year 2000, the equilibrium contribution rate,[3] which equalizes total contributions to total benefits, is set to 21.3 percent. Individuals with low and high education retire at age 62 and receive a

Table 8.1
Simulation results

Year	Case	Median retirement age by educational level			Equi-librium contri-bution rate	Replacement rate by educational level		
		Low	Medium	High		Low	Medium	High
2000		62	60	62	21.3%	67%	51%	65%
2050	Baseline	62	60	62	50.2%	71%	55%	69%
2050	Baseline	62	62	62	49.9%	79%	67%	67%
2050	Baseline	63	63	63	48.8%	86%	71%	72%
2050	Baseline	64	64	64	47.7%	94%	79%	79%
2050	Baseline	65	65	65	46.6%	103%	86%	86%
2050	Silent Reform	62	60	62	49.9%	76%	58%	62%
2050	Silent Reform	62	62	62	49.9%	80%	68%	66%
2050	Silent Reform	63	63	63	48.7%	87%	74%	70%
2050	Silent Reform	64	64	64	47.6%	96%	81%	75%
2050	Silent Reform	65	65	65	46.5%	106%	89%	81%

Note: The first line gives the year 2000 scenario; lines 2 to 6 give the simulations for the social security contribution rate under the 2050 economic, demographic, and political scenario in the baseline case (i.e., with no silent reforms) for different retirement ages. All remaining lines show the simulations for 2050 under the alternative case where a silent reform continues to take place.

higher replacement rate, respectively 67 percent and 65 percent, than individuals with intermediate education, who retire at age 60 and obtain a replacement rate of 51 percent.

The simulations for the year 2050 use the expected demographic, economic, and political scenario for the year 2050 to calculate the contribution rate chosen by a majority of the voters. Together with the changes in the dependency ratio and in the age of the pivotal voter, the partition of the population in the three education groups is modified to account for the overall improvement in the educational level. 2002 data are used from the Spanish Active Population Survey, with the low-, medium-, and high-education groups estimated to include respectively 10.1, 64.5, and 25.4 percent of the total population in 2050.

The second line of table 8.1 describes the baseline simulation for the year 2050, with no silent reform in place. In this case, low-educated individuals receive the minimum pension, while medium- and high-educated individuals receive a normal pension, as calculated in equation (8.1), and no maximum pension is awarded. Under this scenario, with the retirement ages at their 2000 levels—62 years for low and high educated and 60 years for the medium educated—the equilibrium contribution rate is predicted to jump to an impressive 50.2 percent, which commands slightly higher replacement rates than in 2000. This enormous rise in the contribution rate represents the largest projected increase among all simulations, although not the highest forecasted contribution rate (see chapter 7 for the case of Italy), and this is mainly due to the large increase in the age of the pivotal voter.

The simulation results at lines 3 to 6 show that a rise in the retirement age limits the increase in the contribution rate. In the case of Spain, however, this effect remains quite marginal.[4] In fact, even if all workers were to postpone retirement till age 65, the social security contribution rate would still reach 46.6 percent. The replacement rates would however rise with the retirement age, being even above 100 percent for the low-earners, who receive a minimum pension.

The effects of the silent reform described in the previous section on the long-run political sustainability of the Spanish social security system are displayed at lines 7 to 11 of table 8.1. Under this new scenario, low-educated retirees receive the minimum pension, and medium-educated retirees enjoy a normal pension, as calculated in equation (8.1). Highly educated retirees are assumed to have their pension benefits capped by the threshold and hence to receive the maximum pension. This assumption captures the main aspect of this silent reform, which—by not linking the threshold for the maximum pension to economic growth—increases the share of retirees whose benefits are capped by this maximum pension's threshold. The magnitude of this effect may be measured by the share of maximum pensions, which was equal[5] to 3 percent in 2000 and has been set equal to around 25 percent in the 2050 simulations, by assuming that all high-earners receive the maximum pension.[6]

The simulations at table 8.1 suggest that this silent reform—despite introducing some redistributive features—would have almost no impact on the future political sustainability of the system. For instance, with the retirement ages at their 2000 levels, the equilibrium contribution rate under the silent reform is forecasted to jump to 49.9 percent—as opposed to 50.2 percent in the baseline case. Postponing retirement would also have a mild effect in limiting the rise in the contribution rate, which would be equal to 46.5 percent for a retirement age of 65 years.

Although the forecasted contribution rates are virtually identical under the baseline scenario and the silent reform, some differences appear in the replacement rates. In particular, since the threshold on pension benefits becomes binding for the high-earners, they enjoy slightly lower replacement rate under the silent reform than in the baseline case, whereas the opposite occurs for low and medium-educated individuals. The degree of redistributiveness introduced by this silent reform is captured by figure 8.3, which displays the most preferred

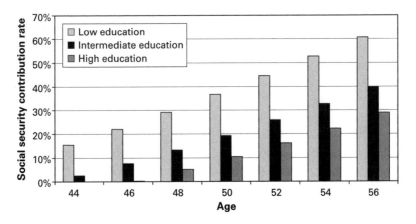

Figure 8.3
Most preferred contribution rates by age and education level in 2050

contribution rate by age and education group in the year 2050 under the silent reform. For a given age, low-educated individuals, who are likely to receive a minimum pension, prefer a higher contribution rate than respectively medium- and high-educated individuals.

These simulation results point at a rather bleak conclusion. The dramatic aging process, by magnifying the political representation of the elderly, will impose significant changes on the Spanish social security system. The future political sustainability of the system will require large increases in the contribution rate, in order to satisfy the political demand of the growing mass of elderly voters. As in all other countries an increase in the retirement age will reduce the effect of the political push on the contribution rate. These gains are limited in the case of Spain because of the enormous underlying jump in the contribution rate. Some scholars argued that a silent reform is currently taking place in Spain that will increase the redistributiveness of the system by capping the pension benefits of the high-earners with a maximum pension that is not tied to the growth of the economy. These simulations suggest that the political effect of aging will dominate after the introduction of this redistributive element from high- to low-earners, hence inducing huge rises in the contribution rates even after the silent reform.

9

Political Sustainability in a
Redistributive System: The
United Kingdom

The British social security system features a rather unique mix of public and private provision of retirement income in the European landscape. Despite being composed of two programs—the Basic State Pension (BSP) and the State Earnings Related Pension Scheme (SERPS) until 2002 or the State Second Pension (S2P) thereafter—the entire public pension system is relatively small and highly redistributive. Most individuals depend also on private pension schemes—typically occupational plans—for their retirement income, and employees are allowed to contract out of the second public pillar (SERPS or S2P) into occupational or private pension plans.

In 2000 public pension spending in the United Kingdom amounted to 4.3 percent of GDP. According to the official estimates provided by the EC and the OECD (see table 2.3) pension spending is expected to decrease to 3.6 percent in 2050. Despite being relatively small, at least by European standards—the public pension system still represents the main program in the UK welfare state. In 2000 old age pensions accounted for 47 percent of total welfare expenditure. However, when survivor and disability pensions are included, this share reaches 58 percent, as displayed in figure 9.1.

Another characteristic feature of the British system is represented by its high degree of redistribution among individuals of the same cohort but with different incomes. The initial design of the system, and the successive reforms, aimed at providing a minimum level of old age income support to the poor, through a combination of flat (i.e., non-earning-related) pension benefits and means-tested programs (e.g., the minimum income guaranteed, MIG). Its redistributive nature is achieved mainly by combining proportional contribution rates on labor earnings with a two-tier benefit scheme featuring a flat pension—the Basic State Pension (BSP)—and a pension that depends

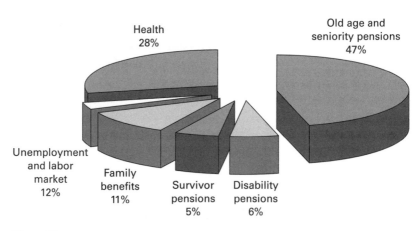

Figure 9.1
Welfare expenditure decomposition in 2000 (Source: OECD)

on the workers' earnings—the State Earnings Related Pension Scheme (SERPS). With the 2002 Blair pension reform, however, the system has become even more redistributive, since SERPS has been replaced by a partially flat benefit pension, the State Second Pension (S2P).

The limited public commitment in the provision of retirement income, with public schemes mainly targeted at replacing the low-income workers' earnings, has always been accompanied by a substantial private provision based, since the end of the nineteenth century, on occupational pensions. All reforms of the British system have managed to accommodate this mix,[1] either by retaining the workers' option of contracting-out of the second public pillar—during the 1975 and 1999 reforms that increased public responsibility for old age income—or by promoting more private arrangements—as in the 1986 Social Security Act by the Thatcher Conservative government.

Since the British public pension system has long been expressively designed to provide sufficient retirement income to low-earner workers, current concerns about poverty among the elderly indicate a major inadequacy of the system. According to a report by the Pension Policy Institute (PPI, 2003), almost a quarter of the retirees are in relative poverty, receiving an income below 60 percent of the median household income. Indeed table 9.1 shows that the risk of poverty among the elderly (defined as people aged 65 years and over) in the United Kingdom is only slightly above the European average and is in line with the data for people aged 0 to 64 years. The difference in the poverty risk between the United Kingdom and the rest of Europe

Table 9.1
Relative poverty risks in 1998 by age group

	Age group		
	0–64	65+	75+
Austria	10%	24%	31%
Belgium	11%	22%	25%
Finland	10%	17%	20%
France	14%	19%	23%
Germany	11%	11%	12%
Greece	18%	33%	39%
Ireland	17%	34%	42%
Italy	19%	14%	14%
Netherlands	11%	7%	8%
Portugal	18%	33%	39%
Spain	10%	8%	12%
United Kingdom	19%	21%	26%
EU 15	15%	17%	19%

Source: European Commission (2003).
Note: For each age group the poverty risk is defined as the share of individuals below 60% of the median income.

becomes more relevant if one concentrates only on the very elderly (people aged 75 years and more). This situation is mainly driven by the lack of indexation of pension benefits to economic growth, which rapidly reduces the relative purchasing power of the benefits after retirement, and by the parsimoniousness of the survivors' pensions, which tend to provide surviving spouses with little retirement income. Unsurprisingly, very old retirees and elderly single women are more often in relative poverty.

At the turn of the twenty-first century the British public pension system hence presents a different set of concerns than most European schemes. Because of the 1986 Thatcher reform, which reduced the generosity of the public earning-related pillar, and because of the widespread use of occupational and private plans, which limits the scope for public intervention in old age retirement income, the future financial sustainability of the system does not represent a hot issue in the political debate (see table 2.3). The use of early retirement provisions is also less pervasive than in other European countries, as the effective median retirement age is around 62 years, and, perhaps more important, aging is less dramatic than elsewhere.

The main element of concern for the public, and private, pension system in the United Kingdom is the expected increase in poverty among the elderly. A 2001 Eurobarometer survey (see European Commission 2003), in which individuals were asked how they expect to get by in their old age with the state pension, captures the public perception on this issue: around 65 percent of the interviewed individuals in the United Kingdom expects some difficulty (almost 30 percent predicts great difficulty), as opposed to around 40 percent in Belgium, France, and Spain, or about 50 percent in Ireland, Italy, and Portugal. These concerns are more common among low- and middle-income retirees, who decided to contract out of the public earnings-related scheme into occupational or private pension plans, following the liberalization of the private pension industry during the 1986 Thatcher reform. The introduction of defined contribution (DC) occupational plan and the subsequent shift of several employees' occupational plans from defined benefits (DB) to defined contributions (DC) will leave many low-income employees to bear the financial risk of their pension plans. Furthermore a massive mis-selling of personal pension plans occurred, leading in 1993 to a major scandal, as several employees were suggested to move to personal plans based on bad judgment by the financial companies. To mitigate these problems, the 1999 and 2002 reforms introduced by the Blair government increased the public involvement in the retirement income provision for low-income individuals. Nevertheless, a large share of the elderly may still be forced to use means-tested benefits that are indexed to average earnings, such as the minimum income guarantee.

This chapter examines the long-run *political* sustainability of the UK public pension system, as shaped by almost three decades of radical reforms. Two features characterize the British system and will be relevant for this analysis: the expected process of mild population aging— as compared to other European countries (see chapter 2)—and the widespread concerns about old age poverty, induced by the expectation of low replacement rates at retirement. The former element indicates that the electoral push toward more public pension spending by an aging population should be moderate in the United Kingdom—at least as compare to other societies. However, the latter aspect suggests that intragenerational redistributive motives may be relevant in shaping the future political sustainability of this social security scheme.

The next section introduces a brief historical detour of the public and private provision of retirement income in the United Kingdom and provides a description of the public scheme at the turn of the century;

while the mild aging process and its impact on the political representation by age are discussed in section 9.2. Section 9.3.1 analyzes the British public pension system as shaped by the 1999 and 2002 reforms, which replaced SERPS with a new, partially flat, pension benefit scheme (S2P). The simulation results, presented in section 9.3.2, suggest that the political equilibrium in this new system will be characterized by a large increase in the contribution rate and more generous pension benefits for low-educated retirees, as measured by the replacement rate.

9.1   An Overview of the British Social Security System

The first public old age income provision, introduced in 1908, constituted a form of financial help for the very elderly—those aged 70 years or more—and was made contingent on a "test of good character." A few years later, in 1911, the National Insurance Act instituted a basic state pension for the elderly, disabled, and unemployed. This system provided a minimal safety net for very low-income individuals but was means-tested.

The British public pension system was completely re-shaped after WWII by the Beveridge Report, which argued in favor of more income protection to the elderly. In particular, the Report explicitly suggested abolishing means-testing to eliminate the stigma from drawing benefits, which had characterized the previous pension scheme. Pension benefits were still to be flat, and contributions not earnings related. A pension reform inspired by the Beveridge Report was implemented in 1946. Unlike the scheme suggested by the Report, pensions were immediately awarded, with no transition period.

The system shaped by the Beveridge Report soon faced two major problems: a diffused poverty among the retirees, many of whom had to recur to additional means-tested schemes, and lack of funding. These financial troubles were mainly due to the growing number of retirees entitled to a pension, and to the financing method, which relied on a flat contribution, clearly designed so as to be payable also by the poorest workers. In 1959 the National Insurance Act tackled these issues by introducing earnings-related contributions, which made the system highly redistributive. Middle- and high-income workers received low value for their contributions. Yet, since they typically enjoyed additional coverage through occupational plans, the Conservative government[2] allowed for contracting out of the public system into occupational plans. The low return on the public scheme for these richer workers implicitly encouraged their contracting-out to occupation plans (see Hannah 1986).

By the seventies occupational schemes had become widespread among all but low-earnings workers and the private pension industry was well developed. As a consequence the 1969 White Paper drafted by the Labour Party did not envisage any reduction in the private provision—via occupational plans—of retirement income. The 1975 Social Security Act, however, increased public involvement in the British old age pension system by introducing a second public pillar along with the existing Basic State Pension (BSP). While BSP paid out a flat rate pension, which only depended on the years of contribution, the new public pillar—called State Earnings Related Pension Scheme (SERPS)—provided a pension benefit based on the workers' earnings. Both schemes' pension benefits were indexed to the higher value between inflation and wage growth. The interests of the existing occupational plan industry were nevertheless preserved with the introduction of a partial exit option from the new public pension pillar: workers were allowed to contract out of SERPS toward occupational plans, by substituting part of their social security contribution to the public system with contributions to occupational plans. The government also regulated the occupation plan industry: in order to qualify as a contracting-in plan, an occupational fund was required to guarantee at least a minimum pension (GMP), which, however, did not need to be indexed to inflation or wage growth.

The following decade was characterized by the Conservative Party effort to retrench the welfare state.[3] The commitment building phase of the 1986 social security reform featured publications by several think-tanks close to the government and the issue of the Green Paper "Reform of Social Security" (DHSS 1985) by a government-appointed committee. All these publications emphasized the urgency of reforming the social security system—due to the demographic trend—and hence endorsed a reduction of the state intervention in the pension industry, to be achieved by eliminating completely the newly born SERPS, by deregulating this industry and by providing a more prominent role to financial institutions.

Already in 1980 the adjustment criterion for the pension benefits had shifted to inflation only; however, the major retrenching measures were adopted with the 1986 Social Security Act. Because of internal opposition by the Treasury Minister within the Conservative government (see Bonoli 2000), SERPS was not abolished, but its replacement rate decreased from 25 to 20 percent of the worker's earnings. The number of years of calculation for the reference wage was increased from the best twenty years to the entire working history, thereby inducing a reduction in the average replacement rate, and survival pensions were limited to 50 percent of the retiree's pension. The 1986 Social Security Act also weakened the requirements for contracting-out. Individuals were allowed to opt out to defined contributions (DC) occupational plans and to the newly introduced personal pension plans; these DC plans were not forced to guarantee a minimum pension (GMP) but only minimum requirements on the contributions to the plan. The scope for private involvement in the pension market largely increased, since the reduced generosity of the public system encouraged workers to opt out, while lower requirements on occupational plans and the introduction of personal pension funds revitalized the private pension industry.

The evolution of the British private pension industry in the following years has drawn large attention by the media and the academia due to the frequent and substantial mismanagements and scandals[4] (e.g., see Blake 2003). To tackle these problems, the 1995 Pension Act introduced a 5 percent maximum limit on self-investment and the obligation for the trustees to control on these limits, launched a new Occupational Pension Regulatory Authority, and instituted a compensation fund to cover cases of insolvency.

When the Labour government was appointed in 1997, several low- and middle-income workers had already been damaged by their use of this contracting out option, often because of mis-information and mis-selling of private plans. The 1998 Green Paper hence put forward two proposals to improve the retirement income of the low-income workers. The State Earnings Related Pension Scheme (SERPS) was to be replaced, along a transition period, by a partially flat state pension, called the State Second Pension (S2P), and Stakeholder Pensions were to be introduced among the private contracting-out options. In order to qualify as a stakeholder pension, a scheme had to obey some rules, such as government-set maximum charge, no entry or exit fees, and no penalties for missing payments.

9.1.1 A Description of the System at the Turn of the Century
The British social security system is composed of two relevant layers. The first pillar—called the Basic State Pension (BSP)—is public and provides a flat pension, which is not related to the worker's earnings.

The pension level depends, however, on the length of the contribution period, with at least 11 years needed to become eligible. To achieve the largest BSP, a worker has to feature a period of contribution equal at least to 44 years for men and 39 for women. Workers with fewer years of contribution receive a smaller pension,[5] while deferring retirement increases pension benefits by 7.5 percent a year.

The public pension system provides also an earning-related pillar, which individuals may choose to opt out of, in order to enroll in occupational or private pension plans. From the 1975 Social Security Act till 2002—when the program was abolished—the State Earnings Related Pension Scheme (SERPS) awarded pension benefits to those workers whose past earnings had been above the lower earning limit (LEL) for at least one year since April 1978. Originally SERPS was designed to provide 1.25 percent of band earnings for each of the 20 years of contributions with the largest earnings, where band earnings were defined as the earnings included between 52 times the weekly Lower Earning Limit (LEL) and 53 times the weekly Upper Earning Limit (UEL). The 1986 Social Security Act decreased the accrual rate to 1 percent of band earnings per year—and hence the maximum replacement rate to 20 percent—and increased the years of contribution in the benefit calculation to the entire working history.

In 2002, a new public scheme—called the State Second Pension (S2P)—was introduced to replace SERPS. During the initial phases—until 2007—S2P will provide partially flat pension benefits, which only loosely depend on the worker's labor earnings. Starting in 2007, however, this second public pillar is expected to provide a flat pension benefit, on the top of BSP.

The financing of these two benefits is based on a complex system of contributions on labor earnings. The Primary National Insurance contribution, which is due by the employee, amounts to 10 percent of the income between the Primary Threshold (PT), corresponding to GBP 87 a week in 2001, and the Upper Earnings Limit (UEL), corresponding to GBP 575 a week; the rights to SERPS benefit actually accrue for all earnings exceeding the Lower Earnings Limit (GBP 67 a week). If the worker contracts out of SERPS into occupational or private pension schemes, the contribution is rebated to 8.4 percent of income between the PT and the UEL. The Secondary National Insurance contribution is instead paid by the employer. No contribution is due for labor income below the Secondary Threshold (ST), GBP 87 a week, while the tax rate is equal to 12.2 percent for the income above the ST.[6] If the employee

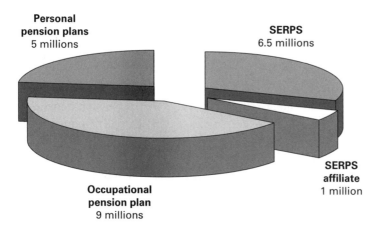

Figure 9.2
Second pension pillar affiliates in 1999 (Source: Emmerson and Johnson 2001)

contracts out, the Secondary National Insurance contribution is rebated to 9.2 percent.

Ever since the introduction in 1975 of a second state pension pillar, employees have been allowed to contracting out of this program into occupational or private pension plans. By opting out, individuals give up their claims to a future pension benefit under SERPS or S2P in exchange for a rebate in their contributions—called National Insurance Contributions (NICs)—to the public pension system. However, these reductions in the NICs have to be dedicated to build up alternative retirement funds, in occupational or private pension plans. The relative share of each type of second pension pillar in 1999 and the number of retirees enrolled to each program are displayed in figure 9.2.

Occupational pension schemes are provided by the employers to their employees and typically cover all workers in a firm or industry (see Blake 2003): for an employee who contracts out of the public program into an occupational plan, the accumulation in this scheme takes the form of contributions paid by the employer on top of labor cost and/or employee direct contributions from their earnings. There exist four types of contract-out schemes: COSRS—contracted-out salary-related scheme; COMPS—contracted-out money-purchase scheme; COMBS—contracted-out mixed-benefit scheme; and COHS—contracted-out hybrid scheme. The first occupational fund is a defined benefit (DB) plan that promises a pension expressed as a percentage of the wage, based on the number of years spent within the scheme. In a

DB plan employers are responsible for underwriting the costs of the plan; moreover, in order to be considered for contracting-out, a COSRS has to ensure a minimum pension at retirement. The second fund is defined contribution (DC) plan. Individuals are required to contribute to this scheme in order to build up investment funds that are converted into a stream of income at retirement. The level of pension benefits is not defined in the contract—employers are hence not responsible for underwriting the costs of the plan—and the uncertainty due to the market value of the funds at retirement is beard by the employees. The only requirement for a COMPS to be available for contracting-out is to receive as contribution at least the contracted-out rebate. The other two schemes, COMBS and COHS, are mixed systems.

After the 1986 Social Security Act, employees may also contract out into private pension plans, by contributing their NICs rebates to these funds, and on some occasions employers may offer to contribute to personal pension plans instead of offering an occupational scheme. Contributions to pension schemes approved by the Inland Revenue are tax relieved, and any buildup in the fund value due to investment returns is free of personal tax. Upon retirement and vesting of the fund, a proportion of the benefits can be taken as a tax-free lump sum (up to a maximum of 25 percent of the fund value), while the remainder is to be used to purchase an annuity.

9.2 Aging in the United Kingdom

The aging phenomenon in the United Kingdom is more limited than in most European countries, and hence the repercussion on the public pension spending should be less sizable. This discrepancy is due to a less dramatic reduction in the fertility rate, but also to a lower increase in the life expectancy at birth. Different magnitudes of the migration flows have also played a role in this difference. In the United Kingdom, the fertility rate—measuring the number of children per woman between 18 and 45 years—has dropped from 2.7 in the sixties—the years of the baby boom—to 1.8 in the eighties and nineties. Analogously, longevity has increased, but less than in many other OECD countries, as life expectancy at birth for females has soared from 73.7 years in 1960 to 80 in 2000 (from 67.9 to 75.2 years for males).

Estimates by the European Commission for the next 50 years suggests additional, mild aging, as further reductions in the old age mortality are forecasted, while the fertility rate is expect to remain rela-

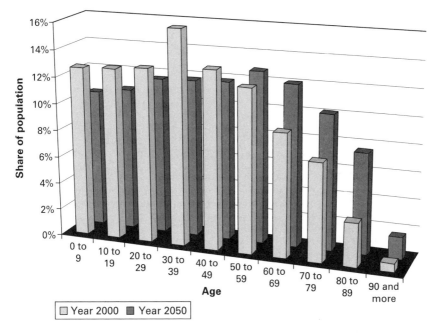

Figure 9.3
Aging in United Kingdom: Population by age group in 2000 and 2050 (Source: Eurostat)

tively constant around 1.8 children per woman. The expected population profile by age for the year 2050 and the actual profile for the year 2000 are shown in figure 9.3. The effect of the aging process is clearly visible. In the year 2000, the single largest generation in the population was composed of individuals in their thirties—the last of the baby boomers, and there was a clear decay in the share of the population at older ages. In the year 2050, population is instead expected to be distributed more evenly across the different age groups, with individuals in their fifties becoming the most numerous generation.

Aging will thus have some effect on the financing of the current public pension system because of the decrease in the share of individuals in the active population and the contemporaneous increase in the fraction of elderly persons. In 2050 there will be slightly more than two individuals of working age for every elderly person, as compared to four workers in 2000.

The shift in the political representation due to population aging is characterized for all countries in figure 2.2 by the median age among the voters. In 2050, individuals in their fifties are expected to form the most numerous generation, and the median age among the voters is expected to rise to 53 years, from 45 years in 2000. According to the theoretical framework presented in chapters 3 and 4, these individuals will use their political power to defend their vested interests in pension issues.

9.3 Challenges for the Future

Unlike in most other European countries, the future financial sustainability of the public pension system in the United Kingdom does not look gloomy. As shown at table 2.3, the mild population aging is expected to increase pension spending only by 1.7 percent of GDP. However, if the effects of the 2002 Blair reform and the forecasted increase in the employment rate are considered, future pension spending in the United Kingdom may actually decrease.

Several studies have argued that the main challenge for the future of the British social security system is in fact to ensure an adequate retirement income to all retirees (e.g., see PPI 2003 and EC 2003). At the turn of the century the British system featured a mix of private and public provision of retirement income, which varied according to the agent's income, as shown at table 9.2. Low-income retirees—in the lowest quintile of the retirees' income—receive more than 70 percent of their income from state pension and an additional 10 percent from means-tested programs. High income retirees—in the highest quintile—obtain less than 25 percent of their income from state pensions, almost 40 percent from private plans and more than 20 percent

Table 9.2
Retirees' income by composition and income quintile in 1996

	Quintile				
	1	2	3	4	5
State pension	71.4%	59.9%	50.1%	38.8%	23.4%
Means-tested benefits	9.4%	13.5%	19.9%	11.3%	5.5%
Other benefits	6.4%	8.3%	8.9%	12.3%	9.6%
Private pensions	8.0%	13.4%	15.1%	26.6%	38.1%
Investment income	3.8%	3.6%	3.7%	6.7%	13.2%
Earnings	1.0%	1.4%	2.3%	4.3%	10.2%

Source: Emmerson and Johnson (2001).
Note: Other benefits include non–means-tested benefits, such as invalidity or incapacity benefits.

from earnings or capital income. The public sector has then to address mainly the needs of low-income individuals, as high-income persons rely more on private arrangements for their retirement income.

The future level of the low-earners' retirement income will likely depend on the evolution of the public pension schemes. According to Emmerson and Johnson (2001), the replacement rate for a low-income single male, whose labor income equals 50 percent of the median earnings, will drop from 62.5 percent in 1998—when the individual was receiving BSP and SERPS benefits—to only 37.6 percent in 2045—when he will enjoy BSP and S2P benefits—or to 35.8 percent—in the hypothetical case where BSP and SERPS are still in place in 2045. These dismaying figures suggest that despite the introduction of a more redistributive program (S2P), public retirement income provision will not be sufficient to support low-income elderly. Furthermore, since pension benefits are indexed to the inflation, rather than to the average growth of the economy, the relative purchasing power of the elderly will decrease even more over time.

The expected increase in poverty suggested by Emmerson and Johnson's (2001) calculations may affect the future political sustainability of the British public pension system, since low-income middle aged and elderly individuals may be willing to provide strong support to a larger system in order to increase its generosity. The next section provides a more detailed description of the public system, and section 9.3.2 addresses its future political sustainability.

9.3.1   A Closer Look at the British System

Until 2002 the British public pension system was composed of two programs: BSP and SERPS. To an agent with education level (or income) q, the Basic State Pension provided a flat benefit that depends on the number of years of contribution, N_q, and on a reference wage, $\tilde{w}_t$, corresponding for all retirees to the lower earning limit, LEL:

$$P^q_{B,t} = \frac{\tilde{w}_t N_q}{44}.$$ (9.1)

The SERPS pension benefits for an agent with education level q retiring at time t with a retirement age J^q were instead computed according to the relevant portion—the difference between the agent's earnings not exceeding the upper earning limit (UEL) and the lower earning limit (LEL)—of the agent's average earnings over her entire working

history, to the number of years of contribution, and to a conversion coefficient α, which was equal to 25 percent:

$$P_{S,t}^q = \frac{\alpha[\sum_{i=s^q}^{J^q-1}(w_{t-J^q+i}^{i,q} - \tilde{w}_{t-J^q+i})]}{N_q} \quad (9.2)$$

$$\text{with} \quad w_{t-J^q+i}^{i,q} = \begin{cases} w_{t-J^q+i}^{i,q} & \text{for } w_{t-J^q+i}^{i,q} \leq w_{t-J^q+i}^u, \\ w_{t-J^q+i}^u & \text{for } w_{t-J^q+i}^{q,i} > w_{t-J^q+i}^u, \end{cases} \quad (9.3)$$

where $w_{t-J^q+i}^{i,q}$ represents the earnings at time $t - J^q + i$ of a type-q agent
born at time i, $w_{t-J^q-i}^u$ is the upper earning limit (UEL), and s^q characterizes the initial period in the working career of an agent of education
q.

Employees may contract out of SERPS, in which case they do not receive any SERPS benefit but obtain a rebate on their contributions (and
on their employer's contributions). Since 1980 both BSP and SERPS
benefits were indexed to inflation.

After the 2002 Blair reforms newly retired individuals had their
SERPS benefits replaced by a partially flat State Second Pension (S2P).
Under S2P an agent with education level q retiring at time t with a
retirement age J^q receives a pension benefit, which is still computed
according to the agent's relevant earnings, meaning between the lower
(LEL) and upper earning limit[7] (UEL):

$$P_{P,t}^q = \frac{\gamma(\sum_{i=s^q}^{J^q-1}(w_{t-J^q+i}^{i,q} - \tilde{w}_{t-J^q+i}))}{N_q} \quad (9.4)$$

with $w_{t-J^q+i}^{i,q}$ as characterized in equation (9.3), and where the conversion coefficient γ is defined as

$$\gamma = \begin{cases} 40\% & \text{for } w_{t-J^q+i}^{i,q} \in [LEL, LET], \\ 10\% & \text{for } w_{t-J^q+i}^{i,q} \in [LET, UET], \\ 20\% & \text{for } w_{t-J^q+i}^{i,q} \in [UET, UEL]. \end{cases} \quad (9.5)$$

In equation (9.5), LET and UET are respectively the lower and upper
earning thresholds. S2P benefits are indexed to inflation. Moreover
employees may choose to contract out of S2P—thereby forgoing
any S2P benefit but receiving a rebate on their National Insurance
contributions.

Employees and employers contribute to the public pension system a
fraction of the worker's labor earnings, which may vary according to
the worker's earnings and to the use of the contracting-out option, as

discussed in section 9.1.1. In each period total contributions thus depend on the employees and employers' social security contribution rates τ_t^W and τ_t^E, on the rebate obtained by contracting out ψ_t^W and ψ_t^E, on the share of workers who do not contract out $\phi_t^{j,q}$, and on the retirement ages J^q. Total contributions to the system at time t are given by

$$T_t(\tau_t^W, \tau_t^E, \psi_t^W, \psi_t^E, J_t^q)$$

$$= \sum_{q=1}^{Q} \sum_{j=1}^{J^q-1} \mu_t^{j,q} [(\overline{w}_t^{j,q} - \hat{w}_t)(\tau_t^W - \psi_t^W(1 - \phi_t^{j,q}))$$

$$+ (w_t^{j,q} - \hat{w}_t)(\tau_t^E - \psi_t^E(1 - \phi_t^{j,q}))], \qquad (9.6)$$

where $\mu_t^{j,q}$ and $w_t^{j,q}$ represent respectively the proportion of agents aged j with education $q \in [1, Q]$, and their actual earnings. The labor earnings for the employee's contribution $\overline{w}_t^{j,q}$ is defined as

$$\overline{w}_t^{j,q} = \begin{cases} w_t^{j,q} & \text{for } w_t^{j,q} \in [\hat{w}_t, w_t^U], \\ w_t^U & \text{for } w_t^{j,q} > w_t^U, \end{cases} \qquad (9.7)$$

with $\hat{w}_t$ corresponding to the Primary Threshold (PT) and w_t^U to the UEL (see section 9.1.1).

In a balanced budget public pension system, the total amount of pensions (BSP and SERPS or S2P) transferred to retirees is equal to the aggregate contributions paid by current workers:

$$T_t(\tau_t^W, \tau_t^E, \psi_t^W, \psi_t^E, J^q) = \begin{cases} \sum_{q=1}^{Q} \sum_{j=J^q}^{G} \mu_t^{j,q}(P_{B,t}^{j,q} + \phi_t^{j,q} P_{S,t}^{j,q}), \\ \sum_{q=1}^{Q} \sum_{j=J^q}^{G} \mu_t^{j,q}(P_{B,t}^{j,q} + \phi_t^{j,q} P_{P,t}^{j,q}), \end{cases} \qquad (9.8)$$

where $P_{B,t}^{j,q}$, $P_{S,t}^{j,q}$, and $P_{P,t}^{j,q}$ refer respectively to BSP, SERPS, and S2P benefits provided at time t to an individual aged j with education level q, and G is the maximum longevity, which in the model is set equal to 95 years.

The simulations on political sustainability discussed in the next section focus on the equilibrium contribution rate, which satisfies equations (9.8). This equilibrium contribution rate determines the total amount of contributions to the system, $T_t(\tau_t^W, \tau_t^E, \psi_t^W, \psi_t^E, J^q)$ and also pins down the total amounts of pension. The sharing of resources, however, is among retirees of different age and income (or education) level, and this depends on the structure of the system (e.g., its composition between BSP, SERPS or S2P). As a result the preferences over the size of the public pension system of individuals who differ in their working history, lifetime earning profile, and retirement age will also depend on the structure of the system.

To analyze the redistributive features that characterize the British public pension system and their impact on the individuals' political decisions, I consider an economy populated by adults who differ in age, education, and income level. Individuals are assumed to live from 18 to at most 95 years, while facing age-specific mortality rates, and to differ within age cohort by education level and, accordingly, by working history, income, and probability of survival. In particular, at every age, agents may be low or high educated. Individuals in the former group have completed secondary education, and according to an average over four waves (1993–96) of the European Commission Household Panel (ECHP), they account for 59.4 percent of the British population. The high-educated have tertiary education and sum up to the remaining 40.6 percent.

Depending on their educational attainments, individuals typically differ in their working history and earning profile by age. According to the 1996 ECHP data, highly educated individuals begin to work at age 22 and retire at 63 years, while featuring a steep earning profile, as shown in figure 9.4. Agents in the low-education group enter the labor market earlier, at age 18, but retire still at 63, and enjoy lower lifetime earnings (see figure 9.4).

9.3.2 Political Constraints

At the turn of the century, the United Kingdom featured a lower level of social security spending than most European countries, but a more complex structure. In 2001, the equilibrium social security tax rate— that is, the contribution rate equating total pension transfers to total contributions—was equal to 17.1 percent. This equilibrium contribution rate refers to the sum of the contribution rates paid by the employee and by the employer on an income between the Second Threshold (ST) and the Upper Earnings Level (UEL) for a worker who chooses not to contract out of the system. The equilibrium contribution rate paid by the employer for the portion of earnings above the UEL is estimated to be equal to 9.4 percent. For individuals who contract out, these contribution rates are respectively 13.5 percent—for the earnings

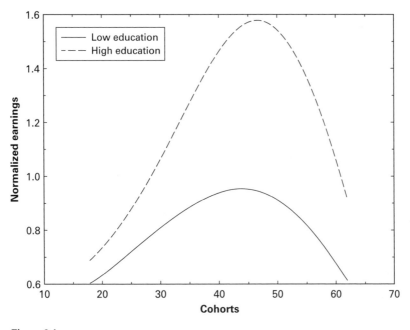

Figure 9.4
Earning profiles by age

between ST and UEL—and 7.1 percent—for the earnings above the UEL. Interestingly these *equilibrium* contribution rates are lower than the statutory National Income contributions, which finance also other social spending beyond public pensions.

EC and OECD official predictions for the year 2050 do not expect the aging process to produce major changes in the British demographic structure and hence in the level of pension spending (see table 2.3). Yet even this mild demographic dynamics and the replacement of SERPS with S2P may significantly affect the future political sustainability of the public pension system. The changes in the British demographic pyramid (see figure 9.3) will moderately reduce the long-term profitability of the social security system, while modifying the identity of the pivotal voter, since the median age among the voters is expected to reach 53 years in 2050. The substitution of an earnings-related scheme (SERPS) with a partially flat S2P will instead increase support for social security among low-educated individuals, while raising the opposition among high-educated agents.

Table 9.3 displays the results of the simulations that evaluate the impact of the aging process and of the 2002 Blair reform on the political

Table 9.3
Simulation results

	Scheme	Effective retirement age	Public pension contribution rate	Replace-ment rate (low)	Replace-ment rate (high)
2000	BSP & SERPS	63	17.1%	66.7%	48.5%
2050	BSP & SERPS	63	39.0%	75.3%	54.5%
2050	BSP & SERPS	64	36.5%	78.1%	58.0%
2050	BSP & SERPS	65	34.3%	81.4%	62.2%
2050	BSP & S2P	63	43.0%	85.4%	55.0%
2050	BSP & S2P	64	40.0%	88.2%	58.5%
2050	BSP & S2P	65	37.6%	92.0%	62.7%

Source: Galasso and Profeta (2004).
Note: The first line gives the year 2000 scenario; lines 2 to 4 give the simulations for the social security contribution rate under the 2050 economic, demographic, and political scenario in a hypothetical scenario with BSP and SERPS (i.e., had the 2003 reform not occurred) for different retirement ages. All remaining lines show the simulations for 2050 in the scenario with BSP and S2P. Contribution rates refer to the sum of the contribution rates paid by the employee and by the employer for an income between the second threshold (ST) and the upper earnings level (UEL) belonging to a worker, who chooses not to contract out of the system; replacement rates refer respectively to low and high educated retirees.

sustainability of the social security system for the year 2050. Several crucial questions may be addressed in this theoretical framework: Which contribution rate will prevail in 2050, after the introduction of a more redistributive scheme (S2P)? How does this contribution rate depend on the effective retirement age? What size would the public pension system have had in absence of the 2002 reform?

The first line of table 9.3 describes the public pensions in the United Kingdom at the turn of the century, as composed by the BSP and SERPS schemes. The equilibrium contribution rate was equal to 17.1 percent and the replacement rate was almost 67 percent for the low-educated individuals but less than 50 percent for the high-educated, thereby showing the redistributive nature of the public pension scheme.

The hypothetical case in which the 2002 Blair reform had not occurred and hence in 2050 the British public system was still composed of BSP and SERPS, is displayed at lines 2 to 4 in table 9.3. Under this scenario the political economy model suggests that with retirement ages at their 2000 levels (63 years), the equilibrium contribution rate would rise to 39 percent, while replacement rates would increase to around 75 percent for the low- and to almost 55 percent for the high-educated individuals. An increase in the retirement age to 65 years would reduce the contribution rate to 34.3%, while replacement rates would increase because of the reduction in the fraction of retirees and to the contemporaneous increase in the share of workers.

The effects of the Blair 2002 reform, which replaced the SERPS with a partially flat S2P, on the long-run political sustainability of the public pension system are displayed in the last three lines of table 9.3. According to these simulations, social security expenditure will increase even further. With retirement ages at 63 years, the equilibrium contribution rate will jump to 43 percent—hence being four percentage points higher than the equilibrium rate under BSP and SERPS. This additional increase in the public pension spending is clearly due to the more redistributive nature of S2P vis-à-vis SERPS, which induces low-educated agents to support a larger system. This effect emerges clearly in table 9.3, in the difference between the replacement rate of low- and high-educated individuals that widens under a BSP-S2P public system. Furthermore, as displayed in figure 9.5, the most preferred contribution rates by low-educated voters—calculated for the 2050 expected economic and demographic scenario—is always larger under a BSP-S2P system than under BSP-SERPS. As in the previous case, postponing retirement age to 65 years reduces public pension spending and the contribution rate drops to 37.6 percent.

These simulations portray a rather unconventional future scenario for the British pension system. Despite the mild population aging the existence of a substantial redistributive component in the design of the system leads to a strong political demand for more pension spending—and hence to a larger system. The associated increase in the pensions' generosity clearly attenuates the current concerns about old age poverty, but at the cost of a large rise in the contribution rate, and thus in the financial burden of the system.

However, the economic scenario used in these simulations did not account for the likely changes in the education composition of the population from the year 2000 to 2050. Plausible modifications of the education structure would be particularly relevant for the political sustainability of the UK public pension system because of the highly redistributive nature of the pension system by income (or education) groups. Table 9.4 presents the results of the simulations carried out under the year 2050 demographic and economic scenario, with a

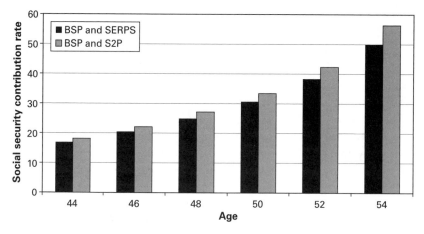

Figure 9.5
Most preferred contribution rate by age for low-educated individuals

Table 9.4
Simulation results with expected education groups in 2050

	Scheme	Effective retirement age	Public pension contribution rate	Replace-ment rate (low)	Replace-ment rate (high)
2050	BSP & S2P	63	37.4%	86.5%	55.7%
2050	BSP & S2P	64	35.5%	90.0%	59.7%
2050	BSP & S2P	65	33.8%	94.2%	64.2%

Note: All lines display the simulations for the social security contribution rate under the 2050 economic, demographic, and political scenario in the scenario with BSP and S2P for different retirement ages. Contribution rates refer to the sum of the contribution rates paid by the employee and by the employer for an income between the second threshold (ST) and the upper earnings level (UEL) belonging to a worker who chooses not to contract out of the system; replacement rates refer respectively to low- and high-educated retirees.

BSP-S2P public pension system, but using a different composition of the two education groups. In accordance with 1996 ECHP data on the education composition of the 26 to 35 years age group, low-educated individuals are assumed to amount to 39.5 percent of the population (down from 59.4 percent in the year 2000) and the remaining 60.5 percent to be highly educated. Unsurprisingly, the smaller proportion of low-educated individuals reduces the support for social security stemming from its redistributive nature, and hence the equilibrium contribution rates drops below 34 percent for a retirement age of 65 years.

10 Political Sustainability in a Redistributive System: The United States

Retirement income in the United States is characterized by the co-existence of public and private arrangements. The social security system provides old age, survival, disability, and health insurance (OASDHI) to the covered individuals, which in 2001 amounted to 187.5 millions people. Nevertheless, workers—particularly those employed in large private companies—rely also on occupational plans and private individual retirement accounts for their retirement income: in 2001, 99.5 millions Americans participated to these pension plans. The largest share of income for the aged population comes from the social security system: in 2002, OASDI benefits made up for 39 percent of the aggregate retirement income, private pensions for 19 percent, and investment income for 14 percent, while earnings still accounted for a large share of old age resources, 25 percent (see Social Security Administration 2004).

By European standards, the US social security system features a relatively modest size and provides low replacement of labor earnings at retirement, particularly for high-income workers, since the benefit formula is designed to redistribute among individuals with different earnings and family composition. In 2000, public pension spending in the United States amounted to 4.4 percent of GDP; according to official estimates provided by the OECD, pension spending is forecasted to reach 6.2 percent in 2050, mainly due to population aging (see table 2.3). Projected changes in employment, eligibility, and benefit formula are, however, expected to partially mitigate the impact of the demographic process.

The demographic projections that became available since the eighties—forecasting a rapid increase in pension spending—generated a large debate in the United States.[1] In 1983 concerns about the fall in the labor market participation of elderly workers led to a gradual increase in the normal retirement age from 65 to 67 years, to the introduction of delayed retirement credits, and to more severe penalties for early retirement. Moreover a clear attempt was made to accumulate consistent resources to finance the retirement of the baby boomers. A sizable share of the social security contributions (around 20 percent since 1990) was devoted to the OASI trust fund. This fund was established in the 1937, when the system was fully funded. Since 1960 it had, however, received a yearly average of only 1.5 percent of total contributions. Nevertheless, concerns about the long-run financial sustainability of the system have continued to surface the US politics, and a reform plan was recently proposed by President Bush, in an effort to shift a large share of the retirement income provision from public to private sources.

Despite their relevance pensions do not entirely permeate the US welfare system, which is instead increasingly dominated by health care expenditure—through programs specifically targeted to elderly and low-income individuals. Health care absorbs half of the US welfare resources (see figure 10.1), while old age and seniority pensions (OAI) represent only a quarter of total welfare spending, and survivor (SI) and disability (DI) pensions amount to 17 percent.

Another characteristic feature of the US system is its redistributiveness. Because of the nonlinear benefit pension formula and of the cap on the social security contribution base, this system tends to redistribute among individuals of the same cohort but with different earnings,

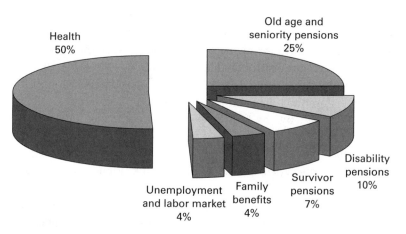

Figure 10.1
Welfare expenditure decomposition in 2000 (Source: OECD)

longevity, and family type. Still several studies suggest that other elements—such as the longevity differential between low- and high-income individuals—may moderate the impact of these redistributive features (see Feldstein and Liebman 2002b).

This chapter examines the long-run political sustainability of the US social security system. As for the United Kingdom, the forecasted aging process for the United States is rather mild. The large differences in the participation rate at elections among US voters of different ages, incomes, and occupational status may magnify the impact of aging on the political process. The electoral push toward more social security of a moderately graying population may hence still be large, while the increase in the dependency ratio—and hence the drop in the profitability of the system—will be of a lower magnitude. The simulations provided in section 10.3, which examine also the redistributive features of the system, suggest that the political equilibrium in 2050 will be characterized by a higher contribution rate and more generous pensions.

The chapter proceeds as follows: Section 10.1 introduces a brief historical detour of the public and private provision of retirement income in the United States and provides a description of the public scheme. It also addresses the redistributive elements of the system, introduces the current debate on its long-term financial sustainability, and discusses some of the recent reform proposals. Section 10.2 presents the demographic trend and analyzes its effects on the political representation of the different generations of Americans. The sustainability issues and the long-run political support for the US public pension system are examined in section 10.3.

10.1 The Current Social Security System: A Brief Description

Initial forms of public retirement program were established already in the nineteenth century to cover some state and local government employees, such as New Jersey teachers and New York policemen and firefighters. Contemporaneously private provisions of retirement income were also introduced, when occupational plans became available to the large companies' employees as formal company pension plans.

Federal government intervention in old age retirement income came into the picture only after the Great Depression. In 1935 Franklin D. Roosevelt, who had strongly advocated the public provision of retirement income during his presidential campaign, launched an Old Age Pension System, charged with providing old age benefits to retired workers previously employed in industry and commerce. This social security system was instituted in order to "give some measure of protection to the average citizen and to his family against the loss of a job and against poverty-ridden old age.... It (the system) will act as a protection to future Administrations against the necessity of going deeply into debt to furnish relief to the needy.... It is, in short, a law that will take care of human needs and at the same time provide the United States an economic structure of vastly greater soundness." (Quoted from President Roosevelt's statement upon signing the Social Security Act, August 14, 1935. Available online at ⟨www.ssa.gov⟩.)

The system was initially conceived as a fully funded scheme that would allow future governments to provide retirement benefits to future retirees without having to resort to more taxes or debt. Yet only few years later, in 1939, the system became PAYG, and coverage was extended to the retired workers' living and surviving dependents.

Later modifications have typically enlarged the coverage of the system and extended the number of programs, but they have not touched its initial architecture (see Miron and Weil 1998). The system has remained unfunded, with its financial cost being borne by covered individuals, coverage is compulsory by law, and eligibility to retirement benefits descents from previous contributions, although pension benefits are not directly linked to these contributions.

A major extension of the social security program occurred in 1956, when disability insurance (DI) was added to the existing old age and survivors insurance (OASI), in order to protect workers and their dependents from the risk of income losses due to injuries during their working life. In 1965, the Social Security Amendment Act re-designed the public health care system by instituting two programs, Medicare—targeted to the elderly and financed by the current workers' contribution—and Medicaid—covering low-income families and financed through general taxation. In 1972, the cost-of-living adjustment (COLA) was automatically linked to the inflation and the earning base for benefit calculation to the average wage growth rate;[2] while previously any indexation had to be explicitly authorized by an Act of the Congress. A delayed retirement credit was also instituted, which increased benefits to the workers retiring after normal retirement age, in an initial attempt to provide incentive for late retirement.

Modifications occurred also in the private provision of retirement income, during a period of large expansion of occupational plans particularly among employees of large companies. In 1974, the Employee

Retirement Income Security Act (ERISA) instituted new individual retirement accounts with generous tax incentives for workers not yet
covered by occupational plans[3] and regulated the eligibility criteria to
obtain tax relieves for the existing occupation plans.

Finally, two more recent modifications of the social security system
took place in 1977 and 1983, when the benefit computation criterion
was changed. The 1977 Social Security Amendments slightly reduced
benefits, while rising payroll taxes. In 1983, following the suggestions
of a bipartisan commission (see Pierson 1996), the retirement age to
achieve a full pension was gradually increased from 65 to 67 years;
delayed retirement credits were increased to 8 percent per year (for
individuals born in 1943 or after), in order to provide incentives for
postponing retirement; taxation was imposed on high-earners' pension
benefits; and the buildup of a large Trust Fund reserve to partially pre-
fund the retirement of the baby boomer generation was initiated.

10.1.1 Main Characteristics

The Old Age, Survivor, Disability and Health Insurance (OASDHI)
system is composed of several programs. Eligibility to old age retirement benefits depends on the retirement age and on the previous
contributions to the system. Pension benefits can be claimed by individuals with at least 40 quarters of coverage upon turning 65 years
old, whereas early retirement benefits can be obtained at age 62.

The amount of Old Age pension benefits awarded is calculated
from a retiree's lifetime earnings through a three-step procedure. First,
all the worker's past labor earnings are converted into current values
through their indexation to the average wage growth. This mechanism
is only partial, since indexation stops when workers turn 60 years old,
thereby leaving out at least two years of labor earnings. Second, the
Average Index Monthly Earnings (AIME) is obtained by computing
the monthly average over the highest 35 years of indexed earnings—
below the maximum taxable level. Finally, the Primary Insurance
Amount (PIA) is calculated from the AIME. Since the 1977 Act, the
benefits structure for obtaining the PIA is computed around two bend
points. The PIA is equal to the sum of 90 percent of the AIME below
the lower bend point, of 32 percent of the AIME between the two bend
points, and of 15 percent of the AIME above the higher band point.
The Primary Insurance Amount (PIA) represents the monthly Old Age
Insurance benefit paid out to a fully insured worker (i.e., the worker retiring at normal retirement age). This normal retirement age has been

gradually increased by the 1983 amendment from 65 to 67 years, starting with those individuals turning 62 in 2000 and will be completed in 2022.

Individuals retiring early receive less then their PIA, as penalties apply for every month of retirement prior to the normal retirement age (5/9 percent each month for the first 36 months of early retirement and to 5/12 for additional months). Since penalizations have been adjusted in accordance with the increase in the normal retirement age, a person retiring at age 62 in 2020 would receive a lower share of her PIA (70 percent) than in 2000 (80 percent). Individuals postponing their retirement after normal retirement age receive instead a delayed retirement credit equal to 5.5 percent per year of deferral, to be increased to 8 percent for those born in 1943 or after.

The OASI system envisages also additional benefits for individuals associated with the insured worker. In particular, Spouse's Insurance Benefits—a peculiar feature of the US social security system—amount to 50 percent of the PIA of the insured worker and are provided to the insured worker's spouse, who is not directly entitled to other pension benefits exceeding this amount. Survivor Insurance benefits, such as Widow(er)'s Insurance, are payable to the dependents of a deceased insured worker; they are equal to the deceased worker's PIA reduced by any amount that the widow(er) may be directly entitled to as insurance benefits. All benefits claimed within a family are subject to a maximum family benefit.

Most OASI benefits are financed through a social security payroll tax—equally shared by employers and employees—although some funding comes also from the income taxation of pension benefits. The social security contribution rate is applied to the wage income up to a maximum taxable base, which increases at the average wage growth rate. In 2000, the combined employer-employee OASI contribution rate was equal to 10.6 percent, the disability insurance contribution (DI) represented an additional 1.8 percent, while health insurance (HI) was financed by a 2.9 percent combined employer–employee contribution rate levied on all wages with no ceilings.

In the last twenty years total contributions have exceeded total pension benefits; this positive surplus has been accumulated in the OASI trust fund and is invested in government securities. According to Congressional Budget Office estimates, the trust fund will begin to be drawn down in 2018, and will be entirely depleted by around 2040. Figure 10.2 displays the actual and expected inflows and outflows

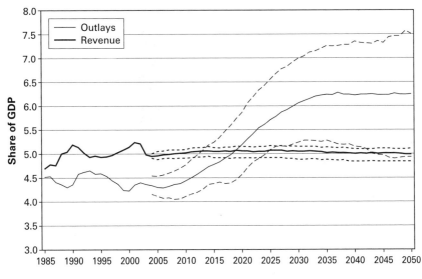

Figure 10.2
OASI trust fund (Source: Congressional Budget Office)

from the trust fund, with a 10 percent confidence interval on the forecasted values.

10.1.2 Redistributive Issues

The contribution and benefits structure of the US social security system described in the previous section generates different redistributive flows among individuals of the same age cohort. The OASDI contribution system is regressive, since the contribution rate is only proportional to wage income up to a maximum (HI contributions are not capped). The benefit scheme instead redistributes in favor of the low-earners, since the ratio of benefits to earnings (or AIME) decreases as earnings rise because of the PIA formula. These redistributive elements hence pull in opposite directions.

Additional within-cohort redistributive features of the OASI system originate from the differential treatment received by the insured individuals (or by their dependents) according to characteristics such as marital status, family composition and within-family earnings distribution. Marital status discriminates among insured, since additional benefits—unrelated to the worker's contribution—are available to the spouse of a covered worker, both during the worker's life and after his death. Because of these spouse's and widow(er)'s insurance benefits,

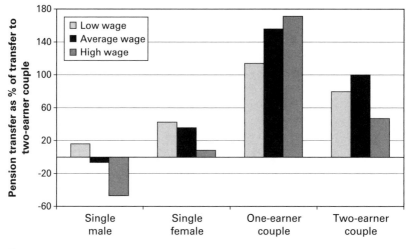

Figure 10.3
Within-cohort redistribution in 1995 (Source: Clark et al. 2004)

the distribution of earnings within the family creates additional disparities, with single-earner families typically receiving larger benefits than
two earners families for a given family income below the maximum
taxable base. Finally, since the system provides gender-neutral annuities, the effective value of the coverage is higher for women than for
men, due to life expectancy differentials.

A large empirical literature (e.g., see Boskin et al. 1987; Steuerle and
Bakija 1994; Gokhale and Kotlikoff 2002) analyzes the overall effect of
these redistributive elements on the treatment received by insured
individuals. The recurrent results are summarized in figure 10.3, which
shows the net transfer obtained from the OASI scheme in 1995 by different individuals as a percentage of the net transfer received by an average wage two-earner couple.

Among single individuals, females enjoy larger net transfers than
males because of their higher longevity, and redistribution takes place
from high- to low-income individuals. Couples receive a better deal
from social security than singles, mainly because of the existence of
survivor pensions and—in the case of one-earner couples—of spouse's
insurance benefits. According to these calculations by Clark et al.
(2004), no income redistribution from rich to poor families seems to
arise, at least within couples. Computations on simulated profiles by
Gokhale and Kotlikoff (2002) show instead evidence of some income
redistribution: merging all family types, for the cohort born between

1945 and 1949, the internal rate of return from OASI ranges from 5.7 percent for the individuals in the lowest earnings quintile to 0.8 percent for people in the highest quintile.

Other studies have stressed the role of life expectancy differentials in creating intra-cohort redistribution. Besides the gender longevity differential, which in Gokhale and Kotlikoff (2002) drives a substantial wedge in the internal rate of return of men and women, life expectancy differs also across income classes. Because of the protective effect of income (see Deaton and Paxson 2001; Smith 1999), richer individuals tend to live longer, thereby enjoying pension benefits for more years, and at the same time their nonworking spouses receive higher benefits than low-income spouses. According to Feldstein and Liebman (2002b), the higher average life expectancy of the high-earners greatly reduces the overall degree of income-related redistribution of the OASI, which is estimated around 5 to 9 percent of total benefits.

The evolution over time of the US social security system—characterized by a gradual, yet steady increase in contribution rates, pension benefits, and share of eligible workers—has also generated substantial redistributive flows across different generations of insured individuals. A large literature has emerged to quantify the value of the social security system to successive generations of Americans, by estimating the returns from social security obtained by workers in different cohorts. These empirical results emphasize that early generations of retirees received better deals than successive cohorts of workers. According to Boskin's et al. (1987) computations, for instance, the internal rate of return from social security for an average wage single-earner couple has dropped from 5.5 percent for individuals in the 1915 cohort to 3.2 percent for the 1930 cohort and to 2.1 percent for individuals born in 1945. In line with the results of Caldwell et al. (1999), Gokhale and Kotlikoff (2002) estimate these average internal rates of returns to remain almost constant—around 2 percent—for individuals in the 1945 to 2000 cohorts, provided that no changes occur to the contribution rates and to the pension benefits calculation. However, in the long run these assumptions are hardly consistent with the financial sustainability of the system. Under every reform scenario proposed by Gokhale and Kotlikoff (2002) to balance the social security system, these average internal rates of return drop substantially. For instance, a tax hike in 2000 would have maintained the returns at 1.7 percent for the individuals in the 1945 cohort, while reducing them to 1.1 percent for those in the 1970 cohort and to 0.9 percent for those in the

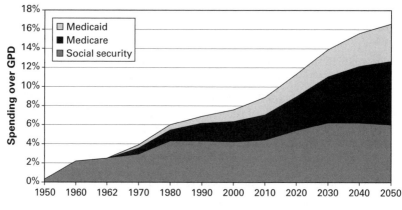

Figure 10.4
Social security and health expenditure (Source: Congressional Budget Office)

1995 cohort. A cut in pension benefits in 2000 would have instead had a more widespread effect, reducing the returns to around 1 percent for all cohorts, while a rapid increase in the normal retirement age would lead to a 1.3 percent return for all generations.

10.1.3 Current Debate

Since its introduction the social security system has played a major role in reducing poverty among the elderly. The percentage of individuals aged 65 years or more below the poverty line has dropped from 59 percent in 1950 to 10.5 percent in 1995 as opposed to a reduction from 39.8 to 13.8 percent in the overall population. However, this impressive record has come at an increasing financial cost, since social security expenditure has been constantly rising after WWII, as displayed in figure 10.4.

While the aging process (see section 10.2) is expected to create financial sustainability problems to the US social security system, expenses for health care provision are forecasted to increase even faster, with the two main health care programs—Medicare and Medicaid—growing respectively from 2.2 and 1.2 percent of GDP in 2000 to 6.7 and 3.9 percent in 2050 (see Bohn 1999, 2005, for a discussion of the long run political viability of health care).

The financial implications of the retirement of the baby boom generation for the social security system have long been debated in the United States. In mid-eighties, a buildup of financial resources in the OASDI trust fund occurred, in an attempt to accumulate sufficient financial resources and accommodate the retirement of the baby boom generation. Nevertheless, as displayed at figure 10.2, the trust fund will begin to shrink around 2018, when outlays will exceed revenues, and is projected to be entirely depleted by 2040. In the long run the OASDI deficit is expected to grow even more (see Lee and Skinner 1999).

Faced with this bleak scenario, the 1994–1996 Advisory Council on Social Security, appointed by President Clinton, proposed three alternative social security reforms,[4] ranging from simple adjustments of the parameters of the system to a partial privatization. The most conservative reform (*maintenance of benefits*) recommended to keep the basic design of the social security system—in particular its defined benefit structure—and to meet the financial constraints through a rise in the contribution rates accompanied by a modest reduction in the pension benefits. The investment of part of the trust fund in private equities was also contemplated. The intermediate reform proposal (*individual accounts*) consisted of introducing individual retirement savings accounts administrated by the government,[5] of reducing pension benefits and of increasing the normal retirement age. Finally, the more radical reform (*personal security account*) suggested a switch to a two-pillar public system composed of a basic pension scheme financed by a flat payroll tax and of private individual savings accounts. Transition cost, arising from the payment of pension benefits to the current generation of retirees, was to be financed through an additional payroll tax.

Disregarding these three proposals, President Clinton drafted an additional reform that contemplated, for the first time in the US social security history, the allocation of general revenues to the social security system. These resources would allow the purchase of private equities and government debt to be redeemed for financing future pension benefits. The use of government debt, in particular, was meant to explicitly recognize the implicit outstanding social security debt toward the insured workers. No reform measure was, however, implemented.

Some few years later a commission appointed by President Bush proposed a reform based on two crucial elements (see Cogan and Mitchell 2003). First, the indexation of the workers' previous wages in the calculation of AIME (see section 10.1.1) was to be shifted from wages to prices, beginning in 2009. This measure would ease the financial requirements of the system through a substantial reduction of the pension benefits. A safety net consisting of more generous benefits for low-earnings long-term contributors was also contemplated and would increase the degree of redistribution of the system. Second, the proposal suggested the introduction of a second pillar made of private individual accounts. Along the lines of the British system (see chapter 9), individuals would have the opportunity of opt out—at least partially—from the public pillar scheme in favor of these private individual accounts: up to 4 percent of the payroll taxes could be devoted to this private pillar, and public pension benefits would be reduced accordingly.

The latter measure was also at the hearth of the reform plan launched by President Bush at the beginning of 2005, which aimed at "strengthening social security for the twenty-first century." The plan envisaged the gradual introduction of personal retirement accounts, to which all workers would eventually be permitted to contribute 4 percent of their payroll taxes. Workers who "opt in" these retirement accounts would experience a reduction in their social security benefits at retirement but would enjoy an annuity and/or lump-sum withdrawals linked to these accounts. The transition cost of the reform was estimated around $664 billion over the initial ten years. The reform proposal—as presented by President Bush at the 2005 State of the Union—also guaranteed to have no effect on individuals aged 55 years or older. Despite this reassuring message the AARP—the US retirees association—has strongly opposed the Bush plan. Indeed, according to an NBC/Wall Street Journal survey conducted in February 2005, 50 percent of the interviewed considered it a bad idea to invest social security contributions in the stock market, while 40 percent were favorable. Moreover, among the latter group, 68 percent were open to change their mind, as opposed to only 39 percent in the former group.

This Bush plan, as well as many of the different reform recommendations put forward in the economic literature (see Lindbeck and Persson 2003), entails a large shift toward a fully—or at least partially—funded system. Indeed, US retirees already rely heavily on private pensions, which in 1997 constituted 20.9 percent of the retirement income for an average couple aged 70 to 74 years old, as opposed to 36.7 percent for OASDI benefits. Among those plans, defined benefit occupational plans—providing the retirees with pension benefits typically linked to the past few wages prior to retirement—had been widespread among large private companies' workers since the beginning of the twentieth century. Yet during the seventies and eighties, following the Employee Retirement Income Security Act, a new form of private pension emerged: the individual retirement accounts. These accounts are typically defined contribution schemes. Individuals contributing to these accounts during their working life receive a pension benefit at retirement that is related to the capitalized values of their previous contributions. In the last three decades the massive move from defined benefit to defined contribution plans[6] has determined a substantial shift of the financial risk related to the workers' retirement income from the companies to the individual workers. The Bush reform would reinforce this trend.

10.2   Aging in the United States

A heated debate is under way in the United States on the effects of aging on the economic environment and on the social security and health care systems (see Clark et al. 2004), despite the aging process being rather mild if compared to most European countries.

The US population has enjoyed moderate longevity gains: life expectancy at birth for females has increased from 73.1 years in 1960 to 79.6 in 2000, with a gain of 6.5 years, vis-à-vis 9.2 years for French females and 9.9 years for Spaniard women. As a result, while in 1960 female longevity in the United States was only second to Scandinavian countries, in 2000 it was in line with the average female longevity among OECD countries. Life expectancy at birth for males has increased from 66.6 years in 1960 to 73.9 in 2000, hence remaining relatively low in both periods. Moreover the United States have always experienced a high fertility rate—as measured by the number of children per woman between 18 and 45 years—despite a long-lasting decreasing trend (see Munnell 2004), moving from 7 children per woman in 1800 to below 3 by 1930 and back to 3.65 in 1960, during the large increase corresponding to the baby boom. Since then, the fertility rate has continued to drop, reaching 2.05 children per woman in 2000.

US Census projections for the next 50 years suggest further moderate aging due to more longevity gains—with life expectancy at birth reaching 79.1 years for males and 83.5 years for females in 2050—and to a modest reduction in the fertility rate, which will drop to 1.95 in 2050. Figure 10.5 displays the projected US population profile by age for the year 2050 and the actual pyramid for the year 2000. In the 2000 profile the effect of the baby boom is clearly visible, with the two largest generations in the population being formed by individuals in their thirties and forties—the baby boomers—and a small fraction of individuals aged 60 years or more. Projections for the year 2050 suggest

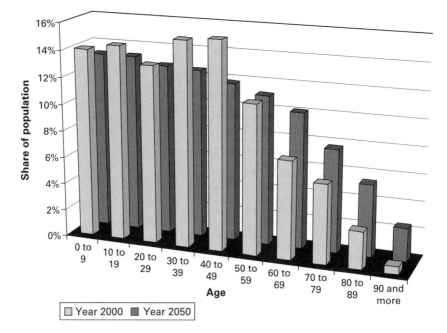

Figure 10.5
Aging in the United States: Population by age group in 2000 and 2050 (Source: US Census Bureau)

instead a more balanced distribution of the population by age. The substantial rise in the share of elderly is, however, less dramatic than elsewhere; for instance, the share of very elderly individuals—those aged 80 years old or more—will increase from 3.3 percent in 2000 to 7.82 percent in 2050, as opposed to a hike from 3.9 to 13 percent in Italy (see table 2.4). Changes in the old age dependency ratio confirm this finding: the increase in the ratio of old individuals (aged 65 years or more) to the potentially active population (individuals aged 18 to 64 years) from 20.5 percent in 2000 to 36.3 percent in 2050 is the smallest among the six countries analyzed (see table 2.5).

The moderate impact of the aging process on the financing of the social security system, as compared to other OECD countries, is also due to the high average retirement age among US workers. The pension dependency ratio computed in chapter 2—which measures the ratio between potential workers and retirees, by partitioning the individuals according to the effective median retirement age in 2000—captures the interaction between early retirement behaviors and aging.

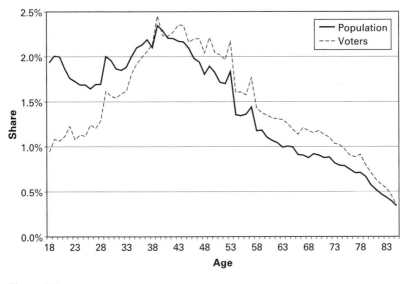

Figure 10.6
Population and voters by age in 2000 (Source: US Census Bureau)

In the United States the pension dependency ratio differs only slightly from its demographic counterpart—the old age dependency ratio: 23.4 versus 20.5 percent in 2000 and 41.5 versus 36.3 percent in 2050. The large participation to the labor market by the elderly workers hence limits the impact of aging on the functioning of the social security system.

The aging process modifies also the future political representation of individuals in the different age groups. This phenomenon may prove particularly strong in the United States, due to the large differences in turnout rates at election by age. With the elderly individuals participating almost twice as much as the young to the political process (see table 2.7), a demographic shift toward more elderly in the population could have dramatic effects on the political representation of different generations—and hence of different interests.

Figures 10.6 and 10.7 show respectively the adult population and the actual voters by age in 2000 and the projections for 2050. In both cases the share of middle-aged and elderly voters largely exceeds the share of middle-aged and elderly individuals in the population. In the year 2000, for instance, while the median age in the adult population is equal to 43 years, the median age among the actual voters is four years higher—47 years.

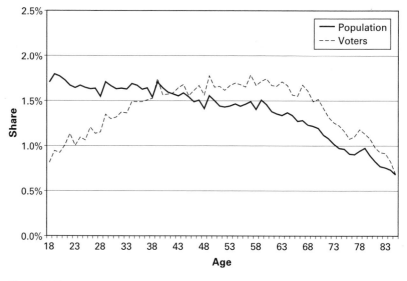

Figure 10.7
Population and voters by age in 2050 (Source: US Census Bureau)

A synthetic measure of the impact of the aging process on the political strength of the different generations is given by the variation in these median ages. In the year 2050 the median age among the adults is expected to be 48 years, while the median age among the actual voters is projected to be 53 years. Hence, while the aging process is accountable for a 5-year increase in the median age of the adult population, due to the high participation rate at election by the elderly, the median age among actual voters is projected to rise by 6 years. This difference suggests that the aging process may have a stronger effect in the political arena, where overrepresented elderly individuals will use their political power to defend their pension benefits, than in the economic environment, where the long-run average profitability of the social security system will mildly fall. Quantifying the relative magnitude of these two effects on the political sustainability of the US system is the task set up for the next section.

10.3 Political Sustainability

Although a heated debate and a flurry of reform proposals have characterized the last decade (see the discussion in section 10.1.3), no major reform has occurred in the United States—therefore suggesting that the pension system is, at least currently, politically sustainable. Yet the aging process, despite being moderate, will clearly modify the economic and political environment. Evaluating how the US social security system will be shaped by these economic and political changes in the year 2050 is the objective of this section.

The current and past political sustainability of the US social security system can be addressed by evaluating the generosity of the social security deal for past and current generations of US voters. According to the theoretical framework introduced in chapters 3 and 4, political sustainability typically requires the expected continuation return from social security to exceed the return from alternative assets for a majority of voters. A measure of the profitability of social security is the continuation internal rate of return (CIRR) from "investing" in social security, which is calculated as the rate of discount that equates the expected present value of current and future social security contributions to the expected present value of future pension benefits. In Galasso (2002), I computed this CIRR for the median voter—defined as the individual with the median age among the voters[7]—at the US presidential elections from 1964 to 1996, using actual contributions and benefits data for the 1964 to 1976 elections, while relying on Social Security Administration's estimates of future contributions and benefits for the remaining elections. The results of these calculations are presented at figure 10.8 for two specifications of the median voter's family: a medium earnings family with a single earner—the husband—and a medium earnings family with two earners—husband and wife—on a 70 to 30 percent earnings split.

The overall assessment from my (2002) calculations is that the US median voter's family received—and may expect to receive—a large (continuation) return from social security (5.7 to 9.8 percent), which compares favorably with ex post returns from alternative assets, such as the Standard and Poor composite index, the Dow Jones industrial average, and US government bonds. In line with the results of the existing literature reviewed in section 10.1.2, computations on actual data (1964 to 1976 elections) show that the CIRR is decreasing over time, thereby suggesting that initial generations of Americans obtained the best deal from social security. Estimated continuation returns for the 1980 to 1996 median voters' family are instead almost constant (around 6 percent for the two-earner family), and, if anything, they tend to increase for the 1992 and 1996 median voters. These surprisingly high returns depend on the two assumptions put forward by the

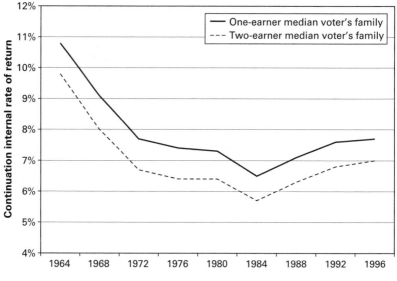

Figure 10.8
Returns from social security for the median voter (Source: Galasso 2002)

SSA, and used in my (2002) calculations, that future contribution rates will be constant at their 1996 value and that future benefits will not be substantially reduced. Any increase in the future contribution rates or reduction in the benefits will clearly decrease these CIRRs. Bohn (1999) provided a complete evaluation of the social security system for future US median voters under the assumption that—whenever needed—future benefits' obligations will be met by increasing social security contribution rates. In this scenario, Bohn (1999) finds that the US social security system will retain the political support of a majority of the voters even if contribution rates will have to rise. The extent to which modifications to future contribution rates and pension benefits will occur depends on the economic and political environment.

The simulations in this section address this issue by analyzing the political constraints that aging will impose on the US social security system.[7] Aging has two major effects on the pension policy-making: it increases the proportion of retiree to workers, thereby reducing the returns from the system, but strengthens the political representation of individuals close to retirement age, or already retired, who hence favor more pension spending. While the mild aging process should limit the former effect (see section 10.2), the impact of aging on the political

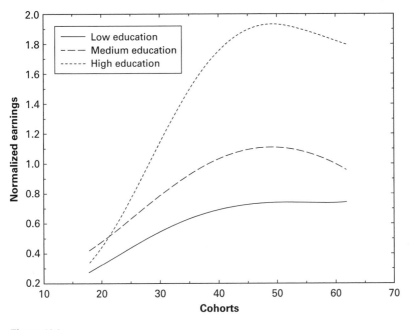

Figure 10.9
Earning profile by age

representation of the different generations is expected to be strong (see figure 10.7) because of the large differential in the turn-out rate at elections among voters of different ages. Were the political effect to dominate even more than in other countries, the increase in the social security contribution rate would be large.

To address the redistributive aspects of the US system (see section 10.1.2), the political economy model described in chapter 4 considers three groups of individuals who differ in their educational attainments, earning profiles, and longevity. According to 2001 US Census data, 12.7 percent of the male earners aged 18 years old or more have not completed high school—and are hence classified as low educated; the medium education group—composed of high school graduates—has a share of 31 percent, while the remaining 56.3 percent have more than high school and are hence regarded as highly educated. The average earning profiles by age for each education group is estimated using mean labor earnings (2001 US Census data). As shown in figure 10.9, high-educated individuals have higher-earnings and a steeper profile than the other two groups.

The main redistributive component of the US social security system is its benefit calculation formula. The monthly pension (PIA) paid out to an individual in the education group q, who retired at time t at normal retirement age, is equal to

$$\bar{P}_t^q = \begin{cases} 0.9w_t^q & \text{for } w_t^q < b_t^l, \\ 0.9b_t^l + 0.32(w_t^q - b_t^l) & \text{for } w_t^q \in [b_t^l, b_t^u], \\ 0.9b_t^l + 0.32(b_t^u - b_t^l) + 0.15(w_t^q - b_t^u) & \text{for } w_t^q > b_t^u, \end{cases} \qquad (10.1)$$

where w_t^q is the average monthly wage of this individual over his best 35 years, and b_t^l and b_t^u are the two bend points for the benefit calculation. This PIA is then reduced (or increased) according to a coefficient $\gamma(J^q)$ that depends on the individual age at retirement, and multiplied by twelve to obtain the actual annual pension benefit for a type-q individual retiring at age $J^q : P_t^q = 12\gamma(J^q)\bar{P}_t^q$. Contributions to the system by employers and employees entail a small redistributive element, since they are proportional to earnings only up to a ceiling. Finally, as discussed in chapter 4, the political economy model considers a balanced budget public pension system in which the total amount of pension benefits equals the aggregate contributions in every period. The simulation results hence concentrate on the equilibrium contribution rate determined at the elections, where voters—according to their age and education level—express their preferences over the size of the system.

The simulations reported in table 10.1 compare the US social security system in the year 2000 with the system that would emerge from the political process in 2050 under the expected demographic, economic, and political environment. The initial scenario for the year 2000 is described in the first line of table 10.1. The social security contribution rate used in the year 2000 simulations represents the actual equilibrium rate computed for the year 2000. The equilibrium rate is set at 9.7 percent, while the effective retirement age is to 63 years, due to the large participation rate among male workers aged 55 or older (see table 2.6). The corresponding replacement rates differ slightly across education groups, thus capturing the mild redistributive element in the benefit calculation formula.

The magnitude of the impact of the aging process on the social security system for the year 2050 is captured in the remaining lines, which report the social security contribution rates arising as political equilibria under the projected 2050 demographic and economic scenarios for

Table 10.1
Simulation results

	Effective retirement age	Social security contribution rate	Replacement rate (low)	Replacement rate (medium)	Replacement rate (high)
2000	63	9.7%	37.7%	34.4%	32.9%
2050	63	23.4%	62.3%	56.7%	54.3%
2050	64	21.7%	60.5%	55.2%	53.0%
2050	65	20.1%	58.8%	53.7%	51.7%
2050	66	18.5%	56.8%	51.9%	50.1%
2050	67	17.1%	55.2%	50.6%	48.9%

Note: The first line gives the year 2000 scenario; all other lines give the simulations for the social security contribution rate under the 2050 economic, demographic, and political scenario for different retirement ages. All replacement rates are calculated using the average earning over the entire working history.

different retirement ages. Unlike in the other countries, since in the US the normal retirement age will be gradually increased to 67 years, simulations are provided for effective retirement age ranging from 63 to 67 years. Regardless of the education group, if the average worker retires at age 63, as in the year 2000, the social security contribution rate is predicted to reach 22 percent, with a substantial increase in the replacement rates. Interestingly the rise in the contribution rate, coupled with the mild aging process, leads to a substantial increase in the generosity of the pension benefits despite the larger share of retirees to workers.

This sizable increase in the US social security contribution rate is only marginally driven by the political push for a larger system stemming from its redistributive design. In line with the redistributive element embed in the benefit calculation formula (see equation 10.1), table 10.1 shows indeed that replacement rates—and hence to some degree the generosity of the pension benefits—tend to differ, at least mildly, across individuals of different income groups. Yet these replacement rates do not capture the additional redistributive feature induced by the higher longevity enjoyed by the richer (or more educated) individuals. This variation in life expectancy tends to compensate the former effect, as rich individuals enjoy less generous pension benefits but for longer years. These two effects are, however, internalized in the voting decisions of the different groups of individuals, which are displayed in figure 10.10. The simulation results suggest that the longevity effect greatly mitigate the redistributive impact of the pension

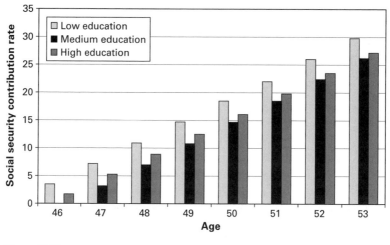

Figure 10.10
Most preferred contribution rate by age and education level in 2050

benefits calculation, as individuals of the same age, but with different levels of education, share similar preferences over the size of the system and thereby reinforce the existing evidence (see section 10.1.2).

The large simulated increase in pension spending depends mainly on the combination of a mild aging process, which reduces only marginally the profitability of the system, and of a significant increase in the political representation of the elderly because of their consistent voting behavior.

Also for the United States, despite of the high initial effective retirement age, the main message arising from table 10.1 is that postponing retirement represents the crucial measure to limit the political incentives toward more pension spending. In particular, if the retirement age rises to 67 years, which constitutes the normal retirement age for individuals born in 1960 or later, the political push will forces the social security contribution rate to reach 17.1 percent, with the associated replacement rates ranging between 48.9 and 55.2 percent. Unlike in other countries, however, in the United States the feasibility of this policy is strictly related to the retirement behavior induced by occupational and private pension plans, since a large majority of the American workers are covered by these schemes. Two interesting findings emerge from the 2004 Retirement Confidence Survey. First, most individuals have little knowledge of the minimum retirement age to obtain full benefits from the social security system, as only less than 20 percent of the interviewed people answered correctly. Second, the individuals' retirement decisions seem to depend on their type of private or occupational plan, whether defined benefit or defined contribution. Interestingly the US retirement policy will hence not be exclusively determined by the social security system, since the design of the private (occupational) scheme—and thus the interests of the large companies—may prove to play a big role. A complete evaluation of this policy option is provided in chapter 11, where the political feasibility of postponing retirement is addressed in a multidimensional voting environment. An encouraging message emerges from these simulations, which suggest the political feasibility of postponing retirement age to 68 or 69 years (see table 11.4).

Demographics, Political
Sustainability, and Reform
Options: A Cross-country
Comparison

Aging will alter the economics, demographics, and politics in every country over the next few decades. The population pyramid will change shape, as the base composed of the young will shrink and the top composed of elderly individuals will expand. The political representation of the different age group will change accordingly, with the elderly enjoying more political power. The economic situation will respond to the demographic process. Because of the higher expected longevity individuals will have to save more to guarantee themselves enough consumption at old age extending to 80 or 90 years old. With more individual savings, economies will accumulate more physical capital. Furthermore, to the extent that longevity gains may turn into longer periods of severe illness and inability of caring after oneself, even more resources will have to be devoted to long-term health care in old age (see Bohn 1999, 2005). Higher longevity may also be associated with longer working carriers, as individuals decide to split the longevity gain between additional working years—by postponing retirement—and more leisure.

The effects induced by the aging process will largely influence the political sustainability of the existing unfunded social security systems. Individual preferences over social security will be modified, since demographic and economic elements change how the system affects the individuals' well-being. Aging increases the proportion of elderly (or retirees) per adult individual (or worker), thereby reducing the average profitability of the system. Longevity gains may instead increase the profitability of the system, since individuals enjoy a longer retirement period. The economic consequences of aging are also relevant. More savings increase the stock of capital and lead to higher wages but to lower returns from private assets, which in turn increase the relative convenience of social security as a saving device. But most important, aging affects the political representation of the different generations and hence the relative importance of the economic well-being of persons in the different age groups to the policy-makers. Clearly, the expected demographic dynamics will lead toward a higher political representation of elderly individuals, as the median age among the voters will largely increase.

Although almost all OECD countries are expected to experience a demographic process of further population aging, the magnitude of this phenomenon will widely vary even among the six countries analyzed here. The negative impact of aging on the social security system, as measured by an increase in the old age dependency ratio, will be particularly large in Italy and Spain, but much less dramatic in the United States, as shown at table 2.5. These differences in the forecasted demographic dynamics carry over to the political representation, as measured by the changes in the median age among the voters: Italy and Spain will feature the largest hike in the age of the pivotal political actor, as displayed at figure 2.3.

How aging will affect the long-run political sustainability of social security depends also on the specific characteristics of the current schemes. Systems inducing early exits from the labor market, typically through generous early retirement provisions, as in France and Italy, magnify the negative impact of aging on the average profitability of the system, since the ratio of retirees to workers becomes even higher than predicted by the old age dependency ratio. Countries already featuring high levels of social security expenditure (e.g., Italy) may have less room for a further expansion of the system, since contribution rates would have to become unbearably high, hence imposing large distortions on economic decisions, particularly in the labor market (see Daveri and Tabellini 2000; Disney 2004). The degree of within-cohort redistribution of each social security system and the reforms underway in several countries may also play an important role in shaping the preferences of an aging electorate over social security.

This chapter provides a comparison of the overall effect of aging on the political constraints that will likely shape the future of the social security systems in six graying societies—France, Germany, Italy, Spain, the United Kingdom, and the United States. The next section discusses the results of the simulations carried out using the political economy model described at chapter 4 for all these countries. The relevance of the country-specific issues analyzed in great details in the previous chapters is surveyed in section 11.2. The political feasibility of postponing retirement—the main policy measures emerging from the simulations of the previous chapters—is addressed in section 11.3, where the results of a multidimensional voting game—on the size of the system and on the retirement age—are presented. Finally, the last section discusses the desirability of delegating pension policy decisions to supranational institutions, such as a pension authority, in order to circumvent the political demand for more pension spending stemming from an aging society.

11.1 Assessing the Political Sustainability of Social Security

The simulations analyzed in this section provide a quantitative evaluation of the impact of aging on social security levels. Current social security schemes—in the year 2000—are compared with the systems estimated to emerge from the political constraints in a scenario featuring the expected demographic, economic, and political characteristics for the year 2050. The simulation results are presented in table 11.1. For each country, the first line describes the main features of the social security system—namely the contribution and replacement rates—the retirement age and the median age among the voters in the year 2000.[1] The following lines report the simulated social security contribution and replacement rates in the year 2050 for different retirement ages.

These simulations give a gloomy picture of the future of social security: under the political constrains imposed by a graying electorate, pension expenditure is forecasted to increase in all countries. Were retirement ages to remain at their initial (year 2000) level, the largest hike would occur in Spain, the fastest aging country in the sample, where the contribution rate would rise from 21.3 to 45.5 percent. Nevertheless, Italy would still experience the largest contribution rate, 50 percent. Interestingly, in Germany, Italy, and Spain, the increase of the contribution rates would not yield higher replacement rates. Despite higher social security contributions the reduction in the relative share of workers contributing to the system and the increase in the proportion of retirees drawing pension benefits in fact diminish the overall generosity of the system. In the United Kingdom and the United States, where the demographic process is expected to be less dramatic (see chapter 2), but also in France, the expected rise in the contribution rate would instead guarantee higher replacement rates.

These changes will also alter the mix of private and public provision of retirement income. Table 11.2 presents the actual composition of the

Table 11.1
Direct impact of aging: Simulation results

		Median voter's age	Effective retirement age	Social security contribution rate	Replace-ment rate
France	2000	47	58	22.4%	49.2%
	2050	56	58	40.8%	54.6%
	2050	56	65	29.7%	72.2%
Germany	2000	46	61	23.8%	68.3%
	2050	55	61	37.7%	55.4%
	2050	55	65	32.6%	81.2%
Italy	1992	44	58	38.0%	73.6%
	2050	56	58	50.0%	55.5%
	2050	56	65	38.0%	74.2%
Spain	2000	44	62	21.3%	67.9%
	2050	57	62	45.5%	64.6%
	2050	57	65	40.7%	77.3%
United Kingdom	2000	45	63	14.5%	75.8%
	2050	53	63	33.2%	95.2%
	2050	53	65	31.1%	114.3%
United States	2000	47	63	9.7%	41.9%
	2050	53	63	21.6%	55.7%
	2050	53	65	18.3%	53.9%

Source: Galasso and Profeta (2004) and author's calculations.
Note: For each country, the first line gives the year 2000 scenario; 2050 simulation results for contribution and replacement rates—using the model described in chapter 4, with exogenous labor supply—are at lines 2 and 3.

retiree's average income for 2000 and the model's estimates for 2000 and 2050. The simulations suggest that the rise in the contribution rate will induce an increase in the share of retirement income provided by the social security system in all countries but Germany and Italy. While in most countries this rebalancing effect is small, in the United Kingdom and the United States the relative importance of private provisions, through occupational plans and personal pension plans, is estimated to fall sharply because of the massive increase in the social security contribution rate.

These simulations validate—in a political economy environment—the conventional wisdom that postponing retirement limits the increase in pension spending. While in most studies (see OECD 2002)

Table 11.2
Actual and simulated composition of retirees' income

		Actual data	Model's predictions	
		1990s	2000	2050
France	Pensions	74.9%	77.7%	81.8%
	Investments	10.4%	22.3%	18.2%
	Earnings	11.0%	—	—
	Other	3.7%	—	—
Germany	Pensions	66.1%	63.2%	61.4%
	Investments and private transfers	11.8%	36.8%	38.6%
	Earnings	14.7%	—	—
	Other	7.4%	—	—
Italy	Pensions	80.0%	85.2%	81.2%
	Investments	9.2%	14.8%	18.8%
	Earnings	10.8%	—	—
Spain	Pensions	—	68.7%	73.2%
	Investments	—	31.3%	26.8%
United Kingdom	Pensions	59.9%	61.7%	88.6%
	Investments and private pensions	33.4%	38.3%	11.4%
	Earnings	6.8%	—	—
United States	Pensions	35.4%	44.4%	67.3%
	Investments and private transfers	38.2%	55.6%	32.7%
	Earnings	26.4%	—	—

Sources: Borsch-Supan, Reil-Held, and Schnabel (2001), Brugiavini and Fornero (2001), Emmerson and Johnson (2001), Joustein (2001), Legendre and Pelé (2001), and author's calculations.
Note: Actual data refer to couples aged 60+, except in France (55+) and in Italy (all retirees). Model's predictions refer to retired individuals, with retirement age being as in table 11.1 for 2000 and at 65 years for 2050.

this policy implication emerges from accounting exercises,[2] the simulations in this book highlight the relevance of this measure even in a political economy context where a change in the effective retirement age alters the voting behavior of individuals.[3] Clearly, postponing retirement is beneficial in those countries with a low effective retirement age, such as France and Italy. In Germany and Spain, the impact would still be sizable, and in the United Kingdom and the United States, raising the retirement age would only induce a reduction of about 3 percent. Interestingly in all countries but the United States, an increase in the effective retirement age is also forecasted to increase the pension replacement rate because of a reduction in the ratio of retirees to workers, which would counterbalance the population aging process. Despite the mitigating effect of postponing retirement, for all countries but Italy the simulations presented in table 11.1 nevertheless forecast a sizable increase in pension spending. These results raise a crucial question. Young workers may represent a minority in the political arena, but will they be willing to continue working, even though their labor earnings are so heavily taxed? The simulations in table 11.3 address this issue by explicitly analyzing the individual working decisions in a more comprehensive economic environment, in which workers of any age may choose to respond to a large increase in the social security contribution rate by reducing their labor supply. By

Table 11.3
Model with labor market distortions: Simulation results

		Median voter's age	Effective retirement age	Social security contribution rate	Replace-ment rate
France	2000	47	58	22.4%	51.8%
	2050	56	58	39.0%	53.6%
	2050	56	65	27.2%	61.6%
Germany	2000	46	61	23.8%	67.6%
	2050	55	61	35.7%	50.0%
	2050	55	65	29.2%	55.4%
Italy	1992	44	58	38.0%	75.7%
	2050	56	58	46.2%	48.4%
	2050	56	65	35.5%	64.0%
Spain	2000	44	62	21.3%	89.7%
	2050	57	62	37.5%	65.2%
	2050	57	65	33.8%	89.8%
United Kingdom	2000	45	63	14.5%	74.8%
	2050	53	63	31.7%	91.6%
	2050	53	65	29.0%	104.2%
United States	2000	47	63%	9.7%	46.4%
	2050	53	63%	20.7%	57.3%
	2050	53	65%	18.7%	60.0%

Source: Galasso and Profeta (2004).
Note: For each country, the first line gives the year 2000 scenario; 2050 simulation results for contribution and replacement rates—using the model described in chapter 4, with endogenous labor supply—are at lines 2 and 3.

focusing on the labor market,[4] these simulations allow for an endogenous response within the economic environment to the political push for more pension spending. The quantitative analysis reported in table 11.3 thus evaluates whether the political pressure of a graying electorate prevails also in presence of labor market distortions.

Even the picture emerging from these simulations is gloomy, as social security spending is still forecasted to increase, albeit less than in the previous analysis. Surprisingly, the conservative effect played by the labor market distortion on the political decision is rather small in magnitude: the hike in the social security contribution rate is reduced at most by 8 percent in Spain, and by less than 1 percent in the United States. The explanation of this counterintuitive—and perhaps disappointing—result is in the role played by the real wages. Aging alters individuals' savings behavior and ultimately leads to an increase in real wages because of the increase in the stock of capital. If this phenomenon is sizable, the positive (substitution) effect due to the rise in wages may compensate the distortionary effect of higher taxation, and the labor supply may actually increase. Social security contributions may then fail to decrease substantially.

Also this set of simulations is in line with the conventional economic wisdom: postponing retirement age leads to lower social security contribution rates and may increase the pensions' replacement rate. Again, France and Italy, the countries featuring the lowest effective retirement age in 2000, would gain the most from this policy. In Italy an increase in the retirement age to 65 years, in line with the measures legislated by the Amato and Dini reforms, would be sufficient to reduce the size of the system, as compared to the 2000 scenario.

11.2 Country-Specific Features

The simulations discussed in the previous section emphasized age as the main line of redistribution in unfunded schemes—from young to elderly individuals—to quantify the effect of aging on social security. However, other redistributive flows of resources exist in many social security systems among individuals of the same cohort, for instance, from rich to poor or from two-earner to one-earner families in the United States. Although these elements of intragenerational redistribution can largely affect individuals' preferences over social security and hence shape a coalition of voters in favor of the system, they need not be influenced by the demographic process.

In recent years some countries have undertaken reform processes that will largely modify the redistributiveness of their system, thereby affecting also individuals' well-being and their preferences over social security. In 1995, Italy implemented the Dini reform (see chapter 7 for details), which converted a defined benefit system into a notional defined contribution scheme. This radical reform altered the generosity of the pension benefits mainly according to the individual lifetime income profile and contribution history, thereby modifying the redistributive characteristics of the Italian system. In 1999, the British Welfare Reform and Pension Act substituted an earnings-related program (SERPS) with a nearly flat rate scheme (S2P), thus increasing the redistributiveness of the British pension system (see chapter 9). Finally, the Spanish "silent reform" described in chapter 8 is extending the degree of redistribution of the system by slowly increasing the share of high-earnings individuals whose pension benefits are capped by the maximum pension. All these reforms are likely to create different political constraints from the ones analyzed in the previous section, and hence to lead to different requirements for the long-term political sustainability of these systems.

A comparison between the simulations' results presented in chapter 7 for Italy and those in table 11.1 confirms this view. When the intragenerational redistribution elements of the Amato and Dini reforms are explicitly considered, the simulations yield a larger social security system. For retirement ages at their 1992 (pre-reforms) level, the contribution rate projected for 2050 is a striking 61.1 percent, as opposed to 50 percent in table 11.1. Analogously, postponing retirement limits the hike of the contribution rate to 48.9 percent, as opposed to 38 percent. These higher estimates are due to the existence of a within-cohort redistributive element in the reform,[5] which increases the political support among the low- and middle-income individuals, and hence creates more political demand for pensions.

In 1999, the Welfare Reform and Pension Act increased the redistributive nature of the British pension system and replaced an earnings-related scheme (SERPS) with a nearly flat rate program, the State Second Pension. The goal of the reform was to guarantee additional pension benefits to low-income retirees in order to reduce their poverty rate. The simulations' results at chapter 9 suggest that this measure will have a major impact on the future political sustainability of the system, leading to higher contribution rates than predicted in table 11.1. Because of its stronger redistributive nature, the British system will draw additional political support among low-educated agents, while high-educated individuals will continue to exercise their option of contracting out of (part of) the system.

The silent reform of the Spanish system analyzed in chapter 8 goes in the direction of creating a more redistributive system, by altering the dynamics of the minimum and maximum pensions that provide respectively a floor and a cap on pension benefits. The simulations that account for this intragenerational redistributive element estimate higher contribution rates than those in table 11.1, again, because of the strong preferences induced among low-earners—who typically receive a minimum pension (see figure 8.3).

The difference in the magnitude of the results obtained by the two types of simulations suggests that any reform that modifies the redistributiveness of the system—making it more Beveridgean or more Bismarckian—may affect its long-term development. In particular, simulations in tables 11.1 and 11.3 may underestimate the effect of aging on those systems featuring a relevant within-cohort redistributive component and where reforms to the redistributiveness of the system have been implemented. The inference is that more Beveridgean systems will experience larger increases in the contribution rate.

However, this inference should be taken with some caution. The peculiar nature of these Beveridgean systems alters the composition of the voting coalition supporting social security. Contrary to the argument in chapters 3 and 4, Conde Ruiz and Profeta (2007) suggest that in a country featuring a Beveridgean system the voting majority supporting social security will not be composed of elderly and low-income middle-age workers. Because of their flat pension benefits these systems are often able to target low-income individuals at low cost, that is, for low social security contribution taxes. While low-income individuals clearly favor this highly redistributive program, also high income individuals may support an inexpensive pension scheme that allows them to save on contributions and hence to invest their resources in the private market. Conde Ruiz and Profeta (2007) in fact conclude that these Beveridgean systems may be supported by a voting coalition of the extreme, composed of low- and high-income individuals.

11.3   The Political Feasibility of Postponing Retirement

Despite the grim picture the simulations presented so far validate in a political economy setting the conventional view that some reform measures may be effective in keeping social security expenditure under control. A rise in the retirement age tends to mitigate the hike of the contribution rates, while increasing the disposable income for old age consumption. In this political economy environment the magnitude of this effect is large: in Italy and France, postponing retirement from 58 to 65 years would decrease the contribution rate by respectively 12 and 11.1 percent; similar results apply to the other countries where the reductions would range between 2.1 and 5.1 percent (see table 11.1).

Postponing retirement mitigates the growth in social security expenditures by weakening the impact of aging on the economic and political environment. The economic effect is reduced by a higher retirement age in that it increases the ratio of workers to retirees, counterbalancing the negative consequence of aging on the average return from social security. An increase in the retirement age also moderates the political pressure for a larger system stemming from an older electorate. In fact, postponing retirement expands the contribution period and reduces the length of retirement (see figure 3.1), thereby lowering the continuation return from the system for all individuals and hence also for the median voter. The simulation results suggest that, on average, a one year increase in the effective retirement age induces a reduction in the contribution rate by almost a one and half percentage point.

This section addresses the political feasibility of this policy measure. Will future voters be willing to support an increase in the retirement age? To provide an answer to this question, I consider a political environment in which agents determine the social security contribution rate, but also the effective retirement age. To retain the relevance of the policy-makers' electoral concerns (see chapter 3), a political regime of majority voting is still adopted. Yet in elections with multidimensional policy spaces, political equilibria in simple majority voting typically fail to exist, since voters are constantly induced to switch among alternative bundle of policies (see section 4.2.1). To overcome this well-known problem, while preserving the median voter framework in this more complex scenario, I introduce a bi-dimensional voting game, in which voters determine simultaneously, yet separately—that is, issue by issue—the two policies (see a detailed description at section 4.2.2 and in the appendix). This political environment (characterized as structure-induced equilibrium; see Shepsle 1979) effectively allows separate decisions on retirement age and social security contributions. In particular, individuals determine respectively their most preferred social security contribution rate, for any given retirement age, and their most preferred retirement age, for any given contribution rate. For each issue, a typically different median voter may hence be identified. The social security contribution rate and the effective retirement age supported by a majority of the voters—meaning the median voter for each issue—represent the equilibrium outcomes of the voting game.

Do individual preferences over the effective aggregate retirement age[6] for a given level of the social security contribution rate[7] differ according to the voter's age? And how do preferences depend on the social security contribution rate? In voting over the effective retirement age, for a given contribution rate, agents consider the individual labor–leisure trade-off associated with their retirement decision and evaluate also the impact that the overall retirement age will have on their own pension benefits, through changes in the dependency ratio and general equilibrium effects on rate of return and wages (see chapter 3). Elderly workers or retirees will typically favor setting the retirement age so as to maximize their own benefits. For instance, every retiree would potentially like to be the youngest of the group in order to minimize the number of people with whom to share resources. Younger individuals may be induced to set lower retirement ages to accelerate their retirement time, but they then would enjoy lower pension benefits at retirement. Which factor prevails cannot be determined a priori. Therefore, unlike the social security contribution rate, preference ordering over retirement age does not need to be monotonic with age.

Variations in the social security contribution rate typically induce the voters to modify their decision over the retirement age, because of substitution and income effects. In particular, a higher contribution rate reduces the net labor income and increases the pension benefit; the opportunity cost of retiring thus decreases, and voters prefer a lower effective retirement age. However, since in this economic environment social security is a dominated asset, a higher contribution rate reduces the overall income of the young, hence inducing them to postpone retirement. Again, which effect prevails cannot be established a priori.

The effect of population aging on these individual preferences over retirement—given the social security contribution rate—comes through two main channels. First, aging reduces the average profitability from social security. Given the large size of the system experienced by most countries, which an older median voter over the social security contribution rate may decide to expand even further, the drop in the social security returns generates a reduction in the lifetime income of future generations. This negative income effect will encourage individuals to postpone retirement. Second, in the context of a balanced budget system, for a given social security contribution rate, aging will reduce the pension benefits' replacement rate, as fewer resources will have to be shared among more retirees. This amounts to a negative substitution effect, which reduces the pecuniary incentives to retire early and leads to an increase in the retirement age. To summarize, while a graying population will exert political pressure to achieve more pension spending—because of an increase in the age of the pivotal voter over the social security contribution rate—aging will also generate political support for postponing retirement[8] through these negative income and substitution effects.

Table 11.4 presents the results of the simulations carried out within the framework, which allows for the contemporaneous political determination of social security contributions and retirement age. For each country, the first line describes the main features for the year 2000 (see also table 11.1), while the following lines characterize the equilibrium outcomes of this bi-dimensional voting game for the year 2050. A crucial result immediately emerges: in all countries the estimated effective retirement age increases with respect to the initial equilibrium in 2000.

Table 11.4
Postponing retirement: Simulation results

		Age of the median voter over contribution rate	Effective retirement age	Social security contribution rate
France	2000	47	58	22.4%
	2050	56	67	29.1%
Italy	1992	44	58	38.0%
	2050	56	67	34.9%
United Kingdom	2000	45	63	14.5%
	2050	53	70	27.1%
United States	2000	47	63	9.7%
	2050	53	68	13.5%
	2050	53	69	11.9%

Source: Galasso (2006).
Note: For each country, the effective retirement age and the social security contribution correspond to the political economy equilibria of the bidimensional voting game described in section 11.3.

Future voters will be willing to support a rise in the retirement age because of the negative economic impact of the aging process.

The largest increase in the effective retirement age—from 58 to 67 years—is forecasted to occur in France and Italy—the two countries featuring the smallest initial retirement age. In Italy, the dramatic aging process will create a sizable, negative income effect. For a retirement age of 67 years, the social security contribution rate will correspond to 34.9 percent, hence leading to a reduction in pension spending, in line with the EC-OECD estimates in table 2.3. Unlike in Italy, where the system in 1992 was notably large, in France the strong increase in the age of the median voter over the contribution rate will induce more pension spending, and thus higher contributions and more pension benefits. The reduction in the net labor income and the contemporaneous increase in the pension benefits create a pecuniary incentive to retire (a positive substitution effect), which partially compensates the negative (income) effect of aging. Overall, the retirement age will largely be postponed in France, but the social security contribution rate will still increase—from 22.4 to 27.1 percent. In the United Kingdom, the aging of the median voter over the contribution rate will lead to a substantial increase in the social security contribution rate and generate a positive substitution effect. Retirement age will increase by seven years, and the contribution rate will reach 27.1 percent. In the United States, the negative income effect of aging is expected to be more moderate, but also the increase in the age of the median voter over the contribution rate is estimated not to have a massive impact on the contribution rate (see table 11.1). Interestingly the United States features multiple equilibria, with the retirement age ranging from 68 to 69 years, while the corresponding contribution rates remain between 11.9 and 13.5 percent. The simulation results in table 11.4 do not include Germany and Spain, where the political equilibrium fails to exist, since the preferences of the voters over the retirement age are not single-peaked (see the appendix).

The simulations presented in this section on the simultaneous political determination of social security contribution rate and retirement age (see table 11.4) shed a new light on the political viability[9] of the most commonly endorsed reform measure: postponing retirement. When all political constraints are considered, the retirement age is expected to increase in all countries, thereby mitigating the rise in the social security contribution rates. According to these simulations, Italy will benefit the most from this policy, whereas France and the United

Kingdom are still estimated to experience a large increase in pension spending.

11.4   Delegating Pension Policy: A Role for the European Commission?

In recent years there has been a growing attention among EU institutions to the challenges posed by an aging population to the EU pension systems. The 2001 Laeken European Council launched the so-called open method of co-ordination on pensions, featuring eleven common objectives for country member's social security systems on such topics as social protection and financial sustainability. A year later each country submitted a National Strategy Report on Pension to detail its individual plan on how to meet these common objectives. These reports were then analyzed by the European Commission in an effort to assess the degree of achievement of these common goals.

Is there any sound economic motive behind this desire for coordination? Aside from concerns on portability of pension claims, which may reduce labor mobility across EU countries, one may argue that there is indeed little role for EU coordination. Social security systems around Europe—albeit all PAYG—differ in several crucial characteristics, such as size, benefit calculation formulas, eligibility requirements, and effective retirement age (see chapter 2). Most systems also differ in their goals. In the United Kingdom and the Netherlands, for instance, rather small Beveridgean schemes are designed to reduce poverty among the elderly, whereas in most other countries large Bismarckian systems represent forced savings schemes aimed at guaranteeing sufficient old age consumption, in which any redistributive element, such as minimum noncontributory pensions, is typically financed through general taxation. To the extent that these disparities may reflect different attitudes toward the welfare state or a different organization of the society—perhaps related to the role of the family—local governments should be in a better position to design redistributive schemes that best suit each country's needs. Hence EU coordination may only aim at targeting each system's financial sustainability, possibly by including the social security implicit debt in the existing Stability and Growth Pact criteria on the public sector deficits and debts.

There may, however, be political reasons behind this recent interest for a common European policy on pensions.[10] As suggested by the simulations in this chapter, the effects of aging on national politics are likely to induce the policy-makers, who are politically accountable toward their graying electorate, to increase the size of the system. The position of the politicians may, however, be more complex than acknowledged by these simulations. Politicians may face a trade-off: an increase in the social security contribution rate needed to keep the pension's replacement rate constant will please a graying electorate, thus boosting the politicians' probability of being re-elected, but may entail some costs. For instance, politicians may have individual preferences in favor of a smaller size of the system, as did the Thatcher government in the United Kingdom during the eighties. Perhaps more important, a large pension system and its likely distortionary effects on labor and financial markets may reduce economic growth, thereby negatively affecting another crucial determinant of re-election. In such scenarios national governments may be willing to delegate pension policies to supranational institutions, such as the European Commission, in order to shift the political cost of a reform decision onto these institutions. National governments, acting to meet EU criteria on pension's financial sustainability, could blame the Europe for any unpopular reform and hence reduce their political accountability.

The European economy history of the last two decades suggests that this delegation of decisions to the EU has proved successful in many instances, such as monetary, exchange rate, and competition policy, in order to "tie the (national) government hands." The use of external constraints allowed many European countries to pursue long-term goals, despite short-term loses, and sensitive redistributive issues (see Boeri et al. 2006). The shift of political burden to the European Union —in particular, to the European Commission—is partially facilitated by the deficit of democratic representation featured by the EC. In fact the Commission needs not be composed of political representatives, such as the members of the European Parliament, and hence is not directly accountable to the European voters. This lack of "political accountability" may also give the Commission enough room to impose some common criteria to reform the EU pension systems along the suggestions contained in the EC reports on adequate and sustainable pensions. The Commission would give voice and political weight to those young, or yet to be born, individuals who cannot vote today but will be asked to foot the bill tomorrow.

All these changes come at the cost of undermining the popularity of European institutions. The recent failures to ratify a European constitution at the referendum held in France and the Netherlands in spring

2005 illustrate the limits of this delegation strategy. External constraints may allow policy-makers to buy time, but the long-term gains of reforming need eventually to be identified by the population at large, or a majority of the voters will oppose delegating powers to the European Union, whenever given the opportunity to express their views. The sensitiveness of the redistributive issues involved and the likely long time horizon of the potential gains from reforming—for instance, in terms of reducing the distortions in the economy and enhancing growth—suggest that delegation may be ill suited for social security issues.

Technical Appendix

This appendix describes the political economy model used in section 11.3 to simulate the political sustainability of postponing retirement. To allow the voters to express their preferences over two issues—the social security contribution rate and the retirement age—the basic model described in chapter 4, and used throughout the book, has been somewhat modified.

The Economic Environment

The economic environment still consists of an overlapping generations general equilibrium model, with no heterogeneity among individuals of the same age. Additionally labor supply decisions are assumed to be exogenous—thereby corresponding to the first specification of the model at chapter 4—with no labor market distortions. The model is enriched by introducing a linear utility from leisure: if individuals decide to work one additional year, they have to give up this annual utility level v. The relevant period utility function thus becomes

$$U(c_{t+j}^t, v_{t+j}^t) = \frac{(c_{t+j}^t)^{1-\rho} - 1}{1 - \rho} + v_{t+j}^t, \tag{A.1}$$

where v_{t+j}^t, which denotes annual leisure at time $t + j$ for an individual born at time t, is a binary variable taking value zero if the individual works at $t + j$, and a positive value if she does not (e.g., if she retires). The remaining description of the economy is analogous to the one in chapter 4.

The Political System

The major departure from the model introduced at chapter 4 is in the political system. To assess the political feasibility of postponing retirement, political decisions on both the social security contribution rate τ and the retirement age J are examined. To retain the relevance of the electoral concerns, as discussed in chapter 3, a political regime of majority voting is still used, but unlike in chapter 4, I will only discuss a once-and-for-all voting game. I leave to the reader the consideration on the implicit social contract among successive generations of voters that may emerge in a repeated voting environment, and cause some workers to support the system, with a certain retirement age (see also Galasso 2006).

A well-known result in the voting literature is that when the policy space over which individuals vote on is multidimensional, a Nash equilibrium of the voting game may fail to exist unless restrictive assumptions on the preferences of the electors are imposed. To overcome this problem, I follow Shepsle (1979) in analyzing voting equilibria[1] induced by institutional restrictions, meaning structure-induced equilibria.

To characterize how the political system aggregates individual preferences over the alternatives into a political outcome (τ, J) under this structure-induced equilibrium, an institutional arrangement has to be introduced that allows issue-by-issue voting.[2] An arrangement is composed of a committee system, a jurisdictional arrangement, an assignment rule, and an amendment control rule. The committee system separates the electorate—namely the set of all voters—into committees. The jurisdictional arrangement divides the issues (τ, J) into jurisdictions. Jurisdictions are then relegated to committees, according to an assignment rule. This way the political system directs the decision over a subset of the issue space (e.g., a single issue) to a particular committee. Every committee is entitled to make a proposal to change the current value of the issue (the status quo) that falls into its jurisdiction. The amendment control rule determines how proposals can be further modified (amended) by the electorate before the final stage is reached, and the (possibly amended) proposal is then voted in a majority rule, pairwise comparison against the status quo by the entire electorate.

The political system that allows the contemporaneous, yet separate vote on the two issues is characterized by the following arrangements:

• *Committee of the whole.* There exists only one committee, which coincides with the electorate.

• *Simple jurisdictions.* Each jurisdiction is a single dimension of the issue space, $\{\{\tau\}, \{J\}\}$. In other words, one jurisdiction has the power to deliberate on the social security contribution rate τ and another on the retirement age J.

• *Assignment rule.* Every simple jurisdiction is assigned to the committee of whole.

• *Germaneness amendment control rule.* Amendments to the proposal are permitted only along the dimensions that fall in the jurisdiction of the committee. That is, if the proposal regards τ, only amendments on τ are permitted, and vice versa.

In this political system the entire electorate has jurisdiction (it is entitled to make proposals) on the two issues, but only separately, which is issue by issue. The restriction that each issue is on the floor separately is achieved through simple jurisdictions and the germaneness amendment rule, and this restriction is needed to overcome the possible lack of Nash equilibrium. No further restrictive jurisdictional arrangements are imposed. The choice of a committee of the whole, for example, guarantees that no subset of the electorate that constitutes a committee is effectively awarded veto power over an issue. Any such committee can block an alternative to the status quo that is preferred by a majority of the electorate but not by a majority of the members of this committee.

This notion of structure-induced equilibrium retains the flavor of the median voter theorem—the political workhorse of this book. The next proposition characterizes the structure-induced equilibrium used in the simulations at section 11.3 (for a proof, see Shepsle 1979).

Proposition Let X_i^* be the set of ith components from the induced ideal points of all voters in the direction i from the status quo x^o. For one-dimensional (simple) jurisdictions, a germaneness rule for amendments, a committee of the whole, and single-peaked preferences, x^o is a structure-induced equilibrium outcome if and only if, for all i, $x_i^o = \text{median } X_i^*$.

Calibration

To evaluate quantitatively the political feasibility of postponing retirement, in the new economic framework, the annual utility level from retirement, v, has to be calibrated to obtain the effective retirement age observed in 2000, as the structure-induced equilibrium outcome of the voting game. The calibrated parameters used in the simulations of section 11.3 are 1.7 for France, 1.8 for Italy, 2.9 for the United Kingdom, and 0.75 for the United States.

Data Appendix

This appendix presents the sources of the demographic, economic, and political data used throughout the book, as well as the source of information on the structure and the reforms of the social security systems.

Demographics

The actual and forecasted life expectancy at birth for all countries are taken from OECD (2002), Health Data, and from the EC Economic Policy Committee (2000). The actual and the forecasted structure of the population by age, the percentage of elderly in the population, and the old age dependency ratio were obtained for the European countries from the Eurostat Data shop (Population projections version v.1999 DE base) and for the US online from the US Census Bureau at ⟨www.census.gov⟩. For the European countries, the 2050 expected old age dependency ratio are taken from the EC Economic Policy Committee (2000) and from EC (2003). The latest survival probabilities by age were obtained from the national statistical institutes, which, in the case of France and the United States, provide also projections on survival probabilities by age for the year 2050.

Labor Market

For the European countries, the average employment rate by age is calculated using (1998) European Commission Household Panel (ECHP) data, while for the United States, I use the Bureau of Labor Statistics, *Employment and Earnings*. Analogously, the wage rates by age—needed to construct the labour efficiency unit profile by age—are obtained from ECHP data for the European countries, and from US Census Bureau, *Current Population Report*, for the United States. Working histories by education are calculated from the Bank of Italy Household Panel for Italy, from INE's Active Population Survey for Spain, from ECHP for the United Kingdom and from the US Census Bureau, *Current Population Survey*, for the United States. Information on male retirement age in the 1990s and in the 1950s is taken from ILO data (Latulippe 1996). Data on effective retirement age for the year 2000 are obtained from the Bank of Italy Household Panel for Italy (for 1992), from EC (2003) joint report for France, Germany, Spain, and the United Kingdom, and from Gruber and Wise (1999) for the United States.

Political and Economic Data

In the calculation of the median age among voters, we include the election's turnout rates by age, taken from IDEA (1999), *Young Voters Participation*, for European countries, from US Census Bureau, *Reported Voting and Registration* ⟨www.census.gov⟩ for the United States, and from Abacus (1999) survey data for Italy. Regarding economic data, values of the average capital share are taken from national accounts. The long-term characteristics of each economy, as characterized by the capital–output ratio, are taken from several sources: for France, Germany, the United Kingdom, and the United States from Maddison (1995); for Italy, from D'Amato and Galasso (2002); and for Spain, from Puch and Licandro (1997). Also the exogenous productivity growths, which are measured by the average per-capita GDP growth rate, are taken from different sources: the EC Economic Policy Committee (2000) for the 1990s average value for France, Germany, and the United Kingdom; D'Amato and Galasso (2002) for Italy; national accounts for Spain, and Galasso (1999) for the United States. In the simulations, I use the projections for the year 2050 in the EC Economic Policy Committee (2000) and keep the 1990s average value for the United States.

Pension Systems

Most of the information on the pension systems of the European countries is obtained from the SSA publication *Social Security throughout the World* from the EC Economic Policy Committee (2000) and from the Economic Policy Committee (2002), *Reform Challenges Facing Public Pension System*. Information on the US social security system can be obtained online from the US SSA Web site. Additional information on pension reforms are taken mainly from the EC DG Employment and

Social Affairs (2002) *Social Protection in Europe 2001*, from the Economic Policy Committee (2002), *Reform Challenges Facing Public Pension System*, and from a Rodolfo De Benedetti report (2001), *Monitoring Slow Pension Reforms in Europe* ⟨www.frdb.org⟩. Official pension spending projections are from OECD (2002). Composition of retirement income (see table 11.2) is taken from Borsch-Supan, Reil-Held, and Schnabel (2001) for Germany, Brugiavini and Fornero (2001) for Italy, Emmerson and Johnson (2001) for the United Kingdom, Joustein (2001) for the United States, and Legendre and Pelé (2001) for France. US data on OASI trust fund and social security and health care are projections from the Congressional Budget Office available online at ⟨www.cbo .gov⟩.

Notes

Chapter 1

1. In a defined benefit scheme, pension benefits are based on the individuals' average wage prior to retirement, and possibly on the number of years of contribution and on the retirement age.

Chapter 2

1. In France, additional contributions are made to a second tier, unfunded scheme: namely 6 percent for the employees belonging to ARRCO and 16 percent for those under the AGIRC scheme. More details are provided in chapter 5.

2. Since 2002, people older than 66 years retiring with at least 35 years of contributions may receive more than 100 percent.

3. The 2004 reform rises the minimum retirement age to 60 years beginning in 2008 for the workers still under the defined benefit scheme.

4. This measure differs from the actual ratio between contributors and beneficiaries, since it does not consider the activity rate among the potential workers and does not single out the actual recipients among the elderly.

Chapter 3

1. The more comprehensive economic and political environment used in the simulations at chapters 5 to 11 is presented in the next chapter.

2. An exception is the environment proposed by Tabellini (2000), in which (low-income) workers are willing to support the system, because of their weak altruism toward their parents, even in the absence of a future transfer.

3. A formal argument is provided at section 4.2.2.

4. Whether some young or adults individuals decide to comply with this implicit contract depends on the economic reasons analyzed in the previous section.

5. Pierson (1996) also notices that the rapid decrease in the political relevance of unions and left parties in some countries was not matched by corresponding cuts in social spending.

6. A more complex voting model—known as issue-by-issue voting or structure-induced-equilibrium (see Shepsle 1979)—which retains the flavor of the median voter, is instead applied to the multidimensional voting issues analyzed at section 11.3 (see also section 4.2.1 and the appendix).

Chapter 4

1. In a different specification of the model, agents vote on the social security contribution rate and also on the retirement age (see section 4.2.1, the appendix and the simulation results at section 11.3).

2. Despite the demographic dynamics in the last decade of the twentieth century can hardly be viewed as stationary, the modeling choice of considering the year 2000 as the initial steady state for the analysis is based on the observation that—as argued at chapter 3—the initial social security policy response to the first stages of the aging process has been rather mild. The bulk of the adjustment to aging is hence yet to come, and may be captured by the simulations for the year 2050.

3. It is straightforward to compact the notation for the simulations with no horizontal heterogeneity, that is, with a unique education group, $Q = 1$, as in chapters 5, 6, and 11.

4. The simulations carried out with this specification provide an upper bound on the distortionary effect of social security on the labor supply, since the entire contribution rate is considered as a distortionary tax rate regardless of the degree of redistributiveness of the system (see Disney 2004).

5. In Galasso's (1999) calculations, the results are not qualitatively different under these alternative specifications.

6. In section 4.2.2 a multidimensional policy environment is discussed, in which agents determine also the retirement age. The results of the associated simulations are presented in section 11.3.

7. The theoretical model presented at section 4.1 abstracts from any altruistic considerations; hence, preferences over social security are a pure expression of self interest. Yet individuals may also be altruistic—or simply fair—for instance, because they dislike large inequality in the society (see Galasso 2003). The introduction of fair agents, who averse inequality among the elderly—or consider retirement as a merit good (see Profeta 2002a)—increases the political support for social security. However, even in this altruistic environment the effect of aging on the political support for pensions is likely to be qualitatively similar to the one analyzed in the book, since young individuals will have to trade off their fairness toward an increasing number of elderly with the self-interest associated with the rising cost of the system.

8. Notice that throughout the book the calculation of the share of voters in each generation and education group considers the different participation rates at elections of individuals by age and education. This theoretical framework, however, abstains from modeling the individuals' decision of whether to vote or to abstain. For a discussion of this "voting paradox," see Wolfinger and Rosenstone (1980).

9. Notice that—due to the balanced budget assumption—the contribution rate determines also the average replacement rate of the system.

Chapter 5

1. Bonoli (2000) argued that the role of the unions in running these supplementary schemes was crucial in the reform processes in the 1990s—see also section 5.1.1.

2. An assessment by gender shows that female workers enjoy on average 26.4 years of retirement, if employed in the public sector, and 21.2, if in the private sector. These differences in the average length of retirement by sector and gender tend to introduce some redistributive features in the French pension system, which is otherwise mainly designed as a Bismarckian, nonredistributive scheme.

3. One quarter's insurance is acquired when the remuneration equals at least 200 hours of the minimum wage.

4. The reference period has increased by one year for every year of birth from 10 years in 1992, and is set to reach 25 years in 2008, regardless of the year of birth of the insured.

Chapter 6

1. In the literature, nonredistributive pension schemes are often referred to as Bismarckian, after the founding father of the German system.

2. Börsch-Supan and Reil-Held (2001) indeed estimate the magnitude of the intragenerational redistribution element in the German system to be around 18 percent of total pension budget.

3. This was meant to eliminate the perverse effect of an increase in the contributions needed to finance the pensions leading to even higher pension benefits.

4. For a detailed explanation of the working of this "sustainability factor," see Börsch-Supan and Wilke (2004).

5. According to Börsch-Supan et al. (2004) survey, 60 percent of the respondents would favour opting out of the system.

6. Several additional and more generous early retirement schemes were made available to middle-aged workers in specific sectors, such as textile and automobile.

7. Aging leads to higher wages, but also to lower returns from savings because of an increase in the stock of capital. In the case of Germany, the overall estimated effect for a young individual is a reduction in lifetime wealth.

8. See the discussion of the model in chapter 4.

9. The forecasted replacement rates reported at table 6.2 are sensibly lower than in the previous scenario, in part because of the lower contribution rates and in part because of the increase in the number of hours worked prior to retirement, which increase the reference labor earnings in the calculation of the replacement rate.

Chapter 7

1. A survey carried out in Italy in 2000 by Boeri et al. (2002) shows that almost three out of four interviewed individuals expected a pension crisis to occur in the next ten to fifteen

years, when the government will become unable to pay current pension levels, and hence expected a reform to take place in the next ten years to reduce pension benefits.

2. Also the 2004 reform featured a transition period, which protected from these measures the same workers already shielded in the 1995 reform.

3. Married women employed in the public sector could retire with only fifteen years of contributions, regardless of their age.

4. In periods of medium to high inflation, this provision hence constituted a source of inexpensive internal funding for the firms.

5. Several scholars have highlighted the novelty of these reform measures, which represented a major change with respect to the past legislation. See, among others, Brugiavini and Fornero (2001), Brugiavini and Galasso (2004), Castellino (1995), Castellino and Fornero (1997), Franco (2002), Giarda (1998), Gronchi (1998), Gronchi and Aprile (1998), Peracchi and Rossi (1998), and Tumbarello (2000).

6. The replacement rate remained equal to the number of years of contribution multiplied by a 2 percent rate of return, but because of the typical hump shape of the earnings profile, this enlargement of the calculation period typically reduced the average reference wage, and hence the average pension.

7. Gronchi and Aprile (1998) also criticize the choice of capitalizing the contributions at a predetermined rate equal to 1.5 percent and emphasize that the new system may experience financial troubles if the average GDP growth drops below 1.5 percent for some time.

8. In the Italian scenario before the reforms, the existence of a deficit violates this assumption, albeit it greatly simplifies the analysis. The main drawback of this assumption is to disregard the redistributive effects induced by the two main alternative instruments used to finance the social security deficit: general taxation and public debt.

9. See Peracchi and Rossi (1998), Giarda (1998), Gronchi and Aprile (1998), and Brugiavini and Galasso (2004).

Chapter 8

1. Public employees are covered by the *Régimen de Clases Pasivas* and by other special schemes financed by general revenues. For a detailed treatment of the Spanish social security system, see Boldrin, Jimenez, and Peracchi (2000).

2. There actually exist four different floors applying to separate classes of workers, displaying similar trends.

3. Notice that the statutory contribution rate is actually equal to 28.3 percent, due to additional nonpension benefits being financed through social security contributions.

4. This small effect is partly due to the large reduction in the earning profile by age of all individuals, who have reached their fifties. Hence postponing retirement increases total contributions, but less than elsewhere, because of the more moderate labor income of the Spanish elderly workers.

5. The simulations for the year 2000 do not consider the existence of maximum pensions, as all high-earners are assumed to receive regular old age pension benefits.

6. This represents a conservative assumption; Conde-Ruiz and Alonso (2004) forecast the share of these maximum pensions to reach 40 percent by 2050.

Chapter 9

1. Conde-Ruiz and Profeta (2007) suggest that this mix of private and public involvement in the provision of old age pensions represents a stable politico-economic equilibrium supported by a coalition of the extreme. Low-income workers enjoy the redistributive nature of the British social security system, whereas high-income individuals appreciate its relatively small fiscal burden and the opportunity of contracting out of its earnings-related pillar into more profitable occupational or private plans.

2. See Conde-Ruiz and Profeta (2007) for a discussion of the political coalition, which may support a highly redistributive system with contracting out.

3. For a discussion of the politics of retrenching and specifically of the Thatcher reforming experience, see chapter 3.

4. For instance, in the Maxwell scandal, Robert Maxwell, the owner of Mirror Group newspapers, used his company pension scheme money to ease the financial problems of his falling empire.

5. Since 1997, retirees eligible to BSP with no private income may, however, be brought up to a full pension by the Pension Credit Guarantees.

6. Notice that LEL and UEL are adjusted for the inflation, while primary and secondary thresholds have only recently been equalized.

7. Notice that earnings below the lower earning threshold (LET), but above the LEL, are counted as being equal to the LET in the benefit formula of equation (9.4). This provides an additional element of intragenerational redistribution.

Chapter 10

1. Concerns for its financial sustainability have been present since the early days of the US system. In his message to the congress on social security (in January 1935, seven months before the establishment of the social security system), Franklin D. Roosevelt stated his crucial principle: "First, the system adopted, except for the money necessary to initiate it, should be self-sustaining in the sense that funds for the payment of insurance benefits should not come from the proceeds of general taxation."

2. This double procedure contained a flaw, which led to a large increase in pension benefits. This problem—known as the "notch"—was later addressed by the 1977 amendment.

3. In 1981 individual retirement plans were made available to all workers.

4. For more details on these proposals see the *Report of the 1994–1996 Advisory Council on Social Security, vol. 1: Findings and Recommendations*, 1997, available at ⟨www.ssa.gov⟩.

5. Individuals were left with little options in terms of portfolio composition choice.

6. In 1980, participants in defined contribution plans amounted to 19.9 millions Americans, as opposed to 38 millions in defined benefit plans, whereas in 1998, 41.6 millions individuals participated in defined benefit plans and 57.9 in defined contribution.

7. Different specifications of the median voter in terms of marital status, income, and family structure are also considered.

8. A similar analysis was also in Galasso (1999).

Chapter 11

1. For Italy the initial scenario is taken to be the year 1992, in order to evaluate the political sustainability of the 1992, 1995, and 2004 reforms.

2. In countries where pensions are not actuarially fair at the margin (see Fenge and Pestieau 2006), an increase in the effective retirement age reduces pension spending, as the decrease in the early retirement benefits is not compensated by an associate rise in the old age pensions.

3. Section 11.3 addresses the political feasibility of this policy.

4. The responsiveness of labor decisions—as well as of investment decisions—to fiscal pressure is analyzed in Daveri and Tabellini (2000). Disney (2004) examines the specific distortionary effects of social security contribution on employment decisions.

5. Replacement rates increase from 59 to 69 percent and from 69 to 77 percent for low- and medium-educated people but drop from 69 to 61 percent for high-educated individuals.

6. Notice that all individuals are forced to retire at the same age.

7. Individual preferences on social security contribution rate for a given retirement age are extensively discussed at chapters 3 and 4.

8. Aging will also increase the share of very elderly individuals—who are likely to support late retirement—and of middle-aged agents. However, since preferences over retirement age are not monotonic with age, the overall effect of the change in the political representation by age on the retirement age decision is uncertain.

9. See also the political economy analysis in Conde-Ruiz, Galasso, and Profeta (2005).

10. On the eve of the EU presidency in the second semester of 2003, the Italian government often argued in favor of introducing pension policies among the topics to be decided at the European level.

Appendix A

1. Conde-Ruiz and Galasso (2003 and 2005) generalize this methodology to repeated games to obtain a subgame perfect structure-induced equilibrium.

2. See Shepsle (1979) for a formal discussion.

Bibliography

Aaron, H. 1966. The social insurance paradox. *Canadian Journal of Economics and Political Science* 32: 371–74.

Abacus. 1999. Exit—poll, European elections.

Acemoglu, D., and J. Robinson. 2000. Why did the West extend the franchise? Growth, inequality and democracy in historical perspective. *Quarterly Journal of Economics* 115: 1167–99.

Acemoglu, D., and J. Robinson. 2001. A theory of political transition. *American Economic Review* 91: 938–63.

Alonso, J., and J. A. Herce. 2003. Balance del sistema de pensiones y boom migratorio en España. Proyecciones del modelo MODPENS de FEDEA a 2050. Documento de trabajo de FEDEA 2003-02.

Azariadis, C., and V. Galasso. 2002. Fiscal constitutions. *Journal of Economic Theory* 103: 255–81.

Bank of Italy. 1995. *Survey on Consumption and Wealth.*

Banting, K., and R. Boadway. 1997. Reform of retirement income policy: International and Canadian perspectives. Kingston (Canada), Queen's University, School of Policy Studies.

Barbi, E. 2001. Aggiornamento ed analisi delle caratteristiche strutturali dei coefficienti di trasformazione previsti dalla legge 335/1995, in Commissione per la Garanzia dell'Informazione Statistica, Presidenza del Consiglio dei Ministri, Completezza e Qualità delle Informazioni Statistiche Utilizzabili Per La Valutazione della Spesa Pensionistica. Rapporto di Ricerca coordinato da F. Peracchi, Rome.

Béland, D. 2001. Does labor matter? Institutions, labour unions and pension reforms in France and the United States. *Journal of Public Policy* 21: 153–72.

Beltrametti, L. 1995. Le Pensioni tra Solidarietà e Sostenibilità. *Il Ponte* 2–3: 71–94.

Beltrametti, L. 1996. *Il Debito Pensionistico in Italia.* Bologna: Il Mulino.

Blake, D. 2003. The UK pension system: Key issues. *Pensions* 8: 330–75.

Blanchet, D., and F. Legros. 2002. France: The difficult path to consensual reforms. In M. Feldstein and H. Siebert, eds., *Social Security Pension Reform in Europe.* Chicago: Chicago University Press.

Blanchet, D., and L.-P. Pelé. 1999. Social security in France. In J. Gruber and D. Wise, eds., *Social Security and Retirement around the World*. Chicago: University of Chicago Press.

Blöndal, S., and S. Scarpetta. 1998. The retirement decision in OECD countries. OECD Working Paper AWP 1.4.

Boeri, T., A. Börsch-Supan, and G. Tabellini. 2002. Pension reforms and the opinions of European citizens. *American Economic Review* 92: 396–401.

Boeri, T., A. Brugiavini, and L. Carmfors. 2001. *The Role of the Unions in the Twenty-first Century*. Oxford: Oxford University Press.

Boeri, T., M. Castanheira, R. Faini, and V. Galasso. 2006. *Structural Reforms without Prejudices*. Oxford: Oxford University Press.

Bohn, H. 1999. Will social security and medicare remain viable as the U.S. population is aging? *Carnagie Rochester Conference Series on Public Policy* 50: 1–53.

Bohn, H. 2005. Will social security and medicare remain viable as the U.S. population is aging? An Update. In R. Brooks and A. Razin, eds., *The Politics and Finance of Social Security Reform*. Cambridge: Cambridge University Press.

Boldrin, M., and A. Rustichini. 2000. Political equilibria with social security. *Review of Economic Dynamics* 3: 41–78.

Boldrin, M., S. Jimenez, and F. Peracchi. 2000. *Sistema de pensiones y mercado de trabajo en España*. Madrid: Fundacion BBVA.

Boldrin, M., S. Jimenez, and A. Sanchez. 2000. *Incentivos a permanecer en activo y pensiones minimas: Algunas propuesta de reforma*. Madrid: Hacienda Publica Española.

Bonoli, G. 2000. *The Politics of Pension Reform*. Cambridge University Press.

Bordo, M. D., C. Goldin, and E. N. White. 1998. *The Defining Moment: The Great Depression and the American Economy in the Twentieth Century*. Chicago: University of Chicago Press.

Borgmann, C., P. Krimmer, and B. Raffelhuschen. 2001. Rentenreformen 1998–2001: Eine (vorlaufige) Bestandsaufnahme. Universitat Freiburg Discussion Papers 92/01.

Börsch-Supan, A., F. Heiss, and J. Winter. 2004. Akzeptanzprobleme bei Renterreformen: Wie die Bevölkerung überzeugt werden kann. Deutsches Institut für Altersvorsorge, Köln.

Börsch-Supan, A., and A. Reil-Held. 2001. How much is transfer and how much insurance in a Pay-as-you-go System? The German case. *Scandinavian Journal of Economics* 103: 505–24.

Börsch-Supan, A., A. Reil-Held, and R. Schnabel. 2001. Pension Provision in Germany. In R. Disney and P. Johnson, eds., *Pension Systems and Retirement Incomes across OECD Countries*. London: Edward Elgar.

Börsch-Supan, A., and R. Schnabel. 1999. Social security and retirement in Germany. In J. Gruber and D. Wise, eds., *Social Security and Retirement around the World*. Chicago: University of Chicago Press.

Börsch-Supan, A., and C. B. Wilke. 2004. The German public pension system: How it was, how it will be. NBER Working paper 10525. Cambridge, MA.

Boskin, M. J., L. J. Kotlikoff, D. J. Puffert, and J. B. Shoven. 1987. Social security: A financial appraisal across and within generations. *National Tax Journal* 40: 19–34.

Brooks, R., and A. Razin. 2005. *The Politics and Finance of Social Security Reform*. Cambridge: Cambridge University Press.

Browning, E. 1975. Why the social insurance budget is too large in a democracy. *Economic Inquiry* 13: 373–88.

Brugiavini, A. 1999. Social security and retirement in Italy. In J. Gruber and D. Wise, eds., *Social Security and Retirement around the World*. Chicago: University of Chicago Press.

Brugiavini, A., B. Ebbinghaus, R. Freeman, P. Garibaldi, B. Holmund, M. Schludi, and T. Verdier. 2001. What do unions do to the welfare state? In T. Boeri, A. Brugiavini, and L. Carmfors, eds., *The Role of the Unions in the Twenty-first Century*. Oxford: Oxford University Press.

Brugiavini, A., and E. Fornero. 2001. Pension provision in Italy. In R. Disney and P. Johnson, eds., *Pension Systems and Retirement Incomes across OECD Countries*. London: Edward Elgar.

Brugiavini, A., and V. Galasso. 2004. The social security reform process in Italy: Where do we stand? *Journal of Pension Economics and Finance* 3: 1–31.

Brugiavini, A., and F. Peracchi. 2001. Fiscal implications of social security reforms in Italy. Mimeo.

Buffeteau, S., and P. Godefroy. 2005. Conditions de départ en retraite selon l'age de fin d'études: Analyse prospective pour les generations 1945 à 1974. INSEE Working paper G 2005/01.

Caldwell, S. B., M. Favreault, A. Gantman, J. Gokhale, T. Johnson, and L. Kotlikoff. 1999. Social security's treatment of postwar Americans. In J. M. Poterba, ed., *Tax Policy and the Economy*. Cambridge: MIT Press.

Casamatta, G., H. Cremer, and P. Pestieau. 1999. The political economy of social security. CORE Discussion paper 9955.

Castellino, O. 1995. Redistributions between and within generations in the Italian social security system. *Ricerche Economiche* 49: 317–27.

Castellino, O., and E. Fornero. 1997. From PAYG to funding in Italy: A feasible transition? Mimeo.

Clark, R. L., R. V. Burkhauser, M. Moon, J. F. Quinn, and T. M. Smeeding. 2004. *The Economics of an Aging Society*. Oxford: Blackwell Publishing.

Colin, C., F. Legros, and R. Mahieu. 2000. Des spécificités institutionnelles aux rendements des régimes de retraite: Une comparaison des secteurs public/privé par microsimulation. *Revue économique* 51: 97–114.

Conde-Ruiz, J. I., and J. Alonso. 2004. El futuro de las pensiones en España: Perspectivas y lecciones. *Información Comercial Española, Revista de Economía* 815: 155–173.

Conde-Ruiz, J. I., and V. Galasso. 2003. Early retirement. *Review of Economic Dynamics* 6: 12–36.

Conde-Ruiz, J. I., and V. Galasso. 2004. The macroeconomics of early retirement. *Journal of Public Economics* 88: 1849–69.

Conde-Ruiz, J. I., and V. Galasso. 2005. Positive arithmetic of the welfare state. *Journal of Public Economics* 89: 933–55.

Conde-Ruiz, J. I., V. Galasso, and P. Profeta. 2005. The evolution of retirement. CEPR Discussion paper 4863.

Conde-Ruiz, J. I., and P. Profeta. 2007. The redistributive design of social security systems. *Economic Journal*, forthcoming.

Cogan, J. F., and O. S. Mitchell. 2003. The role of economic policy in social security reform: Perspective from the President's Commission. *Journal of Economic Perspective* 17: 149–72.

Congressional Budget Office data available at ⟨www.cbo.gov⟩.

Cooley, T. F., and J. Soares. 1996. Will social security survive the baby boom? *Carnegie Rochester Conference Series on Public Policy* 45: 89–121.

Cooley, T. F., and J. Soares. 1999. A positive theory of social security based on reputation. *Journal of Political Economy* 107: 135–60.

Cukierman, A., and A. Meltzer. 1989. A political theory of government debt and deficits in a neo-Ricardian framework. *American Economic Review* 79: 713–32.

Cutright, P. 1965. Political structure, economic development and national social security programs. *American Journal of Sociology* 70: 537–50.

D'Amato, M., and V. Galasso. 2002. Assessing the political sustainability of parametric social security reforms: The case of Italy. *Giornale degli Economisti e Annali di Economia* 61: 171–213.

D'Amato, M., and V. Galasso. 2003. Aggregate risk, political constraints and social security design. In M. Weale, ed., *Pension Reform: Redistribution and Risk*. London: NIESR.

Daveri, F., and G. Tabellini. 2000. Unemployment, growth and taxation in industrial countries. *Economic Policy* 15: 47–104.

Deaton, A., and C. Paxson. 1998. Economies of scale, household size, and the demand for food. *Journal of Political Economy* 106: 897–930.

Deaton, A., and C. Paxson. 2001. Mortality, education, income, and inequality among American cohorts. In D. Wise, ed., *The Economics of Aging*, vol. 8. Chicago: University of Chicago Press.

Diamond, P. 1996. Proposals to restructure social security. *Journal of Economic Perspectives* 10: 67–88.

Disney, R. 2004. Are contributions to public pension programmes a tax on employment? *Economic Policy* 39: 267–311.

Disney, R., and P. Johnson. 2001. *Pension Systems and Retirement Incomes across OECD Countries*. London: Edward Elgar.

Duval, R. 2003. The retirement effects of old-age pension and early retirement schemes in OECD countries. Mimeo. OECD.

Emmerson, C., and P. Johnson. 2001. Pension provision in the United Kingdom. In R. Disney, and P. Johnson, eds., *Pension Systems and Retirement Incomes across OECD Countries*. London: Edward Elgar.

Esping-Andersen, G. 1990. *The Three Worlds of Welfare Capitalism*. Cambridge: Polity.

Esping-Andersen, G. 1999. *Social Foundations of Postindustrial Economies*. Oxford: Oxford University Press.

European Commission. 2000. Progress report to the Ecofin Council on the impact of aging population on the public pension systems. Economic Policy Committee.

European Commission. 2003. Joint report by the Commission and the Council on adequate and sustainable pensions.

European Commission, Economic Policy Committee. 2002. Reform challenges facing public pension systems: The impact of certain parametric reforms on pension expenditure. Brussels: EC.

European Commission, DG Employment and Social Affairs. 2002. *Social Security in Europe—2001*. Brussels: EC.

European Commission, Household Panel—several issues.

Feldstein, M., and J. B. Liebman. 2002a. Social security. In A. J. Auerbach and M. Feldstein, eds., *Handbook of Public Economics*. Amsterdam: North-Holland.

Feldstein, M., and J. B. Liebman. 2002b. The distributional aspects of social security and social security reform. Chicago: Chicago University Press.

Feldstein, M., and H. Siebert. 2002. *Social Security Pension Reform in Europe*. Chicago: Chicago University Press.

Fenge, R., and P. Pestieau. 2006. *Social Security and Early Retirement*. Cambridge: MIT Press.

Ferrera, M. 1985. *The Welfare State in Italia*. Bologna: Il Mulino.

Ferrera, M. 1996. The southern model of welfare in social Europe. *Journal of European Social Policy* 6: 17–37.

Franco, D. 2002. Italy: A never-ending pension reform. In M. Feldstein and H. Siebert, eds., *Social Security Pension Reform in Europe*. Chicago: Chicago University Press.

Galasso, V. 1999. The US social security: What does political sustainability imply? *Review of Economic Dynamics* 2: 698–730.

Galasso, V. 2002. Social security: A financial appraisal for the median voter. *Social Security Bulletin* 64: 57–65.

Galasso, V. 2003. Redistribution and fairness: A note. *European Journal of Political Economy* 19: 885–92.

Galasso, V. 2006. Postponing retirement: The political push of aging. IGIER Working paper.

Galasso, V., and P. Profeta. 2002. Political economy models of social security: A survey. *European Journal of Political Economy* 18: 1–29.

Galasso, V., and P. Profeta. 2004. Lessons for an aging society: The political sustainability of social security systems. *Economic Policy* 38: 63–115.

Giarda, P. 1998. La revisione del sistema pensionistico nel 1997: Come avrebbe potuto essere. *Economia Politica* 15: 267–94.

Giavazzi, F., A. Penati, and G. Tabellini. 1998. La costituzione fiscale. Bologna: Il Mulino.

Gokhale, J., and L. J. Kotlikoff. 2002. Social security's treatment of postwar Americans: How bad can it get? In M. Feldstein and J. B. Liebman, eds., *The Distributional Aspects of Social Security and Social Security Reform*. Chicago: Chicago University Press.

Gramlich, E. M. 1996. Different approaches for dealing with social security. *Journal of Economic Perspectives* 10: 55–66.

Gronchi, S. 1998. La sostenibilità delle nuove forme previdenziali ovvero il sistema pensionistico tra riforme fatte e da fare. *Economia Politica* 15: 295–315.

Gronchi, S., and R. Aprile. 1998. The 1995 pension reform: Sustainability and indexation. *Labor.* 12: 67–100.

Gruber, J., and D. Wise. 1999. Social security and retirement around the world. Chicago: University of Chicago Press.

Hammond, P. 1975. Charity: Altruism or Cooperative Egoism. In E. S. Phelps, ed., *Altruism, Morality and Economic Theory*. New York: Russell Sage Foundation, pp. 115–31.

Hannah, L. 1986. *Inventing Retirement*. Cambridge: Cambridge University Press.

Herbertsson, T. T., and J. M. Orszag. 2003. The early retirement burden. Mimeo.

Herce, J. A. 2002. Pensions in Spain. Mimeo. FEDEA, Madrid.

IDEA. 1999. *Youth Voter Participation*. International IDEA, Sweden.

ISTAT. Italian Population data at ⟨www.istat.it⟩.

Jackson, R. 2003. Germany and the challenge of global aging. Center for Strategic and International Studies.

Jackson, R., and N. Howe. 2003. The 2003 aging vulnerability index. Center for Strategic and International Studies.

Jessop, B., K. Bonnet, S. Bromley, and T. Ling. 1988. *Thatcherism: A Tale of Two Nations*. Cambridge: Polity Press.

Jimeno, J. F. 2002. Incentivos y desigualdad en el sistema español de pensiones contributivas de jubilación. Documento de Trabajo 2002-13. FEDEA, Madrid.

Jousten, A. 2001. Pension provisions in the United States. In R. Disney and P. Johnson, eds., *Pension Systems and Retirement Incomes across OECD Countries*. London: Edward Elgar.

Latulippe, D. 1996. Effective retirement age and duration of retirement in the industrial countries between 1950 and 1990. ILO Issues in Social Protection Discussion paper 2.

Lee, R., and J. Skinner. 1999. Will aging baby boomers bust the federal budget? *Journal of Economic Perspectives* 13: 117–40.

Legendre, D., and L.-P. Pelé. 2001. Pension provision in France. In R. Disney and P. Johnson, eds., *Pension Systems and Retirement Incomes across OECD Countries*. London: Edward Elgar.

Lijphart, A. 1999. *Patterns of Democracy*. New Haven: Yale University Press.

Lindbeck, A., and M. Persson. 2003. The gains from pension reform. *Journal of Economic Literature* 41: 74–112.

Maddison, A. 1995. *Monitoring the World 1820–1992*. Paris: OECD.

Math, A. 2002. Reformes des retraites et revenues des personnes agees: Un apercu comparative. IRES Document de travail 02.04.

Miron, J. A., and D. N. Weil. 1998. The genesis and evolution of social security. In M. D. Bordo, C. Goldin, and E. N. White, eds., *The Defining Moment: The Great Depression and the American Economy in the Twentieth Century*. Chicago: University of Chicago Press.

Myles, J. 1984. *Old Age in the Welfare State*. Boston: Little Brown.

Myles, J., and J. Quadagno. 1997. Recent trends in public pension reform: A comparative view. In K. Banting and R. Boadway, eds., *Reform of Retirement Income Policy: International and Canadian Perspectives*. Kingston (Canada): Queen's University, School of Policy Studies.

Mulligan, C. B., and X. Sala-i-Martin. 1999. Gerontocracy, retirement and social security. NBER Working paper 7117. Cambridge, MA.

Munnel, A. H. 2004. Population aging: It's not just the baby boom. Issue in Brief 16, Center for Retirement Research, Boston College.

Natali, D., and M. Rhodes. 2004a. Reforming pensions in Italy and France: Policy trade-offs and redistributive effects. Paper presented at the ESPAnet Conference on European Social Policy: Meeting the Needs of New Europe, Oxford.

Natali, D., and M. Rhodes. 2004b. The "new politics" of the Bismarckian welfare state: Pension reforms in continental Europe. European University Institute Working paper 2004/10.

OECD. 2002. Policies for an aging society: recent measures and areas for further reforms. Working Paper 1 on Macroeconomic and Structural Policy Analysis.

OECD: Goverment Expenditure Data at ⟨www.oecd.org⟩.

OECD. Health Data at ⟨www.oecd.org⟩.

OECD. Labor statistics at ⟨www.oecd.org⟩.

Ordershook, P. C. 1986. *Game Theory and Political Theory*. Cambridge: Cambridge University Press.

Peracchi, F., and N. Rossi. 1998. Nonostante tutto è una Riforma. In F. Giavazzi, A. Penati, and G. Tabellini, eds., *La Costituzione Fiscale*. Bologna: Il Mulino.

Persson, T., and G. Tabellini. 2000. *Political Economics—Explaining Economic Policy*. Cambridge: MIT Press.

Pierson, P. 1994. *Dismantling the Welfare State?* Cambridge: Cambridge University Press.

Pierson, P. 1996. The new politics of the welfare state. *World Politics* 48: 143–79.

Pierson, P., and R. K. Weaver. 1993. Imposing losses in pension policy. In R. K. Weaver and P. Rockman, eds., *Do Institutions Matter? Government Capabilities in the Unites States and Abroad.* Washington, DC, Brookings Institution.

Poterba, J. M. 1999. *Tax Policy and the Economy.* Cambridge: MIT Press.

PPI. 2003. *The Pensions Landscape.* London: Pension Policy Institute.

Profeta, P. 2002a. Retirement and social security in a probabilistic voting model. *International Tax and Public Finance* 9: 331–48.

Profeta, P. 2002b. Aging and retirement: evidence across countries. *International Tax and Public Finance* 9: 651–72.

Profeta, P. 2004. Aging, retirement and social security in an interest groups model. *Mathematical Population Studies* 28: 93–120.

Puch, L., and O. Licando. 1997. Are there any special feature in the Spanish business cycle? *Investigaciones Economicas* 21: 361–94.

Rodolfo Debenedetti Foundation Report. 2000. Monitoring slow pension reforms in Europe. Mimeo.

Rürop, B. 2002. The German pension system: Status quo and reform options. In M. Feldstein and H. Siebert, eds., *Social Security Pension Reform in Europe.* Chicago: Chicago University Press.

Samuelson, P. A. 1958. An exact consumption-loan model of interest with or without the social contrivance of money. *Journal of Political Economy* 66: 467–82.

Shepsle, K. A. 1979. Institutional arrangements and equilibrium in multidimensional voting models. *American Journal of Political Science* 23: 27–59.

Sinn, H. W., and S. Uebelmesser. 2002. Pensions and the path to gerontocracy in Germany. *European Journal of Political Economy* 19: 153–58.

Sjoblom, K. 1985. Voting for social security. *Public Choice* 45: 225–40.

Smith, J. 1999. Healthy bodies and thick wallets: The dual relation between health and economic status. *Journal of Economic Perspectives* 13: 145–66.

Steuerle, C. E., and J. M. Bakija. 1994. *Retooling Social Security for the 21st Century.* Washington, DC: Urban Institute Press.

Tabellini, G. 2000. A positive theory of social security. *Scandinavian Journal of Economics* 102: 523–45.

Tumbarello, P. 2000. The Italian pension system: a case for notional accounts. Mimeo. IMF.

US Census Bureau. Reported Voting and Registration at ⟨www.census.gov⟩.

US Census Bureau. US Population at ⟨www.census.gov⟩.

US Social Security Administration at ⟨www.ssa.gov⟩.

Weaver, R. K. 1986. The politics of blame avoidance. *Journal of Public Policy* 6: 371–98.

Weaver, R. K., and P. Rockman. 1993. Do institutions matter? Government capabilities in the Unites States and abroad. Washington, DC: Brookings Institution.

Wilensky, H. 1975. *The Welfare State and Equality*. Berkeley: University of California Press.

Wolfinger, R. E., and S. J. Rosenstone. 1980. *Who Votes?* New Haven: Yale University Press.

World Bank. 1994. *Averting the Old-Age Crisis: Policies to Protect the Old and Promote Growth*. New York: Oxford University Press.

Index